An Introduction to Syntactic Theory

Also available from Continuum:

An Introduction to Syntax, Edith Moravcsik

An Introduction to Syntactic Theory

Edith Moravcsik
University of Wisconsin-Milwaukee

continuum
LONDON • NEW YORK

To the memory of my brother
Michael J. Moravcsik

Continuum

The Tower Building
11 York Road
London SE1 7NX

80 Maiden Lane
Suite 704
New York
NY 10038

British Library Cataloguing-in-Publication Data
A catalogue record for this book is available from the British Library.

ISBN: 0–8264–8943–5 (hardback)
        0–8264–8944–3 (paperback)

Library of Congress Cataloging-in-Publication Data
Catalogue record of this book is available.

Typeset by Servis Filmsetting Ltd, Manchester
Printed and bound in Great Britain by MPG Books Ltd, Bodmin, Cornwall

Contents

Preface

1 Main points

Why are there so many different approaches to syntactic description? What it is about sentence structure that keeps on inviting new attempts to analyse it? The answer proposed in this book centres on the existence of conflicts in the data.

In the recent linguistic literature, there has been increasing attention paid to the nature and the resolution of conflicts in grammatical descriptions, also referred to as mismatches. Conflicts arise between syntax and meaning, between syntax and phonetic form, and among various aspects of syntax itself. Such mismatches and the problems that they pose have been central to Autolexical Grammar, Cognitive Grammar, Construction Grammar, Functional Grammar and Lexical-Functional Grammar, and have been seminal in Optimality Theory.

That the attempt to resolve conflicts is an overarching theme across syntactic theories has been suggested by Ray Jackendoff. As he considers various accounts of tense in English, which is morphologically marked on the verb even though it has the entire proposition in its semantic scope, Jackendoff notes that there is a mismatch here between phonology and meaning and he remarks:

> Much dispute in modern syntax has been over these sorts of mismatch and how to deal with them. (I don't think most linguists have viewed it this way, though.)
> (Jackendoff 2002: 15)

A step in the direction of surveying various syntactic theories from the point of view of how they accommodate conflicts has been taken by Elaine J. Francis and Laura A. Michaelis (2003) in their introduction to a collection of studies on mismatches and in some of the papers in that volume. This book, *An Introduction to Syntactic Theory*, may be viewed as a further exploration of this idea. Drawing upon the theoretical literature of the past few decades, it presents selected analyses from different syntactic frameworks and makes two main points.

(1) Many of the various conceptual tools employed by syntacticians are designed to resolve conflicts in the data.

(2) Given that there is a limited range of the logically available ways of conflict resolution, the range of syntactic theory types is limited as well and their diversity can be systematically characterized in terms of the conflict-resolving constructs they employ.

The book is meant for undergraduate and graduate courses. An introductory linguistics course and basic familiarity with syntactic analysis are presupposed. Illustrative data are taken from English and several other languages.

2 Overview

Chapter 1 'Parameters of syntactic theories' surveys various ways in which syntactic theories may differ and states the goals that all syntactic theories must share, including consistency of descriptions. On two examples – English imperatives and wh-questions – it is illustrated how accounts that strive to be both empirically correct and general can run afoul of the consistency requirement. An overview is provided of the major types of conflict and the logically possible ways in which they can be dealt with. Each alternative analysis of English imperatives and wh-questions is identified as an instance of a general type of conflict-resolution.

Chapter 2 'Alternative analyses of syntactic structures' discusses conflicts that arise in the analysis of syntactic form. Examples of discontinuous linear order and 'long-distance' verb agreement are taken up along with their resolutions found in the literature.

The next two chapters turn to conflicts between syntactic form and meaning. In Chapter 3 'Alternative analyses of symbolic correspondence relations: co-ordination', the problem is illustrated on co-ordinate structures; various suggestions are gleaned from the literature on how to solve them. Chapter 4 'Alternative analyses of symbolic correspondence relations: grammatical functions' discusses mismatches between semantic participant roles and grammatical functions, with the focus on 'double-object' constructions and their various analyses.

In Chapter 5 'Alternative analyses of syntactic variation and change', data on cross-linguistic variation of constituent order are presented; various resolutions of the conflicts in this domain are surveyed as they emerge from the typological literature. Syntactic change is discussed as it takes place in individual development: the acquisition of relative clause structures by children. Conflicts in the data are made explicit and alternative resolutions presented.

While the preceding chapters used analyses of specific aspects of syntax taken from different approaches, Chapter 6 'Four contemporary approaches to syntax' provides overall characterizations of four families of contemporary syntactic approaches: transformational grammars, dependency grammars, construction grammars and optimality theory.

Each chapter is followed by a set of exercises. Some of the questions are based on the language data in the appendix, which contains a set of 18 sentences given in six languages. There is a list of symbols and abbreviations following the preface and a glossary in the back of the book.

3 Acknowledgements

Many people have provided indispensable help for this project. First and foremost, it is with very special gratitude that I think of Joseph H. Greenberg and Gerald A. Sanders whose views on language and linguistics will be apparent throughout the book.

Joseph Greenberg's pioneering oeuvre encompassing many fields of linguistics and anthropology is well known. In this book, I have mostly relied on his work in language typology, major highlights of which are the recognition and fruitful use of implicational statements as the principal means of capturing constraints on language variation, and the elaboration of the claims of markedness theory.

Gerald Sanders' 1972 book *Equational Grammar* presented a comprehensive theory of grammar. In it, several ideas that have since been independently proposed and now figure prominently in various current syntactic approaches were first put forth and synthesized within a coherent and principled framework. These include the insights that syntactic and phonological rules, just like lexical entries, express symbolic correspondence relations between meaning and form; that rules of syntactic selection and linear order must be separately formulated; that linear order be recognized as a feature of phonetic form; that linear order statements be surface-true and thus invariant in the course of grammatical derivations; that the application of rules should be motivated by the requirement of full phonetic and semantic interpretability; and that the discourse, rather than the sentence, is the proper domain of linguistics.

I also want to thank my other professors and mentors in linguistics as well as my teachers of Hungarian grammar in elementary and high school in Budapest for all that I learnt from them.

From among my colleagues and friends, I am particularly grateful to my present and past linguist colleagues at the University of Wisconsin-Milwaukee: Mark Amsler, Michael Darnell, Pamela Downing, Fred Eckman, Michael Hammond, Ashley Hastings, Gregory Iverson, Patricia Mayes, Michael Noonan, Bozena Tieszen, Bert Vaux and Barbara Wheatley; and especially to Jessica R. Wirth for her encouragement, for many stimulating discussions, for her sense of orderly argumentation and for her keen insights. For stimulating discussions over many years, I am grateful to the members of the Cognitive Science Reading Group at UWM. For stimulation and encouragement, my heartfelt thanks go to colleagues and friends at the Linguistic Research Institute of the Hungarian Academy of Sciences, the Department of Linguistics at the Eötvös Lóránd University in Budapest, the Max Planck Institute for Evolutionary Anthropology in Leipzig, the

EUROTYP programme, and the World Atlas of Language Structures (WALS) project.

I am much indebted to Konrad Koerner, who steadfastly encouraged me to complete the book over several years. Eun Hee Lee has provided a thorough and perceptive commentary on several of the chapters, for which I am particularly grateful. Many thanks to András Kertész for his thoroughgoing and insightful suggestions. My sincere thanks also to Jenny Lovel and her colleagues at Continuum for their help and encouragement.

Finally, I am profoundly grateful to my relatives and friends for their unflagging support; and to all my students in Stanford, Los Angeles, Vienna, Salzburg, Honolulu, Giessen, Budapest and Milwaukee for their ideas and for providing the basic motivation for writing this book.

Edith A. Moravcsik
July 2005

Department of Foreign Languages and Linguistics
University of Wisconsin-Milwaukee
Milwaukee, WI 53201-0413, USA
(edith@uwm.edu)

Symbols and Abbreviations

Symbols

In interlinear glosses:

- – indicates morpheme boundaries
- : indicates morpheme boundaries in the English gloss that are not shown in the object-language words
- . indicates two words in English for one word in the object language
- & indicates temporal precedence: 'A & B' means 'A immediately precedes B'
- , indicates co-occurrence in some unspecified linear order: 'A, B' means 'A and B co-occur'
- * indicates ungrammatical constructions
- ? indicates constructions of questionable grammaticality

Abbreviations

These abbreviations mostly follow those given in the Leipzig Glossing Rules (http://www.eva.mpg.de/lingua/files/morpheme/html). They stand for grammatical markers of the categories indicated.

ABL	ablative case
ABS	absolutive case
ACC	accusative case
ADJ	adjective
ADP	adposition
ANT	anterior tense
ART	article
AUX	auxiliary
CL1	noun class 1
CL2	noun class 2
CM	case marker
DAT	dative case
DECL	declarative sentence
DEF	definite

DEM	demonstrative
DET	determiner
DO	direct object or direct object case marker
ERG	ergative case
FEM	feminine gender
FOC	focus
GEN	genitive case
GER	gerund
INDEF	indefinite
INF	infinitive
InfM	infinitive marker
INS	instrumental
IO	indirect object or indirect object case marker
M	modality
MSC	masculine gender
NEG	negative
NEU	neuter gender
NOM	nominative case
NP	noun phrase
NPST	non-past tense
OBJ	object or object marker
P1	first person plural
P2	second person plural
P3	third person plural
PART	participle
PASS	passive
PERF	perfective
PL	plural
PP	prepositional phrase
PREP	preposition
PROG	progressive aspect
PRS	present tense
PST	past tense
Q	question particle
REFL	reflexive
REL	relative clause
S1	first person singular
S2	second person singular
S3	third person singular
SBJ	subject case
SG	singular
TOP	topic
TRANS	transitive
you(r)$_\text{P}$	plural 'you(r)'
you(r)$_\text{S}$	singular 'you(r)'

Chapter One

Parameters of Syntactic Theories

Please signal in one direction only.

> (Elevator sign in the Memorial Library of the University of
> Wisconsin-Madison, 2001)

1 Preliminaries

The goal of grammatical descriptions is to characterize the well-formed sentences of a language. There are different ways in which sentences can fail to be well-formed; accordingly, different kinds of rules are needed to describe well-formedness. Here is an example.

Suppose you want to say the English sentence *The plane landed safely.* In (1)–(5) are shown various ways in which the sentence may be ill-formed:

(1) (a) **The **rplane** landed safely.*
     (b) **The **lpane** landed safely.*

(2) (a) **The plane **land-ed-s** safely.*
     (b) **The plane **ed-land** safely.*

(3) (a) **They the plane landed safely.*
    (b) ****Plane the** *landed safely.*

(4) **The **Flugzeug** landed safely.*

(5) **The **generosity** landed safely.*

In (1) phonological ill-formedness is illustrated: a word-initial consonant cluster containing /r/, /p/ and /l/, as in (1a), is not pronounceable in English regardless of the order in which they appear. Word-initial clusters consisting of /p/ and /l/ are pronounceable but only if /p/ precedes /l/ and not if /l/ precedes /p/, as is the case in (1b). To exclude sentences such as those in (1), **phonological rules** are needed to specify the permissible selection and ordering of phonetic segments.

The problem with the sentences in (2) is different. The choice and ordering of the phonetic segments comply with English pronunciation constraints; here the cause of ungrammaticality is the choice and ordering of morphemes. *Land-ed-s* (as in (2a)) consists of a verb stem, a past tense affix and the third person singular agreement marker. This combination of morphemes does not make a well-formed English word in any order. The morphemes of *ed-land* (as in (2b)) – verb stem and past tense affix – are properly chosen for making a word but are not correctly ordered. The rules responsible for excluding forms such as those in (2) that state the proper selection and order of morphemes are called **morphological rules**.

The sentences in (3) also illustrate the illegitimate choice and ordering of meaningful units but here, these units are entire words rather than morphemes: (3a) has an extra word in it – *they* – which makes the sentence ungrammatical; (3b) has the right words in the wrong order. Specifying what words can go together in a sentence and in what order is the minimal task of **syntactic rules**.

The sentence in (4) fails because it includes a word that is not part of English vocabulary: *Flugzeug* is the German word for 'plane'. The sentence thus violates a rule that states what word form can express what meaning in English. Such rules are called **lexical rules**.

Finally, (5) is ill-formed because the meaning that it conveys is non-sensical: abstract nouns like *generosity* cannot land. Rules that characterize well-formed meanings are called **semantic rules**.

For a sentence to be fully well-formed, all its various kinds of components – sounds, morphemes, words and meaning elements – have to be selected and arranged correctly. While all the various types of rules surveyed above are concerned with the choice and arrangement of components of one kind or another, the examples in (2) highlight the special contribution that syntactic rules make to the entirety of a grammar. These rules address well-formedness as it depends on the choice and the ordering of words and of larger units that words are parts of, such as phrases and clauses.

The syntactic structure of the sentence *The plane landed safely*, stated in terms of word classes and phrase classes, is as follows (& means 'immediately precedes'):

(6) [[Article & Noun]$_{NP}$ & [Verb & Adverb]$_{VP}$]$_S$

The rules characterizing this sentence as having a well-formed syntactic structure are given in (7):

(7) (A) INVENTORY OF SYNTACTIC CATEGORIES
article, noun, verb, adverb and so on.

(B) SELECTION OF SYNTACTIC CATEGORIES
(a) Article and noun may be selected to form a noun phrase.
(b) Verb and adverb may be selected to form a verb phrase.
(c) Noun phrase and verb phrase may be selected to form a sentence with the noun phrase as subject.

(C) ORDERING OF SYNTACTIC CATEGORIES
(a) Given that an article and a noun have been selected for a noun phrase, the article must precede the noun.
(b) Given that a verb and an adverb have been selected for a verb phrase, the verb may precede the adverb.
(c) Given that a subject noun phrase and a verb phrase have been selected for a sentence, the subject noun phrase must precede the verb phrase.

In addition to accounting for well-formed syntactic structures, rules of syntax also need to relate these structures to sentence meanings, on the one hand, and sentence pronunciations, on the other. In our example sentence above, syntactic structure and meaning, and syntactic structure and phonetic form match, but this may not always be the case.

For example, in the sentence *Bill entered and sat down*, Bill is understood as the subject of the second verb as well – *sat down* – even though it does not appear in syntactic structure. This illustrates a gap between syntax and meaning. Similar gaps exist between syntax and phonetic form. For example, in the sentence *I wanna go to a café*, the single phonetic form *wanna* corresponds to two syntactic constituents: *want* and *to*. Rules that state the permissible pairings of syntactic structures and meaning, on the one hand, and syntactic structures and phonetic form, on the other, are called **symbolic correspondence rules**.

Based on this discussion, syntax appears to be a straightforward matter. It would seem that there was only one way of describing syntax: by specifying the inventory of syntactic categories available, constraints on selecting categories from this inventory to form sentences, constraints on the linear order of the categories, and symbolic correspondence relations connecting syntax with meaning and pronunciation.

However, this is certainly not the case: syntax has been described in many different ways by many different theories. A 1979 conference on syntactic theories featured 14 different frameworks: Cognitive Grammar, Corepresentational

Grammar, Daughter-Dependency Grammar, Epiphenomenal Grammar, Equational Grammar, two versions of Functional Grammar, Functionally-Interpreted Base-Generated Grammar, Montague Grammar, Relational Grammar, Role and Reference Grammar, Stratificational Grammar, Tagmemics and Trace Theory. This roster actually fell quite a bit short of covering the entire then-current scene: a number of approaches – among others Tesnière's Dependency Grammar, Bar-Hillel's Categorial Grammar, Halliday's Systemic Grammar, Shaumyan's Applicative Grammar and Starosta's Lexicase – remained unrepresented at the meeting.

Since that time, new developments have taken place within these frameworks and a number of additional approaches have entered the field. They include Noam Chomsky's Government and Binding Theory and his Minimalist Theory, Paul Postal's Arc-Pair Grammar, Richard Hudson's Word Grammar, Ronald Langacker's Cognitive Grammar, Joan Bresnan's Lexical-Functional Grammar, Gerald Gazdar, Ewan Klein, Geoffrey Pullum and Ivan Sag's Generalized Phrase Structure Grammar, Ivan Sag and Thomas Wasow's Head-Driven Phrase Structure Grammar, Igor Mel'čuk's Dependency Grammar, Ivan Sag's Unificational Theory, Jerrold Sadock's Autolexical Syntax, the Columbia School approach, William McGregor's Semiotic Grammar, as well as various versions of Construction Grammar, Optimality Theory and Usage-Based Models. The *Concise Encyclopedia of Syntactic Theories* published in 1996 presents about thirty frameworks (Brown and Miller 1996). And even this number may account for only a small subset of the possible theories of syntax: in a not-completely tongue-in-cheek manner, James McCawley titled a collection of his articles *Thirty Million Theories of Grammar* (McCawley 1982a).

An illustration of the range of differences among the various frameworks is provided below by representations of the English sentence *Susan expected him to succeed*, as proposed by Government and Binding Theory, Relational Grammar and Word Grammar.

(8) Government and Binding Theory (see Horrocks 1987: 108)

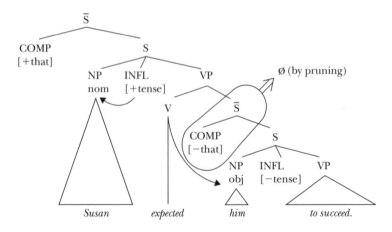

Notation:
- triangles indicate lack of detail on phrase-internal structure
- single arrows point from governor to governee
- the double arrow indicates a transformational rule

(9) Relational Grammar (see Blake 1990: 96, 97)

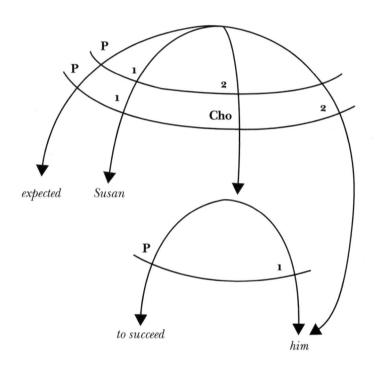

Notation:

P	=	predicate
1	=	subject
2	=	direct object
cho	=	chomeur (i.e., a syntactic constituent that bears no grammatical relation to the verb)

(10) Word Grammar (see Hudson 1984: 112)

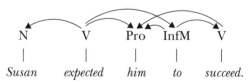

Notation:

Arrows point from heads to dependents.

The three diagrams are alike in some ways and different in other ways. While none of them tell the whole story about the analysis of the sentence in the given framework, each shows some of the salient features of the approach. Let us see what the diagrams have in common and how they differ.

First, all three diagrams represent sentences as **partonomic** – whole–part – structures but, whereas Government and Binding assumes a multi-layered partonomy (called constituent structure), with sentences containing clauses, clauses in turn containing phrases, and phrases broken down into words, Word Grammar has only two layers: words are immediate parts of sentences. Word Grammar does not represent sequences of words that 'act together' as wholes – that is, phrases; instead, it represents **head-dependent** relations among words. The unitary behaviour of head and dependents is accounted for by a principle that requires that the dependents be adjacent to their heads.

Second, all three diagrams reflect a **taxonomy** (type-token relations) of syntactic constituents. However, the category types employed are different. The node labels in the Government and Binding tree are S, NP, V and so on, all of which are non-relational categories. The nodes in the Relational Grammar tree – predicate, subject, direct object and chomeur – are of the relational kind: a subject is a subject of a predicate, unlike a noun phrase which is not 'the noun phrase of a predicate', and so are those of Word Grammar, which, as noted above, assumes a division of words into the relational categories of heads and dependents. In the Government and Binding diagram, one constituent – COMP(lementizer) – has no phonetic form; in the other two frameworks, all syntactic constituents are phonetically realized.

Third, while both Government and Binding and Word Grammar represent the **linear ordering** of the constituents as they actually appear in the sentence, Relational Grammar shows the sentence in a more abstract form in terms of the mere presence of constituents but not how they are arranged.

Fourth, the three approaches differ in whether they assume **single or multiple levels** of syntactic representation. Note that the crux of the construction is the grammatical function of the word *him*: is it an object or a subject? Its oblique form makes it look as if it is the direct object of the main verb *expected*; however, it functions as the subject of the infinitive *to succeed*. Its linear position is consistent with both analyses: it directly follows the main verb as direct objects are wont to and it immediately precedes the infinitive as subjects do.

The three approaches deal with this conflict in different ways. In Word Grammar, there is a single level and the double allegiance of the word *him* is shown by multiple dependency arrows. Government and Binding and Relational Grammar both posit multiple levels to do justice to the double nature of *him* although they do this in different ways. Relational Grammar represents various levels within the same diagram: they form a single representation. The subordinate clause – *him to succeed* – has only a single-level structure but the main clause – *Susan expected . . .* – has two strata. The top horizontal arch in (9) shows the initial stratum; the second arch shows the final stratum. Here is how the two strata differ.

(11)	predicate:	subject:	direct object:	chomeur:
initial stratum:	*expected*	I	*him to succeed*	0
final stratum:	*expected*	I	*him*	*him to succeed*

The process connecting the initial and the final strata is called ascension: *him,* the initial subject of the subordinate clause, ascends into the main clause to become the direct object of the main verb *expected.* The initial direct object of *expected* – the subordinate clause – then loses its grammatical relation and becomes a 'chomeur' ('unemployed' in French).

In contrast to Relational Grammar, in Government and Binding Theory each of the multiple representations of a sentence is shown in a separate diagram. The tree diagram in (8) is a surface structure except for the circled portion, which is a part of the underlying structure. It is subsequently deleted ('pruned') and thus prevented from appearing on the surface. The pruning operation reduces the syntactic distance between the main verb *expected* and *he,* the subject of the subordinate clause. This enables the main verb to be sufficiently close to the object *him* to serve as *him*'s governor and thus to assign accusative case to it.

Exactly what is it about syntax that is so complex as to call for different ways of describing it? Is there anything that syntacticians all agree on? What are the differences and what drives them? Addressing these questions is the task of this book.

This is how we are going to proceed. In the present chapter, we will first consider logically possible ways in which syntactic theories may and may not differ and then consider actual differences and probe into the general reasons why the various options are resorted to. In the three chapters to follow, we will look at some proposals in the literature regarding various aspects of syntax: proposals regarding syntactic structure (Chapter 2) and regarding the symbolic correspondence relations between syntax and meaning (Chapters 3 and 4). Chapter 5 will present alternative analyses of syntactic variation and change. Chapter 6 gives brief overall characterizations of four contemporary approaches to syntax. Chapter 7 provides some thoughts on the roots of conflicts in syntax.

2 How can syntactic theories differ from each other?

2.1 NECESSARY SIMILARITIES

Theories of syntax – as theories of anything else – are human artifacts created in the pursuit of the goal of making sense of the world. Thus, the character-istics of theories can conveniently be viewed as **goal-related** and **means-related**. In both domains, there are some necessary resemblances across theories: goals and tools that all syntactic theories must share, and a limited range of differences. We will start with the similarities.

2.1.1 Shared goals

A theory is a scientific tool that consists of a set of generalizations. The aim is the comprehensive description and explanation of some set of observa-tions about the world. A theory of syntax aims at describing and explaining the structure of utterances in human languages. The descriptions derived from the theory should mirror commonalities and differences among utter-ances of a language and among utterances of different languages, as well as commonalities and differences between the syntax of natural languages and things outside it.

Theories in general, and linguistic theories in particular, can therefore be viewed as a kind of language: they serve to make it possible to talk about things. Natural languages express the speaker's ideas about the world; theo-ries of natural languages express the analyst's ideas about natural languages. The language of linguistic theories is called **metalanguage** (the Greek mor-pheme *meta* means 'after'). Just like natural languages, syntactic metalan-guages, too, can be compared and classified into types.

Users of natural languages are constrained by the grammar of their lan-guage in what they can say and how they can to say it. Similarly, theory-builders are constrained in formulating their metalinguistic statements. These constraints are dictated by two factors: external reality – as perceived by the observer – and the goals and means of the human mind.

The first constraint on theory-building is the requirement of **empirical adequacy**. A sculptor faces a block of marble and he attempts to carve out the likeness of a person. In the same way, the theorist faces a block of logical possibilities regarding what things could be like and he needs to find the true image of his object within that block by chiselling off just the right amount of material for that image to emerge. His description should neither under-represent nor over-represent reality. What syntactic theories have to repre-sent are the well-formedness of strings of words that make up sentences and the symbolic correspondence relation between these strings of words and meaning, on the one hand, and phonological form, on the other.

While the facts greatly contribute to defining the nature of theories, they do not fully determine it. As Albert Einstein said about physics: 'Physical con-cepts are the free creations of the human mind and are not, however it may seem, uniquely determined by the external world' (Harrison 1999: 127). This statement highlights the other factor that enters into theory-formation, whether in physics or in other sciences: the **human mind**. Reality itself is free of 'problems' and 'solutions'; it is our minds that formulate problems and look for ways of solving them.

There are three requirements for scientific theories in general and syntactic theories in particular that stem from the aspirations and limitations of the human mind. First, descriptions must be **general**. It is only by means of generalizations that infinite sets of objects can be described and explained by token of a finite number of statements.

The second conceptual constraint on scientific accounts is **consistency**: they have to be couched in the language of the rational mind, which means they have to be free of contradictions. Just as the pea-brain of the elevator cited in the epigraph to this chapter asks not to be instructed to go both up and down at the same time, the much more mighty cognitive apparatus of human beings, too, baulks at contradictions. A statement according to which something is both A and not-A at the same time remains indigestible to human rationality. The conceptual roots of the requirement of consistency are underlined by Nicholas Rescher: 'The quest for consistency is a matter of practical human convenience – a response to the demands of a limited creature with an intolerance to cognitive dissonance and an incapacity to accept inconsistency' (Rescher 1987: 315).

The third requirement imposed on theories by the human mind is **simplicity**. This requirement is also closely tailored to human needs: accounts are best if they are simple so that not too much of the limited time and energy that people have available needs to be spent on grasping them.

Since these four goals are shared by all theories in any science, they form common goal-related denominators for syntactic theories as well. The next question has to do with the means whereby these goals can be achieved.

2.1.2 *Shared tools*

Minimally, there are five conceptual tools that all syntactic theories will necessarily share. In order to characterize any object in a general way, that object must be broken down into component parts and properties so that a unique object can be shown to be a unique combination of non-unique components. Furthermore, these components need to be assigned to categories. Given that the segmenting of larger structures into components and the classification of the latter are therefore indispensable steps in all scientific analyses, **partonomic** and **taxonomic relations** are necessarily part of the conceptual armamentarium of all syntactic theories as well.

Partonomic and taxonomic relations define units such as words, phrases and clauses, and place them into categories such as adjective, verb phrase and relative clause. Since syntactic descriptions have to account for the selection and order of words, two additional relations must be posited to hold among syntactic categories: selectional dependency and linear precedence. **Selectional dependency** is the relationship between two objects where the presence of one requires or allows the presence of another in the same structure. For example, articles and nouns are selectionally related: once an article – such as *a(n)* – has been selected, a noun must be selected as well (e.g. *boy*). **Linear precedence** is the temporal relation that holds between words, phrases and clauses. For example, the linear relation between the English article and noun is article preceding noun: *a boy* and not **boy a*.

Given that we are interested not only in well-formed syntactic structures but also in well-formed symbolic correspondence relations that syntactic structures participate in, namely, how syntactic structures relate to the meanings and sound forms of sentences, rules of **symbolic correspondence** are also called for to characterize these relations. An example of a rule regarding the symbolic correspondence relation between syntactic structure and meaning is one that states that in the sentence *A boy hid behind the tree*, the article & noun structure – *a boy* – is a semantic participant (also called a 'semantic argument') of the predicate that *hid* conveys. An example of a rule regarding the relationship between syntactic structure and sound form is one that takes care of the correct pronunciation of the indefinite article: in front of a consonant-initial word such as *boy*, it has to be *a*, rather than *an*, as it would be in front of vowel-initial words like *apple*.

Let us summarize our discussion about the goals and tools that syntactic theories necessarily share.

A. GOALS

Content:

Syntactic theories must characterize
- well-formed **syntactic structures**
- how syntactic structures convey **meanings**
- how syntactic structures can be **pronounced**

Manner:

Syntactic theories must be
- **true**
- **general**
- **consistent**
- **simple**

B. MEANS

As their conceptual means towards obtaining these goals, syntactic theories must posit the following relations:
- **partonomic relations**
- **taxonomic relations**
- **selectional dependency relations**
- **linear order relations**
- **symbolic correspondence relations**

These necessary commonalities among syntactic theories still leave much room for differences – a topic that we will turn to next.

2.2 ACTUAL DIFFERENCES

2.2.1 *Apparent differences*

First, there may be differences among syntactic approaches that are merely apparent – that is, they do not have to do with truth, generality, consistency or even simplicity. These differences turn out to be likenesses in disguise. For example, whether a particular phrasal category is symbolized as N′ or N in X-bar theory (Cann 1996), or whether a given semantic participant role is termed Patient or Theme makes no difference at all: it is a matter of arbitrary terminology, a matter of packaging rather than of content.

Similarly, within the framework called Categorial Grammar, where grammatical categories are labelled in terms of what other categories they co-occur with and what category results from their co-occurrence, different notational systems yield different representations of intransitive verbs, as shown in (1) (Wood 1993: 12–13). All three notations stand for the same thing: that an intransitive verb is a word that can join a noun to make a sentence.

(1) (a) $\frac{s}{n}$ (b) N\S (c) S\N

The choice between formulaic or discursive ('prose') rules is also notational: whether I say 'The subject immediately precedes the verb' or 'Subject & Verb', the message is the same. The existence of stylistic differences among syntactic approaches points at a similarity between natural language and metalanguage: both allow for synonymy.

In addition to such stylistic, **notational** differences, there is a second type of divergence among syntactic accounts that is equally non-substantive. It has to do with the **actual practice** of the adherents to a theory. For example, Minimalist Theory (Atkinson 1996) adopts the sentence for its domain of analysis and thus it would seem to differ crucially from Tagmemic Theory, whose basic domain is the discourse – that is, entire sets of connected sentences (Jones 1996). But there is nothing in the basic assumptions of Minimalist Theory that would conflict with discourse analysis; it is just that its practitioners have not chosen to exploit this option. The domain difference holds between practices here and not between theories.

A third kind of superficial difference among syntactic approaches has to do with the **choice of factual domains** within syntax. If the claims of different frameworks pertain to different sub-domains of syntax, the frameworks are complementary rather than contradictory. For example, Relational Grammar (see (9) in Section 1 and Blake 1990) analyses sentence structure in terms of its immediate constituents – such as subject, object, indirect object and verb – and makes no claims about the internal structure of these phrases. Thus, when we compare it with, say, Government and Binding Theory (see (8) in Section 1 and Freidin 1996) whose scope does include the internal structure of the Noun Phrase, we find the two frameworks to be different but compatible.

In sum, we have seen that some differences among syntactic approaches are only apparent. This is so if they are notational, or if they result from different practices of their practitioners, or if they pertain to different factual domains. But there are also possible differences among the goals and means of syntactic theories that are real, rather than apparent. This is the topic that we will turn to next.

2.2.2 *Substantive differences*

In Section 2.1, we saw that syntactic theories were alike in some of their goals and in some of the means they use to achieve them. The differences among syntactic theories similarly fall into two kinds: goal-related and means-related.

Syntactic approaches may differ in their choice of **goals**: in addition to those goals that all syntactic theories must by definition subscribe to, other objectives may also be adopted. Examples are practical, interventional applications, such as aiding language pedagogy, remedying pathologies of language, facilitating translation between languages, helping to design orthographies and programming computers for speech production and speech recognition.

More surprising is the tremendous variability of conceptual **tools**. As already seen in Section 1, some approaches posit multi-level derivational accounts of sentence structure while others assume a single level of syntactic representation; some theories make major use of multi-layered constituent structure while others assume minimal sentence partonomies consisting of only two layers: sentences and words; some theories assume that selection and order should be specified together while others assume separate selection and order rules. Some of the variability of theoretical constructs follows, understandably, from differences in goals: different goals cannot be expected to be obtainable with the same means. But even descriptions subscribing to the same goals often use different conceptual devices. Why?

A complete answer to this question would have to take many factors into account, such as the sociological setting within which linguists conduct research, the analyst's philosophical orientation and psychological factors. While such a comprehensive view of the matter cannot be offered in this book, our discussion will highlight one important factor: **conflicts among goals**.

As discussed in Section 2.1.1, theories have to be true, general, consistent and simple. However, when linguists attempt to comply with the first two requirements – truth and generality – they often come up short of one or the other of the two remaining constraints – consistency and simplicity. In Section 3, we will analyse aspects of syntax where such conflicts arise and begin to try to sort out the various ways in which syntacticians have come to grips with the conflicts. We will see that conflicts can be dealt with in different ways and that the differential resolutions of conflicts go a long way towards accounting for the differences among syntactic theories.

3 Why are there different syntactic theories?

3.1 Imperatives in English: the problem

For an example of the conflicts that arise in syntactic analysis and whose alternative resolutions yield alternative descriptions, consider English imperative sentences:

(1) (a) *Go home!*
    (b) *Take your medicine!*
    (c) *Love your neighbour!*

What are the selectional statements that characterize such sentences? At first, one might propose the following:

(2) Imperative sentences consist of a verb and its complement(s). They do not include a subject.

However, although no subject is visible in the sentences of (1), there is syntactic evidence that the subject is there, after all. Compare the following:

(3) (a) *Love **yourself**!*
    (b) *Don't hurt **yourself**!*
    (c) *Mind **your** own business!*
    (d) *Don't stub **your** toe!*
    (e) *Close the door, will **you**?*
    (f) *Pass the salt, won't **you**?*

Taking any one of these sentences by itself, we find no syntactic reason to depart from the assertion that they lack a syntactic subject. Of course, the meaning of a YOU-subject is present: a command is always meant for the addressee of the speech situation, but the syntactic structure bears no trace of this subject if we consider each sentence singly. If, however, we want to subsume these sentences under general rules, a conflict arises: although the sentences lack an actual subject, they act **as if** they had one. Here are three arguments to this effect.

First, the sentences (3a) and (3b) include the reflexive pronoun *yourself* which in other English sentences occurs only if the sentence has *you* for its subject. This is shown in (4).

(4) (a) ***You** will hurt **yourself**.*
    (b) ***I** will hurt **yourself**.*
    (c) ***John** will hurt **yourself**.*

We could of course formulate a rule that says that *yourself* occurs either in the presence of a YOU-subject or in imperative sentences. But this would be a complex rule, not in compliance with the requirements of generality and simplicity.

Second, consider (3c) and (3d). They include the word *your* that occurs elsewhere in such idiomatic sentences only if the corresponding declarative sentences have a YOU-subject:

(5) (a) *You* will stub *your* toe.
    (b) **I* will stub *your* toe.
    (c) **John* will stub *your* toe.

Once again, we could state that the pronoun *your* occurs in idiomatic expressions like *stub one's toe, hold one's mouth* and so on only if either the subject is YOU or the sentence is imperative. But this would be the second time that imperative sentences were said to allow for the selection of an element that in all other cases occurs only in sentences whose subject is an explicit expression of YOU.

Third, sentences (3e) and (3f) add to mounting evidence that, despite appearances, imperative sentences do have a syntactic YOU-subject. This is because (3e) and (3f) include the tags *will you* and *won't you*. These tags can also occur in non-imperative sentences but only if the subject is YOU, as in (6a) and (6b).

(6) (a) *You* will pass the salt, *won't you?*
    (b) **I* will pass the salt, *won't you?*
    (c) **John* will pass the salt, *won't you?*

Let us summarize so far. If we take the absence of the YOU-subject in imperatives at face value, we arrive at the following description:

(7) (a) English **imperative** sentences have **no subjects**.
    (b) The reflexive pronoun is *yourself* in a sentence if **either** it has a YOU-subject **or the sentence is a command**.
    (c) In idiomatic expressions such as *stub one's toe, keep one's mouth shut*, the pronoun *your* occurs if **either** the sentence has a YOU-subject **or the sentence is a command**.
    (d) In tags, the pronoun is *you* if **either** the sentence has a YOU-subject **or the sentence is a command**.

Rules that specify alternative conditions for a single pattern are not satisfactory: they are less general and less simple than rules stating a single condition. And if there are three rules each making reference to the very same disjunction of conditions – a sentence having a YOU-subject or being an imperative – it is very clear that a generalization is being missed: sentences with a YOU-subject and imperative sentences belong to the very same class.

A way to eliminate the offending '*or*-clauses' in (7) is by declaring imperative sentences to actually have a YOU-subject. Here is the alternative account, with the differences from (7) crossed out.

(8) (a) English imperative sentences have no subjects.
    (b) **English imperative sentences have YOU-subjects**.
    (c) The reflexive pronoun is *yourself* in a sentence **only** if it has a YOU-subject ~~or if the sentence is a command~~.
    (c) In idiomatic expressions such as *stub one's toe, keep one's mouth shut*, the pronoun *your* occurs **only** if the sentence has a YOU-subject ~~or if the sentence is a command~~.
    (d) In tags, the pronoun is *you* only if the sentence has a YOU-subject ~~or if the sentence is a command~~.

This description is simpler than the one in (7) since it eliminates disjunctive conditions. But simplicity comes at a hefty price: (8) contains a contradiction. The statement in (8a) says imperative sentences have no subjects but (8b) says they do. Both statements are supported by empirical facts. Since no YOU-subject is pronounced, (8a) is justified; but the fact that a YOU-subject makes itself felt in the structure of the rest of the sentence supports (8b). An imperative sentence is like the figurine of a tennis player in action with the racket missing: every detail of the body posture suggests the image of a racket being swung – yet, the hands are empty.

As noted above, theories must fit reality into the framework of rational human thought and human rationality does not tolerate contradictions. Thus, we cannot put up with a description like (8) that says that imperative sentences both do and do not have subjects. We have reached an impasse: a conflict between generality and consistency. The description in (7) is free of contradictions but is not general; (8) is more general but is contradictory.

Is there a way to formulate an account that is both general and consistent? We will postpone trying to answer this question until Section 3.3 so that we can first consider the ways in which we deal with contradictions outside syntax, in everyday life.

3.2 COPING WITH CONTRADICTIONS

For an example, take the statement in (1).

(1) *Lizards are green and brown.*

On the face of it, (1) is an irresolvable contradiction: what is green cannot be brown and what is brown cannot be green. One reaction to a contradictory statement like (1) is to reject it.

One might reject the entire proposition because it cannot possibly be true; or one might reject one of the two contradictory predicates as untrue. Another reaction might be to accept the statement on grounds that contradictions are tolerable as long as they are a limited phenomenon. Accepting a contradiction on a limited basis would mean viewing it as a statement type that is legitimate with respect to, say, colours but not other attributes, such as shape or location.

More productively, we may attempt to resolve the paradox by re-interpreting it as non-contradictory. There are two basic ways of achieving this. Since a statement is contradictory if its two predicates say contradictory things about a single entity, it can be resolved in either of two ways:

- by reinterpreting the two predicates as one non-contradictory assertion that is thus applicable to a single entity without creating a conflict;
- by reinterpreting the one entity as two entities, with each predicate applying to only one of the two.

Let us consider each option in more detail. To begin with the first: how could two contradictory predicates be re-interpreted as a single self-consistent one? There are three ways that come to mind. First, it may be demonstrated that the two predicates that are seemingly at odds are actually synonyms: they say the same thing. Take for example the statement in (2).

(2) *Jim lives at 234 Plum Street and at 69 Cherry Street.*

Assuming that people generally have a single residential address, this is a contradiction. However, the contradiction is resolved if it turns out that Jim's house has two entrances, one from Plum Street and the other from Cherry Street. If so, the two contradictory predicates are referentially synonymous: they zero in on the same referent.

Second, contradictory predicates may be reinterpreted as a single consistent one if we take the intended meaning to fall between those of the two predicates. Take (1) again.

(1) /repeated/
    Lizards are green and brown.

This seemingly contradictory statement is reconciled if interpreted to refer to a colour that falls between green and brown.

Third, contradictory predicates may be dealt with by ranking the two. This means that both predicates are kept on the docket as valid but one is given priority with the other temporarily suppressed: the importance of one of them overshadows the other. An example, involving multiple predicates that are incompatible, is in (3).

(3) *Work eight hours every day, study for six hours, exercise for two hours, and sleep for ten hours.*

Given that a day has only 24 hours, the four desiderata are in conflict. A resolution is to give temporary priority to one over the others on any given day.

Besides re-interpreting the conflicting predicates as a single consistent one, the other way of re-interpreting contradictory statements is by viewing the single entity of which the contradictory predicates as stated as two things. There are at least four ways of doing so. First, the contradiction melts away if it turns out that the name designating the single entity in actuality refers to more than one thing: the word is homonymous. Take (2) again. Rather than showing that the two addresses refer to the same building, one may be able to show that there are two people named Jim involved, one living on Plum Street and the other on Cherry Street. If so, there is no contradiction.

For a second way of splitting the single entity into two, let us take another look at (1), about lizards being both green and brown. We may interpret the statement as saying that *some parts* of the bodies of lizards are green and other parts are brown. Or, third, we may interpret the statement as saying that *some types* of lizards are green and other types are brown. And, fourth, we may interpret the statement as saying that lizards look green *under some conditions* – perhaps in bright sunshine, or at some stages in their life – while they look brown under other conditions.

Here is a summary of the ways of conflict resolution discussed above:

(4) (a) REINTERPRETING TWO CONTRADICTORY PREDICATES AS ONE SELF-CONSISTENT PREDICATE
   (i) by showing that the two predicates are **synonymous**;
   (ii) by showing that the predicates jointly refer to a property **falling between** the two;
   (iii) by **ranking** them so that at a given point, only one is taken to apply.

(b) REINTERPRETING THE ONE ENTITY AS TWO ENTITIES
   (iv) by interpreting the name of the single entity as **homonymous** and thus referring to two distinct entities;
   (v) by interpreting the name of the single entity as a cover term for **two subparts** of that entity;
   (vi) by interpreting the name of the single entity as a cover term for **two subtypes** of that entity;
   (vii) by interpreting the statement as saying that two things about a single entity apply **under different conditions**.

The last option represents a particularly fruitful way of resolving contradictions. What it means is that we relativize the validity of each of the contradictory predicates to certain conditions: under one set of conditions, one of the two predicates applies and under another set of conditions, the other does. Neither predicate is thrown out as invalid: both are retained but, depending on the conditions, one is allowed to outweigh the other. Is a cone circular or triangular? To say that it is both circular and triangular is contradictory; but to say that, viewed from one angle, it is circular and viewed from another angle, it is triangular, is not.

Physicists in the early twentieth century came to such a conclusion when they encountered a contradiction regarding the basic nature of electrons: are they particles or waves? Since a particle occupies one point in time and space while a wave is spread out in both dimensions, one cannot maintain both analyses at the same time. Here is how the paradox has been resolved in quantum physics:

> Wave and particle behavior mutually exclude each other. The classical physicist would say: if two descriptions are mutually exclusive, then at least one of them must be wrong. The quantum physicist would say: whether an object behaves as a particle or as a wave depends **on your choice of experimental arrangement for looking at it**. He will not deny that particle and wave behavior are mutually exclusive but will assert that both are necessary for the full understanding of the properties of the object.
>
> (Pais 1994: 44; emphasis added)

Armed with an understanding of how contradictory statements may dealt with in general, we will now return to the problem of the paradoxical imperative sentences.

3.3 Imperatives in English: solutions

In Section 3.1, we saw that there was a conflict regarding the presence versus absence of the YOU-subject in the syntactic structure of English imperative sentences: there was evidence pointing in both directions. But to say that YOU is both present and absent is a contradiction – a logical pattern barred by human rationality. In Section 3.2, we surveyed the ways in which contradictions could in principle be eliminated. Let us now see if any of these solutions apply to the case of imperatives.

The three options of re-interpreting the contradictory predicates do not appear promising in this case. First, the assertions that the YOU-subject is present and that it is not present cannot be shown to be synonymous. A second option for resolving the contradiction would require us to re-interpret the predicates by recognizing an in-between point between the two predicates. However, presence is not a gradable notion: we cannot get out of the problem by saying that YOU is present but only to an extent. The third option, that of ranking the two predicates, does not appear helpful, either.

Thus, our options are limited to the four strategies that keep the contradictory predicate unchanged but attempt to re-interpret the paradoxical entity as referring to two different entities, so that each of the predicates applies to one only thing. Two of the analyses available in the literature do indeed solve the problem by 'splitting the entity' albeit in different ways.

Let us first take the Standard Theory of Transformational Generative Grammar (TG). Two assumptions of this framework are relevant. First, as in Government and Binding Theory mentioned in Section 1 – multiple levels of syntactic representations are assumed: starting with an underlying representation, structures are converted into others in the course of syntactic derivations by transformational rules. These rules add, delete, replace and move constituents and thus reshape underlying structures into surface representations. Second, it is assumed that all syntactic constituents must have phonological form on all levels: they must be pronounceable.

Given these assumptions, the transformational account of imperative sentences runs like this: the YOU-subject, complete with phonological form, is present in the initial, underlying structure and, once it has done its job – that is, it has provided the proper condition for the rules that yield the right reflexive pronouns and the right personal pronouns in idioms and tags as in (3) of Section 3.1 – it is deleted. Thus, the both-present-and-absent conflict is solved by saying that this constituent is first present and is subsequently expunged. This rule is paraphrased in (1).

(1) In English imperative sentences, the YOU-subject is present in the underlying structure but, since it is deleted at the end of the syntactic derivation, it is absent in surface structure.

The underlying and surface structures for *Love yourself!*, mediated by the reflexivization and YOU-deletion transformations, are given in (2).

(2)   (a) underlying structure   (b) surface structure

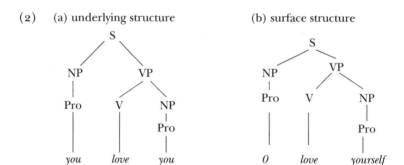

Another syntactic framework called **Head-driven Phrase Structure Grammar** (HPSG) does not have this kind of solution available to it: the framework posits a single level of syntactic representation and thus there is no syntactic derivation in the course of which a constituent can first be present and then be deleted. However, an alternative solution is made possible because HPSG also dispenses with the other assumption of traditional transformational grammar: that syntactic constituents necessarily come equipped with phonological form. In TG, the subject of a command sentence 'starts out' as any other syntactic constituent: complete with phonetic form, and then it is wiped out by a rule. Because a constituent's syntactic and phonological identities are assumed to be inseparable, when the syntactic presence of the YOU-subject is needed, its phonological realization also has to be present; and when its phonological realization needs to be got rid of, the entire syntactic constituent must be deleted. In HPSG in turn, syntactic and phonological identities are separable: some syntactic constituents are allowed to be 'silent' to begin with. After all, there is no evidence for the presence of the phonological form of YOU in imperative sentences, only for its syntactic characteristics: that it is a singular or plural second person pronoun. The relevant part of the imperative rule in this framework can be paraphrased as follows (see Sag *et al.* 2003: 216–18):

(3) If a sentence is a command, its YOU-subject does not have a phonological form.

Both TG and HPSG 'split' the recalcitrant YOU-subject in some way. In TG, the split is between representations: in the underlying representation, YOU is present while in surface structure, it is not. In HPSG, the constituent does not change its 'mode of existence': it has a firm syntactic presence. But HPSG categorizes the subject of imperatives as a special subtype of syntactic constituent: the kind that does not have a sound form.

Here is a summary of the problem and the two solutions:

(4) (a) Contradiction:
- In English command sentences, a YOU-subject is **present**.
- In English command sentences, a YOU-subject is **absent**.
(b) Resolutions:
(i) **Transformational analysis**
The YOU-subject of command sentences has a single, undividable identity that includes syntactic and phonological properties. It is present in underlying structure and absent in surface structure.
(ii) **Head-driven Phrase Structure analysis**
The YOU-subject of command sentences has a syntactic identity but no phonological one. Thus, it is present as a syntactic entity but absent as a phonetic form.

TG's resolution of the conflict is an instance of strategy (4vii) in Section 3.2, which appeals to viewing the paradoxical entity under different conditions: just as a lizard may be 'both green and brown' if it is green in its early life but turning brown later, the YOU-subject is said to be present in the initial period of its derivational career but absent later. HPSG's solution is of type (4v) in Section 3.2: the YOU is conceived as consisting of two parts – its syntactic self and its phonological self. With this split, the contradiction is eliminated since the contradictory predicates 'present' and 'absent' are now stated for different facets of the YOU-subject: it is present as a syntactic constituent but absent as a phonological one.

Note, however, that each analysis requires the positing of a powerful descriptive device. In TG, this descriptive device is multiple levels of syntactic representation: YOU is allowed 'to perform a disappearing act' so that it is there on one level but not on another level. In HPSG, the powerful descriptive device is sound less syntactic constituents: words that are allowed not to have sound form.

If these conceptual devices are left uncurbed, they will lead to over-generalizations: both would allow for any syntactic constituent to remain unpronounced. But this assumption clashes with the criterion of empirical truth: it is in violation of how language really is. The syntactically present YOU of *Go home!* may remain unpronounced; but the YOU of the sentence *You went home* may not. In general, words must be pronounced if they are to convey a meaning: if I want to say *Herman ate the cabbage soup with relish*, I cannot just say *Herman ate the ____ with relish* and expect 'cabbage soup' to be understood.

The way TG attempted to curb the potentially run away assumption of the deletability of words is by placing constraints on deletion rules. One such constraint is that the constituent to be deleted must be a 'constant' – that is an individual word rather than an entire category. HPSG in turn needs to place constraints on words allowed to have syntactic presence but no sound form.

This example illustrates the tension among the requirements of empirical truth, generality, consistency and simplicity. Note that, as pointed out above, the syntactic structure of a command sentence is not self-contradictory when described all by itself; the paradox arises only when we attempt to subsume it under a generalization that also holds for other sentences of the language. It is when we attempt a generalization that it becomes clear that the form of command sentences is out of line with other data and thus an account that is both general and consistent is not possible. In order to resolve the ensuing contradiction, we broaden our conceptual apparatus by finding ways to 'split' the offending entity so that the contradictory assertions can apply to different entities. But were this newly created powerful conceptual tool allowed to apply across the board, it would lead to a clash with empirical adequacy and it needs to be restricted.

Indeed, most – or perhaps all – proposals in syntactic theory either put forth a new conceptual device to accommodate contradictions, or attempt to curb contradiction-accommodating devices. The overall descriptive apparatus must be strong enough to accommodate some types of contradictions that do occur and exclude those that do not.

Let us summarize so far. The central question that we are addressing in Section 3 is why there are different syntactic theories. In (5) are listed the answers that have emerged.

(5) (a) In describing syntactic structure, the four criteria of
      scientific descriptions – truth, generality, consistency and

simplicity – may be at odds with each other. In particular, the attempt to **generalize** about facts may lead to **contradictory** statements.

(b) A description that predicates contradictory properties for a single entity may be altogether **rejected**, or **accepted** as a limited phenomenon, or **resolved** by re-interpretation. Re-interpretation can be achieved in two basic ways:

    (i) By finding a way to show that **the two contradictory predicates** actually amount to a single self-consistent one. This can be done by showing that the two predicates are actually **synonymous**, or that they are meant to describe a property that **falls between** the two, or that they may be **ranked** with one of them temporarily suppressed.

    (ii) By finding a way to show that **the one entity** for which the contradictory properties are predicated is in fact two different entities. This is so if the single entity's name is **homonymous**, or if that entity consists of **different parts**, or it has **different sub types**, or if it can be viewed under **different conditions**.

(c) Conceptual devices introduced to deal with contradictory evidence need to be **constrained** so as to sanction only those types of contradiction that the facts of actual languages pose but not ones that do not occur.

(d) **Differences among syntactic theories** are due, at least in part, to the employment of alternative ways of dealing with contradictions. Since there are limits to the logically possible range of these strategies, syntactic theories are amenable to a systematic overview based on what conflict-resolving strategies they resort to.

3.4 WH-QUESTIONS IN ENGLISH: PROBLEMS AND SOLUTIONS

The example of English imperative sentences has illustrated one type of contradiction in syntactic description – that between a constituent appearing to be both present and absent. Other conflicts may emerge regarding syntactic relations among words.

Normally, we would expect that if a syntactic relation holds between two words, all other syntactic relations also hold within that pair. However, this is not always the case: a word may be connected to one word by one syntactic relation but to another word by another syntactic relation.

Consider the ways in which the wh-words in (1) are related to other words in the sentence:

(1) (a) ***Who(m)*** *did you see in the bar?*
    (b) ***What*** *should we choose?*

(c) ***Where*** *are the porcupines?*
(d) ***When*** *is Jason going to arrive?*

In each sentence of (1), the question pronoun stands in the beginning of the sentences directly preceding the auxiliary. This is surprising in view of the fact that question pronouns are selected as complements of the main verb and that verb complements in sentences other than questions are adjacent to the main verb. This is shown in (2).

(2) (a) *I saw **Jason** in the bar.*
(b) *We should choose **a parrot**.*
(c) *The porcupines are **behind the barn**.*
(d) *Jason is going to arrive **on Wednesday**.*

To be sure, question pronouns do occur adjacent to the verb in so-called echo-questions (questions that simply ask for the repetition of a sentence part that was either not fully heard or that sounded unlikely), such as in (3) (all capitals stand for emphatic stress).

(3) (a) *You saw **WHO(M)** in the bar?*
(b) *We should choose **WHAT**?*
(c) *The porcupines are **WHERE**?*
(d) *Jason is going to arrive **WHEN**?*

But in regular wh-questions, the question pronouns must be separated from the verb.

That the pronouns *whom, what, where* and *when* are indeed verb complements is shown not only by their meaning but also by the fact that their presence and their form match the syntactic selectional constraints of verbs. For example, in (1a) the verb *see* is transitive, requiring a direct object; and this object is supplied by the object form *who(m)*. The question pronoun *whom* would be ungrammatical if the sentence had an intransitive verb, such as **Whom (did you) stand in the bar?* Similarly, **Where did you see in the bar?* is ungrammatical since *see* needs an object. Given that question pronouns are verb complements, they seem displaced in their pre-auxiliary position: they should be adjacent to their selectors rather than separated from them.

At first, the following conflict arises:

(4) (a) **Syntactic relations** of non-subject question pronouns link them to the main verb.
(b) **Syntactic relations** of non-subject question pronouns link them to the auxiliary.

But this conflict is easily resolved if we note that the syntactic relations mentioned in (4a) and (4b) are different: question pronouns are linked to the verb by selection and to the auxiliary by linear order. Thus, by recognizing different types of syntactic relations, the conflict is resolved as follows:

(5) (a) **Selectional relations** of non-subject question pronouns link them to the main verb.

(b) **Linear relations** of non-subject question pronouns link them to the auxiliary.

Even though (5) is an obvious solution of the paradox in (4), it may not be easy to implement in syntactic descriptions. The statement in (5) requires that selectional and order relations be recognized as distinct relations so that there is room for the two to go separate ways. This is a considerable problem in the Standard Theory of Transformational Grammar. As we saw in the example of imperative sentences, in this approach the syntactic and phonological properties of syntactic constituents are inseparable: they are two sides of a single entity like two sides of a sheet of paper. The inseparability of syntactic and phonological properties is assumed to hold not only for constituents but also for the relations among them: the syntactic relation of selection and the phonological relation of temporal precedence are also seen as inseparable: two sides of the same single relation.

Thus, in this theory, the fact that the question pronouns are selected by the verb cannot be stated without also saying that they are ordered next to the verb. But this leads to a contradiction:

(6) (a) Verb complements (including non-subject question pronouns) are both selected by and **immediately follow** the auxiliary-verb complex.

(b) Question pronouns **immediately precede** the auxiliary-verb complex.

In order to resolve this conflict, a rule needs to be posited which, after the question pronouns have been selected, moves them from the verb to pre-auxiliary position. The new account keeps (6a) but replaces (6b):

(7) (a) Verb complements (including non-subject question pronouns) are both selected by and immediately follow the auxiliary-verb complex.

(b) Verb complements that are question pronouns are moved from the position following the auxiliary-verb complex to the position immediately preceding it.

Thus, just as in the case of the YOU-subject of commands discussed above, two rules must be assumed to apply at two different points of the derivation, with the second partially cancelling the output of the first. The first rule ((7a)) selects question pronouns as complements of the verb and at the same time cannot but order them immediately following the verb. The second rule

((7b)) then serves as a corrective step to move the question pronouns to the position immediately preceding the auxiliary. The account says that question pronouns are 'both after the auxiliary-verb complex and before it', but the contradiction is resolved by the first order holding in underlying structure and the second in surface structure – that is, under different conditions.

The transformational solution to the contradiction in (6) is based on the same assumptions as the solution to the problem of YOU-subjects in imperative sentences discussed in the preceding section. Here is the comparison between how TG accounts for imperative subjects and wh-words. In this framework, once constituents are selected, they will also be pronounced unless they are deleted; and if they are selected by a constituent, they have to be ordered relative to that constituent unless they are moved. Because of the inseparability of syntactic and phonological properties of constituents in TG, when selectional and phonological behaviour part ways, the grammar needs to first assign the wrong phonetic form – whether segmental or linear – to a constituent in order to account for its selectional relations. In a second step, it needs to correct the phonological side either by deleting the entire constituent (the YOU-subject) to make sure it is not pronounced, or by moving the entire constituent (the question pronoun) to make sure it is pronounced where it should be pronounced. Both solutions are instances of the type of conflict resolution that reconciles two contradictory properties of an entity by saying that one holds under certain conditions, and the other holds under other conditions ((4vii) of Section 3.2). The different levels in the syntactic derivation represent the different conditions.

3.5 A TYPOLOGY OF CONFLICTS

So far we have seen two kinds of conflict in syntax: in the case of the YOU-subject of imperatives, the conflict pertains to the presence versus absence of a constituent; in the case of wh-questions, it has to do with the relations between constituents.

Additional types of conflicts arise regarding whether a constituent is one or more than one, and whether two constituents are the same or different. Regarding the former kind of conflict involving quantity, consider examples such as in (1).

(1) (a) *I saw **five ripe cherries** on the tree.*
    (b) *He dislikes **the green hat.***
    (c) ***The bread in the fridge** is still fresh.*

Are the expressions in bold 'one' or 'more than one'? On the one hand, they are 'more than one': they consist of more than one word. The syntactic separability of the words in these sequences can be readily shown by three kinds of evidence. First, some of the words can occur without the others in the same context. For example, one could say *I saw cherries on the tree*, where *cherries* occurs without *five* and *ripe*. Second, even if they all occur together in a sentence, some of them may be linearly separated from each other, such as in **The bread** *is still fresh* **in the fridge**. Third, notice that the nouns in these phrases are replaceable by the pronoun *one* with the other members of the sequence staying in place; for example, *He dislikes the green* **one**. Thus, the bold words in (1) are separate syntactic units.

However, each bold sequence of words in the sentences of (1) is also **one** rather than more than one. This is shown by the fact that if a definite pronoun is used in reference to these sequences of words, it will have to replace all the words together: one can say *I saw them on the tree.* but not **I saw five them on the tree* or **I saw five ripe them on the tree.* Also, the word sequences can occur in different parts of the sentence as a unit: *the green hat* is the object in (1b) but it can also be a subject as in *The green hat looks good on you.* Thus, the whole expression is both one and more than one.

One solution to this paradox is provided by the very concept of part–whole relations: **partonomy**. This conceptual device legitimizes something being both one and many if it is a whole that consists of parts. Thus, each of the structures *five ripe cherries, the green hat* and *the bread in the fridge* is analysed as a single noun phrase consisting of a sequence of words.

A somewhat different solution is offered by dependency grammars, such as Word Grammar. As we saw in Section 1 (see example (10)), in this syntactic framework, the only wholes admitted are sentences and the only parts are words: there are no intermediate-size phrase-level and clause-level constituents. What corresponds to a phrase in dependency grammars is a head constituent and its dependents which are required to be adjacent to it. For example, in a noun phrase *five ripe cherries, cherries* is the head and *five* and *ripe* are its dependents. Words in a constituent structure representation form a unit because they are viewed as equal parts dominated by a single whole: a phrasal category. In dependency grammars in turn, words form a unit if they are unequal, with one of them a head and the others its dependents, which are assumed to stick with the head. The operative relationship in the first instance is the 'vertical' relation of partonomy; in the second instance, it is the 'horizontal' relation of **dependency**. If sequences of words are analysed as parts of a whole, they can be jointly called up by reference to the whole. If, in turn, sequences of words are analysed as a head and its dependents, they can be jointly called up by reference to the head; the dependents will follow.

Here is the summary of the problem and its alternative solutions as stated for the examples in (1):

(2) (a) CONTRADICTION:
- The sequence Article & Numeral & Adjective & Noun & Prepositional Phrase consists of **more than one** constituent.
- The sequence Article & Numeral & Adjective & Noun & Prepositional Phrase is **one** constituent.

    (b) ALTERNATIVE RESOLUTIONS:
>   (i) Partonomy: The article, numeral, adjective, noun and prepositional phrase are parts that together make a whole phrase. The parts are in some ways independent, but in other ways, they 'do' what the whole 'does'.
>   (ii) Dependency: The noun is the head, the article, numeral, adjective and prepositional phrase are the dependents. The parts are in some ways independent, but in other ways, the dependents 'do' what the head 'does'.

The examples in (1) posed a conflict in quantity. Conflicts regarding quality can be exemplified by considering nouns and pronouns. Are they the same or are they different? The answer is: they are both the same and different – an apparent contradiction. English nouns and pronouns are similar in that they can show gender, number and case distinctions; but they are also different in that nouns can take articles and adjectives while pronouns cannot.

Similarly to how the concepts of partonomy and dependency serve to resolve some conflicts related to quantity, taxonomy steps in to resolve some conflicts related to quality. Taxonomy allows us to say that things are the same in some respects but different in other respects. This is shown in (3).

    (3) (a) CONTRADICTION:
>   Nouns and pronouns are both the same and not the same.

        (b) RESOLUTION:
>   Nouns and pronouns are the same in some ways and not the same in other ways.

All three of these concepts – partonomy, dependency and taxonomy – amount to legitimizing certain kinds of contradictions by saying that things can have contradictory quantitative and qualitative characteristics viewed from different angles (see (4vii) in Section 3.2).

Even though these three concepts are contradiction-resolving devices, they may themselves be complex if not outright contradictory. Sometimes a constituent is a **part of two distinct wholes**; and a constituent may be a **token of two different types**.

The former is exemplified by the sentence *Susan expected him to succeed* analysed in (8)–(10) of Section 1 of this chapter. In this sentence, a noun phrase – *him* – shows double allegiance: it seems to be both the object of the main verb *expected* and the subject of the subordinate verb *succeed*. The three approaches illustrated in Section 1 deal with this fact differently. In Word Grammar, multiple motherhood is simply accepted as legitimate: a single diagram includes arrows originating both from *expected* and from *succeed* pointing at *him* as their shared dependent. Relational Grammar represents the two functions of *him* on two different strata of the same diagram, while Government and Binding has shows them on different diagrams each representing a different level of syntactic derivation.

The second kind of complexity mentioned above – something being a subtype of different types – is exemplified by numerals in Russian. As shown by Bernard Comrie (1989: 107–10), several numerals in Russian straddle the line between noun and adjective. For example, the numeral *dva* 'two' agrees with the head noun in gender as adjectives do; but it is unlike adjectives in that it requires the (singular) genitive on the head noun – 'two of sheep'. This latter characteristic in turn ties this numeral to nouns since a quantity noun, such as 'flock', would also govern the genitive on the head noun – 'flock of sheep'. Thus, the Russian numeral 'two' is a subtype of both adjectives and nouns.

Are such partonomic and taxonomic patterns – a constituent being a part of two wholes or being a token of two types – just complex patterns or are they outright contradictory? What is the difference between complexity and contradiction?

If a description is complex, this means that it fails in regard to the criterion of simplicity. If a description is contradictory, this means it fails in regard to the criterion of consistency. Complexities are bothersome but tolerable since they can be accommodated within the limits of rational human thinking. For example, the sound effect of a million hands clapping is more complex than the sound of two hands clapping but it is nonetheless readily imaginable. But what about the sound of one hand clapping, mentioned in a Zen koan? This hypothetical event does not only stretch our rationality – it defeats it. The very definition of clapping excludes the option of one hand producing it and thus the assertion that one hand can clap is contradictory.

Complexities and contradictions are distinguishable only relative to the assumptions that we make. What is contradictory within one conceptual framework because it conflicts with the basic assumptions of the framework may be consistent in another framework whose basic assumptions are less restrictive. Thus, if we assume a partonomic framework where every part must belong to only a single whole, a part belonging to two wholes is contradictory; but if 'multiple motherhood' is viewed as legitimate, there is no conflict: examples of it will be viewed as complex but not contradictory.

The same consideration applies to other complex syntactic phenomena, such as when a constituent selectionally depends on more than one constituent, or when a syntactic structure is associated with more than one meaning or more than one sound form. Depending on the assumptions we make, these patterns are either complex or outright contradictory. Contradictions can soften into complexities and complexities can stiffen into contradictions depending on the assumptions that we make.

Since a contradiction involves incompatible predicates stated on a single entity, the crucial assumptions that determine whether something is a contradiction or just a complexity have to do with two things:

- what counts as a single entity?
- what count as incompatible predicates?

The notion '**incompatible predicates**' is clear: A and not-A cannot both be true at the same time and in the same respect. But the notion of a single entity is much more negotiable. For example, a very natural assumption to make is that a sentence makes a single entity. Thus, if the properties of a single sentence are incompatible, that is a contradiction. Since it holds within a single sentence, we call it a **syntagmatic** contradiction.

A second relevant assumption that one might make is that a language is a single entity. Under this assumption, if otherwise similar sentences of a single language show contradictory properties, that is a contradiction. But if a language is not assumed to be a unified entity, non-uniform patterns among sentences only amount to complexities. Contradictions that hold across sentences of a language are called **paradigmatic**.

Third, if we take every language to be a separate entity, cross-linguistic differences are complexities but not contradictions; but if we assume that there is a single entity, Human Language, that unites in itself all languages of the world, differences across languages turn into contradictions on the **cross-linguistic** level.

So far in this chapter, the following kinds of conflicts – contradictions and complexities – have been discussed:

- A constituent is both present and absent in the same sentence (the YOU-subject of English command sentences).
- A constituent is syntactically related to two different constituents in the same sentence (question pronouns in English wh-questions).
- A constituent is both one and many (noun phrase).
- Two constituents are both the same and not the same (nouns and pronouns).
- A constituent is part of two distinct wholes (*him* in *Susan expected him to succeed*).
- A constituent is a subtype of two distinct types (Russian 'two').

There are also others. In (4) are shown ten types of contradictions and complexities that one might encounter in syntax, including the six mentioned above. The left column indicates what is expected and the right column, what might be found.

(4)
(a) CONTRADICTIONS
  1. PRESENCE

Expected:	Observed:
if **X is present**,	**X is present**
then not also:	and
X is not present	**X is not present**

2. QUANTITY

Expected:	Observed:
if **X is one**,	**X is one**
then not also:	and
X **is more than one**	**X is more than one**

3. QUALITY

Expected:	Observed:
if **X is the same as A**,	**X is the same as A**
then not also:	and
X is not the same as A	**X is not the same as A**

4. SELECTIONAL RELATIONS

Expected:	Observed:
if **X depends on A**,	**X depends on A**
then not also:	and
X does not depend on A	**X does not depend on A**

5. LINEAR RELATIONS

(i) Expected: / Observed:

if **X is adjacent to A**,	**X is adjacent to A**
then not also:	and
X is not adjacent to A	**X is not adjacent to A**

(ii) Expected: / Observed:

X precedes A,	**X precedes A**
then not also:	and
X does not precede A	**X does not precede A**

6. SYMBOLIC CORRESPONDENCE RELATIONS

Expected:	Observed:
if **X symbolically corresponds to A**,	**X symbolically corresponds to A**
then not also:	and
X does not symbolically correspond to A	**X does not symbolically correspond to A**

(b) COMPLEXITIES

7. MULTIPLE WHOLES TO A PART

Expected:	Observed:
if **X is a part of A**,	**X is a part of A**
then not also:	and
X is a part of B	**X is a part of B**

(where A and B are not in a whole–part relation)

8. MULTIPLE TYPES TO A SUBTYPE

Expected:	Observed:
if **X is a subtype of A**,	**X is a subtype of A**
then not also:	and
X is a subtype of B	**X is a subtype of B**

(where A and B are not in a type-token relation)

9. MULTIPLE SELECTORS TO A SELECTEE

Expected:	Observed:
if **X selectionally depends on A**,	**X selectionally depends on A**
then not also:	and
X selectionally depends on B	**X selectionally depends on B**

10. MULTIPLE SYMBOLIC CORRESPONDENCE RELATIONS

Expected:	Observed:
if **X symbolically corresponds to A**,	**X symbolically corresponds both to A**
then not also:	and
X symbolically corresponds to B	**X symbolically corresponds to B**

Notice that some of these patterns may apply either syntagmatically or paradigmatically. Take (1) PRESENCE. The YOU-subject in English imperative constructions plays 'hide and seek' in two ways. As we saw earlier, for an imperative sentence with a reflexive pronoun, such as *Don't hurt yourself*, there is evidence that the YOU-subject is both present and absent in the syntactic structure of the same sentence. It is present in the sense that it licenses the reflexive pronoun *yourself*, but it is absent in that it is not pronounced. Here, the paradox of both-present-and-absent applies to the same sentence, that is, **syntagmatically**. But notice also that the YOU-subject has the option of being present: both *Sit down* and *You sit down* are well-formed commands. Thus, the both-present-and-absent paradox also applies across sentences (present in one sentence but not in another), that is, **paradigmatically**.

While the patterns listed under 1–6 in (4) are true contradictions when they hold syntagmatically – that is, for one and the same sentence – they fade into complexities when they apply across sentences. It is logically impossible for an element to be both present and absent at the same time in the same sentence; but it is not logically impossible for it to be present in one version of a sentence and absent in another version. Similarly, the complexities listed under 7–10 in (4) lose some of their force when they apply across sentences. For example, to see the same constituent dependent on two selectors at the same time in the same sentence is complex; but to see the same constituent dependent on alternative selectors in different sentences is less so.

4 Conclusions

In terms of the characterization given in Section 1, the syntax of a sentence may be simply described by formulating a list of syntactic categories and specifying selectional constraints, linear order constraints and constraints on symbolic correspondence relations. It is therefore startling to see the large variety of syntactic frameworks adopting different approaches. If syntax is so simple – then why is it so complicated?

The answer that we have seen emerge is that there are conflicts among the goals that syntacticians adopt in analysing sentences. As we attempt descriptions that are both true and general, we lose out on simplicity or consistency. These conflicts may be dealt with in various ways and this is one reason for the multiplicity of approaches to syntactic description.

The role of contradictions in scientific research is concisely summarized by Albert Einstein (1950: 280):

> Science forces us to create new ideas, new theories. Their aim is to break down the wall of contradictions which frequently blocks the way of scientific progress. All the essential ideas in science were born in a dramatic conflict between reality and our attempts at understanding.

Some examples of such conflicts and their alternative resolutions have already been given. The next chapters will provide more detailed discussions of alternative analyses of selected syntactic constructions that pose complications or conflicts.

Notes

1   Preliminaries

- Figure (8) is reprinted by permission of Pearson Education Inc., Upper Saddle River, NJ.
- The proceedings of the 1979 conference on syntactic approaches mentioned in this section have been published in Moravcsik and Wirth 1980.
- For points of agreement among linguists of various persuasions, see Hudson 1981.
- For a relatively theory-neutral approach to describing syntax, see R.M.W. Dixon's Basic Linguistic Theory (Dixon 1997: 128–38; Dryer 2005). For more detail concerning the theory-neutral approach described here, see Moravcsik 2006.
- Dependency Grammar, Construction Grammar and Optimality Theory will be discussed in Chapter 6 along with various versions of Transformational Grammar. On Usage-Based Models, see Barlow and Kemmer 2000.

- More will be said on constructions such as *Susan expected him to succeed* in Section 3.3. of Chapter 2.

2.1.1   Shared goals

The ban on contradictory statements goes back to Aristotle; for example, 'It is impossible for the same attribute at once to belong and not to belong to the same thing and in the same relation . . . This is the most certain of all principles' (The Metaphysics IV. iii. 1005b). For interesting discussions of contradictions as problem-solving devices in science, see Popper 1962 and Laudan 1977. Philosophers of science of the past couple of decades have actually relaxed the requirement of consistency for scientific accounts and have recognized the legitimacy of contradictory statements in limited ways; see for example Rescher 1987, Meheus 2002, Kertész 2004b (especially 301–21, 357–65).

2.2   Actual differences

For a proposal regarding the interaction of conceptual and social factors in scientific theorizing, including a summary of the relevant literature, see Kertész 2004a, especially chapters 4–7.

3.1 and 3.3   Imperatives in English

The TG analysis of English imperative sentences is based on Postal 1964.

3.2   Coping with contradictions

- I am grateful to Susan Kövesi Domokos for the example of the shape of the cone illustrating the significance of point of view in classifying things.
- On conflict resolution in syntax, see also Moravcsik 1993.
  A somewhat similar discussion of contradictions and the typology of their possible resolutions in found in Goodman 1978: 109–40. Conflicts that arise in domains other than science – such as in interpersonal relations, in societies, in economics and in international relations – have been widely analysed in the past 50 years; for a small sample of the relevant literature, see Coombs and Avrunin 1988; Jeong 1999; and Mayer 2000. On the related psychological concept of cognitive dissonance, see Festinger 1957; Schachter & Gazzaniga 1989; Thagard 2000. On conflict resolution in politics, society and individual life, see Deutsch and Coleman 2000; Jackson 1999; Christie *et al.* 2001; and the *Conflict Resolution Quarterly* – the publication of the Association for Conflict Resolution.

3.4   Wh-questions in English: problems and solutions

For the transformational analysis wh-questions in terms of the Standard Theory, see Stockwell *et al.* 1973: 619–20.

3.5   A typology of conflicts

- In logic, a distinction is made between contradictory and contrary statements. Two statements are contradictory if both cannot be true at the same time or cannot both be false. By this criterion, *All my sisters live in Chicago* and *Some of my sisters do not live in Chicago* are contradictory statements. Two statements are in turn contrary if both cannot be true together but they can both be false, such as *All my sisters live in Chicago* and *None of my sisters live in Chicago*. In this book, however, the terms contradiction and contradictory will be used loosely without distinguishing the two kinds of oppositions.
- On Word Grammar, see Hudson 1984, 1990, 1996.

Exercises

1. Question words are not the only constituents that are sentence-initial even though their selectional relations tie them to the verb. The same wh-words are also sentence-initial when they function as relative pronouns, such as in *the artist **whom** we invited,* and so may be noun phrases that are emphasized, such as in ***Tom** I have not seen in a while* or ***This** I can believe.* What might be the reason for this positional similarity between question pronouns, relative pronouns and emphatic noun phrases?

2. As was seen in Section 3.5, sequences of words may act like a single unit such as a noun phrase. Which word sequences in the following sentences can be shown to form phrases – whether noun phrases or other kinds? What is the evidence?

 (a) *Last night there was a thunderstorm.*
 (b) *The money is lost that I won in the lottery.*
 (c) *The company fired six people.*
 (d) *The radio stations in the area did not broadcast the concert.*

3. As was also discussed in Section 3.5, words may be similar in some ways and different in other ways. Consider the following English words:

 (a) *the*
 (b) *a(n)*
 (c) *this*
 (d) *these*
 (e) *that*
 (f) *those*

Which of these form a single category and why?

4. Check sentences 16–18 in the six languages given in the Appendix. How are question words ordered in each?

5. Find an example outside language of a collection of objects or people that can be considered both 'many' and 'one'.

6. Imagine that you are working for a company and you and your supervisor have a conflict. How would you apply the conflict-resolution methods surveyed in Section 3.2 to this situation?

Chapter Two

Alternative Analyses of Syntactic Structures

It is a rare thinker who keeps two contradictory thoughts simultaneously in mind; yet this is precisely what is often needed to get all the truth.

(de Waal 2001: 7)

1 Preliminaries

This chapter will discuss two syntactic patterns that have given rise to alternative analyses in the literature. In each case, the core of the problem is contradictory or complex data compromising either the generality or the consistency of descriptions. Our goal will be to identify conceptual devices that the various solutions employ in their attempt to come to grips with the conflicts.

Here is a brief preview. Both constructions have to do with syntactic relations: the selection of words and word forms, and linear order. One pattern is **discontinuous order**, illustrated from English in (1).

(1) (a) *Jill forgot to **call up** Aunt Paula.*
    (b) *Jill forgot to **call** Aunt Paula **up**.*

The sentences in (1) present two conflicts, one paradigmatic, the other syntagmatic. The **paradigmatic** conflict has to do with linear order: the word *call* and *up* are adjacent in (1a) but non-adjacent in (1b). This is a contra-diction of type 5 given at the end of Chapter 1, Section 3.5 (point (4): X is both adjacent and non-adjacent to A in the sentences of the same lan-guage). If we assume that a language is a unified system, all patterns will be expected to be one way with no alternatives allowed. If there are alternatives, they pose a conflict.

The other, **syntagmatic** conflict, is internal to sentence (1b): a mismatch between selection and adjacency. The word *up* is selected by the verb *call* but not adjacent to it. If we assume that, in any one sentence, the various syn-tactic relations should hold between the same pair of categories, this is, again, a conflict.

The other construction to be discussed is **long-distance agreement**, illus-trated in (2) from Tsez, a language of the Caucasus. (More detailed gloss-ing will be provided in Section 3.2.)

(2) (a) *Enir   r-iyxo   uža magalu   bac'ruλi.*
    mother **CL4**-know boy bread:**CL3** eaten
    'The mother knows that the boy ate bread.'

(b) *Enir   b-iyxo   uža magalu   bac'ruλi.*
    mother **CL3**-know boy bread:**CL3** eaten
    'The mother knows that the boy ate bread.'

Just like the English sentences in (1), these sentences also present two con-flicts, one paradigmatic, the other syntagmatic. First, consider the main verb 'know'. In Tsez, verb agreement is in terms of gender: CL3 refers to nominal gender class 3, CL4 refers to nominal gender class 4. The difference between the two sentences is the agreement prefix of the verb 'know': in (2a), it is class 4, in (2b), it is class 3. Class 4 agreement is controlled by the entire subordinate clause because clauses are classified as belonging to class 4. Class 3 agreement is in turn controlled by 'bread', a constituent of the subordinate clause. Thus, the agreement prefix on the main verb is alter-natively selected by two different contollers. This is a type of complexity listed under 9 at the end of Chapter 1 (Section 3.5, point (4)): alternative selectors for a single selectee). Since it holds across sentences, it is a para-digmatic conflict.

The other, syntagmatic conflict has to do with sentence (2b). While agree-ment in Class 4 is expected (as in (2a)) since the entire subordinate clause 'that the boy ate bread' is the object of the main verb 'know', in (2b), the verb agrees with the noun phrase 'bread', which is not its own object; rather, it is the object of the subordinate clause. Here is the conflict: the verb selects the clause as its object but it does not agree with the clause; instead, it agrees with a constituent of the clause. The terms of object selection and object agreement are thus not the same. This is another instance of multiple selec-tional dependence, this time applying within a single sentence.

We will start the discussion with linear discontinuity.

2 Discontinuous order

2.1 WHAT IS DISCONTINUOUS ORDER?

Discontinuity is a ubiquitous phenomenon in syntax. Examples are in (1), with the disjointed parts in bold.

(1) SUBJECT . . . PREDICATE
    (a) **Josh** *I believe* **is the best long-distance runner in town.**
    (b) *When they bought the '64 Chevy, they got* **what** *many would say* **was the best bargain at the auto show.**

(2) VERB . . . PARTICLE
    (a) *Herbert* **looked** *the address* **up.**
    (b) Before leaving for the trip, *you should* **check** *the train schedule* **out.**

(3) NOUN PHRASE . . . RELATIVE CLAUSE
    (a) *The man donated* **a book** *to the library* **which he never read.**
    (b) **Many people** *came to the party* **who had not said they would.**

(4) COMPARATIVE ADJECTIVE PHRASE . . . COMPLEMENT
    (a) *The social worker said she had never seen a* **messier** *home* **than Mary's.**
    (b) *Peter wants his children to have a* **better** *life* **than he had.**

(5) QUESTION WORD . . . VERB
    (a) **What** *did the dog* **chew up?**
    (b) **Who(m)** *did they* **fire?**

Why are these constructions considered discontinuous? The term implies two things. First, it implies that the constituents of the construction are not adjacent. This is clearly true for (1)–(5): the sentence segments marked in bold are not next to each other. For example, in (1a), *Josh* and *is the best long-distance runner in town* are separated by *I believe*. Similarly, in (4a), *messier* and *than Mary's* are separated by the word *home*.

But not any two non-adjacent words in a sentence are considered discontinuous. For instance, in (1a) *is* and *runner* are not adjacent, just as the words *seen* and *than Mary's* in (4a), yet they cannot be said to form a discontinuous construction. This is because, in addition to non-adjacency, there is a second component of the meaning of the term 'discontinuous construction': that the non-adjacent words would be expected to occur next to each other.

For an analogy, take Tom and Sue. Tom lives in Illinois and Sue lives in California. Would we consider them 'separated'? Not unless they form a unit of some sort such as being friends or spouses. Discontinuity can be said to hold between two non-adjacent entities only if they are connected by a relationship that would call for proximity. Thus, the bolded expressions in (1)–(5) are justifiably considered discontinuous only if they can be shown to be more closely related to each other than to the words that separate them. Is there evidence that this is so?

The most obvious way in which the non-adjacent sentence parts cohere in these examples is by meaning. Subjects are understood as what predicates are about (1); verbal particles have a meaning only when taken together with the verb (2). Restrictive relative clauses serve to delimit the referent of noun phrases (3). Comparative adjectives make sense only if there is a standard that they express a comparison with (4). And, as was already discussed in the preceding chapter (Section 3.4 of Chapter 1), question words, as in (5), are selected by verbs. Since in general, adjacency tends to iconically mirror semantic cohesion, semantically coherent but non-adjacent words are justly considered discontinuous.

Apart from meaning, there is also syntactic evidence that the disjointed words in (1)–(5) belong together. First, note that the sentence segments which occur non-adjacent in (1)–(5) have alternative adjacent orderings. This is shown in (6b)–(10b), with the discontinuous orders repeated from (1)–(5) for comparison.

(6) SUBJECT + PREDICATE
    (a) ***Josh** I believe **is the best long-distance runner in town.***
    (b) *I believe **Josh is the best long-distance runner in town.***

(7) VERB + PARTICLE
    (a) *Herbert **looked** the address **up**.*
    (b) *Herbert **looked up** the address.*

(8) NOUN PHRASE + RELATIVE CLAUSE
    (a) *The man donated **a book** to the library **which he never read**.*
    (b) *The man donated **a book that he never read** to the library.*

(9) COMPARATIVE ADJECTIVE + COMPLEMENT
    (a) *The social worker said she had never seen a **messier** home **than Mary's**.*
    (b) *The social worker said she had never seen a home **messier than Mary's**.*

(10) QUESTION WORD + VERB
    (a) ***What** did the dog **chew up**?*
    (b) *The dog **chewed up WHAT**?*

However, the alternative adjacent order of these constituents does not prove their close syntactic relationship in and of itself: maybe these words do not in fact syntactically 'belong together', in which case their non-adjacent order is what we should expect. But there is evidence to show that the non-adjacent constituents are syntactically related, just as they are in the continuous versions.

Three pieces of evidence will be cited to show the syntactic relatedness of these constituents regardless of their order.

First, consider selectional relations. Regardless of whether these words are continuous or not, they are in a syntactic selector–selectee relationship: the predicate selects the subject, the particle selects the verb, the relative clause selects the noun phrase, the comparative complement selects the comparative adjective, and the verb selects the question pronoun. For example, a plural subject such as *my brothers* would be an inappropriate subject of the predicate *is the best long-distance runner in town* regardless of whether they are adjacent or not. The constructions **I believe **my brothers is** the best long-distance runner in town* and ****My brothers** I believe **is** is the best long-distance in town* are equally ungrammatical, both violating the subject–verb agreement rule of English.

Second, consider the distribution of pro-forms – words such as *it* or *so* that make brief reference to an entity mentioned elsewhere in the sentence or discourse. Pro-forms have the same distribution as clauses or phrases, which are independently known to be syntactic units. This is shown in (11a), where the antecedent of *it* is the noun phrase *a book that he never read,* and in (11b), where the antecedent of *so* is the clause *Josh is the best long-distance runner in town*. While the grammatical sentences in (11) show that the pro-form *so* replaces a full clause and the pronoun *it* replaces a full noun phrase, the ungrammatical sentences in (12) show that these pro-forms cannot replace only a part of a clause or part of a noun phrase.

(11) (a)   ***it*** replaces a continuous noun phrase:
             *The man donated **a book that he never read** to the library and I much enjoyed reading **it**.*

      (b)   ***so*** replaces a continuous clause:
             *I believe **Josh is the best long-distance runner in town** and his coach thinks **so**, too.*

(12) (a)   ***it*** cannot replace part of a continuous noun phrase, such as *a book*:
             ** The man donated **a book that he never read** to the library and I much enjoyed reading **it that he never read**.*

      (b)   ***so*** cannot replace part of a continuous clause, such as *is the best long-distance runner in town*:
             I believe **Josh is the best long-distance runner in town and his coach thinks **Josh so**, too.*

Consider now (13) and (14). They are like the sentences in (11) and (12) except that the words that jointly serve as antecedents for the pro-forms are now discontinuous. Yet, replacement works the same way: the pro-forms are grammatical in (13) just as they are in (11) and ungrammatical in (14) just as they are in (12).

(13) (a) *it* replaces a discontinuous noun phrase:
　　　　　*The man donated **a book** to the library **that he never read** and
　　　　　I much enjoyed reading **it**.*

　　　(b) *so* replaces a discontinuous clause:
　　　　　***Josh** I believe **is the best long-distance runner in town** and his coach
　　　　　thinks **so**, too.*

(14) (a) *it* cannot replace part of a discontinuous noun phrase, such
　　　　　as *a book*:
　　　　　The man donated **a book to the library **that he never read** and I
　　　　　much enjoyed reading **it that he never read**.*

　　　(b) *so* cannot replace part of a discontinuous clause, such as *is the
　　　　　best long-distance runner in town*:
　　　　　*****Josh** I believe **is the best long-distance runner in town** and his
　　　　　coach thinks **Josh so**, too.*

In other words, pro-forms 'do not care' whether their antecedents are continuous or not. Thus, given the general rule according to which pro-forms replace clauses or major phrases, it is useful to consider the discontinuous sentence parts shown in these examples as forming a single constituent, just as they do when they are adjacent to each other.

A third kind of evidence showing the syntactic coherence between discontinuous words is illustrated from Breton (Anderson and Chung 1977: 11–25). Breton has variable ordering for subjects, objects and verbs but, as illustrated in (15), in neutral sentences – that is, when no constituent is particularly emphatic – the order is VSO.

(15) V　　S　　O
　　　Gwelout a ra Yann e　vignonez.
　　　sees　　　　Yann **his girlfriend**
　　　'Yann sees his girlfriend.'

In (15) it is shown that, in normal order, the verb and the object are non-adjacent: they are separated by the subject. But given that in Breton, as in English, objects are selected by verbs, and assuming that different syntactic relations – such as selection and order – apply to the same pair of constituents, we would expect verb and object to be adjacent. Thus, the Breton sentences where verb and object are not adjacent are examples of discontinuous order.

In addition to selection, there is further evidence for the syntactic relatedness of verb and object in the language. Breton has topicalization constructions: sentence parts – such as adverbs or nouns – can stand in front of the verb if they are understood as the topic of the sentence. Sentences with a topicalized adverb (a) and a topicalized noun (b) are shown in (16) (ibid.: 12; the reason for the different forms of the particle and the verb is not clear).

(16) (a) ***Hiziv*** *e   tebro   Yannig krampouezh e   Kemper.*
     today PRT will:eat Johnny crepes   in Quimper
     'Today, Johnny will eat crepes in Quimper.'

(b) ***Krampouezh*** *a   zebro   Yannig e Kemper   hiziv.*
     crepes   PRT will:eat Johnny in Quimper today
     'Crepes, Johnny will eat today in Quimper.'

Interestingly, verbs themselves can also be topicalized, in which case they stand in front of a 'light verb' such as 'do'. The sentence in (17) illustrates verb topicalization (ibid.: 22).

(17) ***Deskiñ***   *a   reomp Berzhoneg.*
     to:learn PRT do   Breton
     'We are learning Breton.' ('Learning we do of Breton.')

In (16) and (17), the topicalized material consists of a single word. This is not so in some other sentences: the topicalized material can consist of more than one word but there is a general constraint on the topicalized word sequence: it has to be a single syntactic phrase. The sentences in (18) illustrate the topicalization of multiple words. In (18a), the topicalization of two words is grammatical since they form a single noun phrase while in (18b) the topicalization of two words is ungrammatical since the two adverbs do not form a phrase (ibid.: 21).

(18) (a) ***Mab Per*** *a   zo klañv.*
     son Peter PRT is sick
     'Peter's son is sick.'

(b) *****Hiziv e Kemper*** *e   tebro   Yannig krampouezh.*
     today in Quimper PRT will:eat Johnny crepes
     'Today, in Quimper, Johnny will eat crepes.'

The evidence for the phrasehood of verb and object comes from the topicalization of verbs. In verb topicalization, too, there can be more than one word serving as topic in addition to the verb itself. Given that, as noted above, the topicalized material must form a phrase in other instances, whatever other words can be topicalized along with the verb are best considered as forming a single phrase with the verb. In (19) is shown that a verb–subject sequence cannot be topicalized (see (a)) but a verb–object sequence can (see (b)) (ibid.: 22, 23).

(19) (a) **Deskiñ ni*   *a*   *ra Brezhoneg.*
        learn   **we** PRT do Breton
        'We are learning Breton.'

     (b) *Deskiñ Brezhoneg a*   *reomp.*
        learn **Breton**   PRT we:do
        'We are learning Breton.'

Thus, for purposes of topicalization, the verb–object sequence acts as a single phrase and is best analysed as such even in normal non-topicalized sentences where the two are not adjacent. Of course we could also conclude that verb and object form a phrase only in topic position where they are adjacent but that they do not form a phrase when, as in non-topicalized sentences, they are not adjacent. But the requirements of generality and simplicity favour an account according to which verb and object form a phrase in both constructions of this language.

In sum: we have discussed the rationale for proposing that certain sets of non-adjacent words be regarded as forming a discontinuous construction. Based on the discussion, the highlighted words in the English examples in (1)–(5) are indeed properly analysed as discontinuous because even though they are non-adjacent, they are related in other ways. The relationship between these words was seen to be borne out not only by their semantic coherence but also by two syntactic facts: they are in a selector–selectee relationship, and they are jointly replaceable by a pro-form just as when they are adjacent. Evidence cited from Breton shows how topicalization can also support the phrasehood of non-adjacent words.

Discontinuous constructions have been widely discussed in the literature as a problem for syntactic analysis. Exactly what is problematic about them? As already noted in Section 1, they represent two conflicts. One conflict is paradigmatic, holding between alternative linear patterns in different sentences in the same language; the other conflict is syntagmatic, holding between the selectional and linear relations between a pair of constituents within a sentence. The two conflicts are stated in (20).

(20) (a) **Paradigmatic conflict: conflict between alternative orderings**
        A and B are adjacent in some sentences but non-adjacent in other sentences of the same language.

     (b) **Syntagmatic conflict: conflict between ordering and selection**
        A and B are selectionally related but linearly not related in the same sentence.

Syntacticians have chosen various ways of dealing with these puzzles. As an example of discontinuous constructions, the next two sections will discuss verbs and their particles in English already illustrated in (2) above. The paradigmatic conflict they pose will be addressed in Section 2.2; the syntagmatic one will be taken up in 2.3.

2.2 CONFLICT BETWEEN ORDERINGS

One of the two puzzles about verb–particle constructions is that the verb and the particle are alternatively ordered adjacent and non-adjacent in the same language: English. This is illustrated in (1).

(1) (a) Verb . . . Particle: *Megan **wiped** the counter **off**.*
          Verb & Particle: *Megan **wiped off** the counter.*

     (b) Verb . . . Particle: *Joe **called** his aunt **up**.*
          Verb & Particle: *Joe **called up** his aunt.*

     (c) Verb . . . Particle: *Sue forgot to **check** the book **out**.*
          Verb & Particle: *Sue forgot to **check out** the book.*

     (d) Verb . . . Particle: *Mary **called** the man **in**.*
          Verb & Particle: *Mary **called in** the man.*

Like all conflicts, this, too, depends on the assumptions that we make about what is a single entity and what are contradictory predicates. In this case, the paradox arises if we assume that the two order patterns – particle next to the verb and away from it – do indeed involve the same syntactic constituents: verb and particle. However, if it could be shown that, even though the lexical items involved are the same, the syntactic structures are not the same, the conflict would be resolved: there is no reason why different syntactic structures should not be ordered differently.

Two accounts in the literature propose that, in spite of appearances, the terms of the two order patterns are not the same.

One proposal has been offered by Pauline Jacobson, formulated within a **Categorial Grammar** framework (Jacobson 1987: 32–9). The gist of her proposal is that the verb involved in the two order patterns is not the same verb. According to this account, expressions such as *look up, wipe off, call up, check out* and so on are listed in the lexicon as verbs containing verbs. For example, the lexical entry of *wipe off* is $[[wipe]_v \; off]_v$, which means *wipe* is a verb and *wipe off* is also a verb. The rule that is indirectly responsible for determining the order of the verb and the particle puts the object after the verb. Since both *wipe* and *wipe off* are verbs, this rule can apply to either of them. If it applies to the 'larger' verb (*wipe off*), the object will follow the particle; if it applies to the 'smaller' verb (*wipe*), the object will end up wedged in between the verb and the object.

The other proposal regarding the same issue is by Ivan Sag. His framework is **Head-Driven Phrase Structure Grammar**, already mentioned in Chapter 1 (Section 3.3) in connection with the analysis of English imperatives. In Jacobson's account, the particle is not a syntactic constituent at all and thus not a term in any syntactic ordering rule. Sag in turn accounts for the alternative orders of the particle by assuming that it is a syntactic constituent and by assigning it to two different syntactic categories (Sag 1987: 329–33). On the one hand, the particle is a single lexical item: a preposition, and in that case it occurs right after the verb (from the account, it is not clear what general rule is responsible for this order). On the other hand, the particle can be a prepositional phrase, in which case the general rule of English that puts prepositional phrases after direct objects (*John put the book on the shelf*, **John put on the shelf the book*) places the particle after the direct object.

The phrasal nature of the post-object particle is independently borne out by the following data (ibid.: 330).

(2) (a)   *I looked the number* **right up**.
    (b)   **I looked* **right up** *the number*.

In (2) is shown that when the particle follows the object, it can take a modifier such as *right* but the particle directly following the verb cannot. Since *right* in other instances occurs with prepositional phrases (e.g. *right after the lecture*), its co-occurrence with the particle suggests that the particle, when separated from the verb, is a prepositional phrase.

Both of these proposals ascribe the alternative orders to different 'personalities' of the terms of the order patterns and to the particle in particular. For Jacobson, the particle is either part of a verb lexeme or it is not; for Sag, it is either a preposition or a prepositional phrase.

The strategy of resolving contradictions by 'splitting the entity' is familiar from Chapter 1, Section 3.2. It was discussed there that one of the ways in which a contradiction can be resolved is by re-interpreting the single entity of which the contradictory assertions are made so that there are actually two entities involved. The conflict is thus resolved as a case of 'mistaken identity'. Both Jacobson's and Sag's solutions fall into this type: the single entity (the verb–particle construction) is shown to be structurally homonymous: it is analysed as two different entities because of the alternative categorizations of verb, particle or both. This is like resolving the contradiction in the statement *Jim lives at 234 Plum Street and at 69 Cherry Street* by showing that there are two different people named Jim involved.

2.3 Conflict between selection and ordering

Let us now take up the syntagmatic conflict posed by discontinuous ordering: that constituents that are otherwise syntactically related are non-adjacent. Here are some examples, repeated from (1) of Section 2.2:

(1) (a) *Megan **wiped** the counter **off**.*
    (b) *Joe **called** his aunt **up**.*
    (c) *Sue forgot to **check** the book **out**.*
    (d) *Mary **called** the man **in**.*

In these sentences, the verb and the particle are separated even though they are selectionally related. This is a conflict under the assumption that a sentence is a unified object and that therefore all syntactic relations in the sentence are expected to hold between the same pair of constituents. That verb and particle are indeed related syntactically even when they are non-adjacent is shown by selection: the particle is selected by the verb and by no other word in the sentence.

The conflict most acutely arises in descriptive frameworks where the assignment of selection and linear order are inseparable: one cannot be present without the other. In such frameworks – such as traditional Transformational Grammar – the sentence *Megan wiped the counter off* could have one of two representations, shown in (2).

(2) (a)   (b)

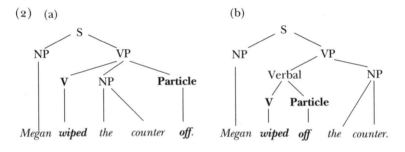

In (2a) is shown the linear discontinuity of *wiped* and *off* but not their phrasehood: they are not uniquely dominated by a single node. In turn, (2b) shows the phrasehood of the two words – they are both dominated by the node Verbal – but not their linear discontinuity. The representation in (2a) is true to the linear ordering of verb and particle but it fails to show their selectional relation; in turn, (2b) shows their selectional relatedness but fails to represent their actual linear order. Thus, each representation is only half-true: in and of itself, neither captures both aspects of the construction – that these words both form a unit and that they are separated. The challenge is to do justice to both facts.

An obvious solution would be to represent the sentence by a single, composite tree structure, such as in (3) overleaf.

This tree has the advantage of single-handedly conveying both points made separately by the two trees in (2): that *off* is both a sister of *wiped* and it is linearly separate from it. But, on the flip side, accepting it would amount to legitimizing a conflict: that a word can be a part of two different wholes. This is because in (3), *off* is a daughter constituent both of Verbal and of the entire verb phrase (VP).

(3)

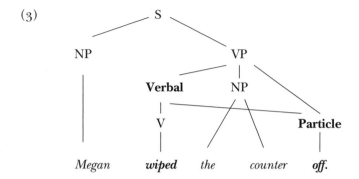

While this solution may be satisfactory in this particular example – it is complex but not contradictory – such composite tree representations are inadequate in other instances because they introduce not only complexity but a contradiction in the account. Mark Baltin points out this problem with composite tree representations for some English sentences that include the reciprocal pronoun *each other* (1987, esp. 22–3; Baltin's examples and discussion are somewhat simplified below). Consider first (4).

(4) *The discussants were too biased to be convinced.*

The sentence in (4) includes a discontinuous constituent: *too* and *to be convinced* form a single unit even though they are separated. Their syntactic relatedness is shown by selection: the presence of *too* is required by the infinitival phrase. Without *too*, the sentence would be ungrammatical: **The discussants were biased to be convinced.*

(5)

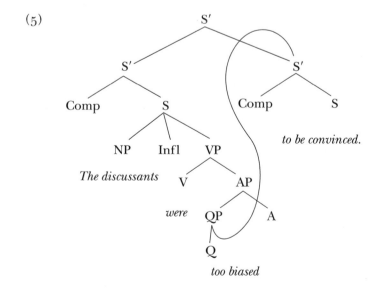

How should this sentence be represented? The challenge is to show both the syntactic relationship of the two constituents *too* and *to be convinced* and their linear separation. Based on (3) as a model, we may attempt a composite tree as in (5) (ibid.: 22). In (5) is shown that, in line with its selectional relation to *too*, *to be convinced* is a sister of *too* and at the same time, in line with its non-adjacent relation to *too*, it is also sister to the entire remainder of the sentence.

However, as Baltin demonstrates, this representation is inadequate for some sentences that are only minimally distinct from (4). Compare the ungrammatical sentence in (6a) with (6b) (repeated from (4)).

(6) (a) **The discussants were too biased for **each other** to be convinced.*
     (b) *The discussants were too biased to be convinced.*

The sentences in (6) have similar structures; yet, (6b) is grammatical but (6a) is not. Why? The offending element in (6a) is the reciprocal pronoun *each other*.

In general, reciprocal pronouns are used in reference to an antecedent (i.e., a phrase that they refer to) if the reciprocal pronoun is either a sister node of the antecedent or a descendant of a sister node. The relationship thus described is called **c-command**: node A c-commands node B if the first branching node dominating A also dominates B and neither A nor B dominates the other. C-command thus refers to 'sister-to-sister', 'aunt-to-niece' and 'aunt-to-(great-(great-))grand-niece' relations.

For example, the sentence *The men praised each other* is grammatical because the *the men* c-commands *each other*: as (7a) shows, the S-node (in bold) immediately dominating *the men* also dominates *each other*. But **The*

(7) (a)

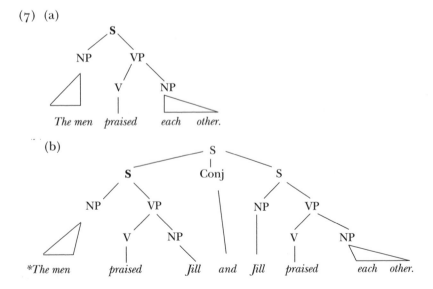

men praised Jill and she thanked each other (with *each other* intended to refer to 'the men') is ungrammatical: (7b) shows that the S-node on the left (in bold) that immediately dominates *the men* does not also dominate *each other*.

Because of the c-command requirement between antecedent and pronoun, an adequate tree structure of the ungrammatical sentence (6a) should represent *each other* as not c-commanded by its antecedent *the discussants* because if it were c-commanded by it, the sentence ought to be grammatical. Let us now consider a tree diagram for (6a) constructed on the pattern of (5).

(8)

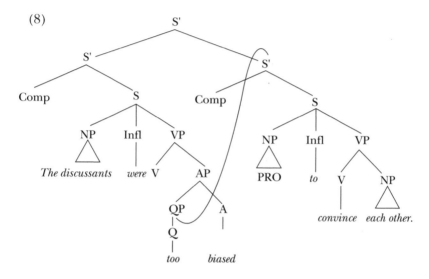

Does this tree show *each other* as not c-commanded by *the discussants* as we would want it to be the case? The answer is: yes and no. The diagram represents *each other* as having two 'allegiances'. On the one hand, it is part of the sentence on the right that *the discussants* is not the subject of. Since *each other* thus appears in a position not c-commanded by the intended antecedent *discussants*, the ungrammaticality of the sentence in (6a) is correctly predicted.

But the problem is that this right-hand-side S-node is at the same time shown as part of the sentence that *the discussants* is the subject of. Thus, this portion of the tree diagram represents *each other* as c-commanded by *the discussants*. In view of this fact, (6a) should be grammatical!

Thus, the tree in (8) is paradoxical: it makes contradictory predictions regarding the grammaticality of the sentence. One of the predictions is correct, the other is not. As Baltin points out, the source of the problem with the diagram in (8) is that when the tree assigns double motherhood to a constituent, it does not specify in what respect the constituent behaves like a part of one phrase and in what other respect it behaves like a part of another phrase. In this particular instance, selectional relations argue for the clause *for each other to be convinced* to be a sister to the quantifier *too*; but facts of 'binding' (i.e., antecedent–pronoun relations) as well as linear order require the clause to be free of domination by the adjectival phrase.

Since it is difficult to tag the two conflicting structures for their differing applicability, Baltin concludes that, instead a single discontinuous tree, what is needed are two separate tree structures each explicitly designated for a particular purpose: one for selectional relations and the other for linear order and binding, such as in (9):

(9)   (a) tree structure for selection:

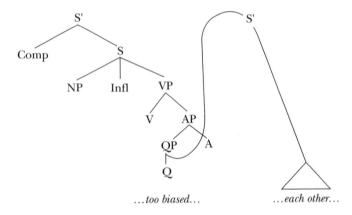

...*too biased...*   ...*each other...*

(b) tree structure for binding and linear order:

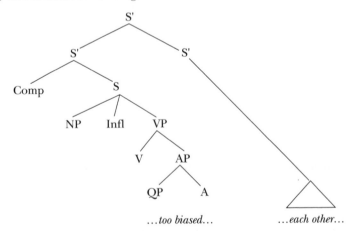

...*too biased...*   ...*each other...*

Let us now return to verb–particle constructions. What does Baltin's argument say about the analysis of non-adjacent verb and particle in sentences such as *Megan **wiped** the counter **off**?* We saw that neither of the two trees in (2) is appropriate **by itself** for representing the sentence *Megan **wiped** the counter **off*** but that a composite tree, as in (3), might. Baltin does not argue that composite trees are inappropriate representations of verb–particle constructions but he does show that composite trees are not appropriate for some other discontinuous constructions and suggests that representations in terms of two distinct trees rather than one composite one are the way to go. Let us therefore apply his idea of having two separate trees for the discontinuous verb–particle constructions.

The basis of labelling the different trees for different syntactic purposes has differed among various approaches in the literature. In Baltin's case, each tree is designated for a particular aspect of syntax: selection, on the one hand, and binding and linear order, on the other. Here, the two structures are not declared to represent different levels in the process of deriving a sentence. Alternatively, in the Standard Theory of **Transformational Generative Grammar** – as seen before in connection with the analysis of imperatives and wh-questions (Chapter 1, Sections 3.3 and 3.4) – the two representations are derivationally sequenced. One representation is called underlying while the other is called surface; and there may be several intermediate-level trees in between.

The notions 'underlying structure' and 'surface structure' have been conceptualized in various different ways in Transformational Grammar but in most approaches underlying structure is closer to meaning, and surface structure is closer to pronunciation. Thus, in the case of discontinuity, the surface structure tree should be true to linear order by showing discontinuity and the underlying structure should be responsible for representing selectional relations.

Accordingly, in this framework, the two tree structures of (2) are useful not as alternative accounts but as parts of a single account. While neither by itself provides a proper representation of the sentence, the two together do, one serving as underlying structure showing the selection relation between verbs and particle, and the other serving as surface structure showing their linear precedence relation. In (10a) is shown a copy of (2a), in (10b) is a copy of (2b), the two now forming parts of a single analysis.

Given that the two structures are parts of the account of a single sentence, they need to be connected somehow. As discussed in Chapter 1, in Transformational Generative Grammar, the rules that link the two representations are called transformations. More specifically, they model the

(10) (a) UNDERLYING STRUCTURE: (b) SURFACE STRUCTURE: ·

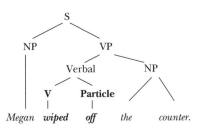
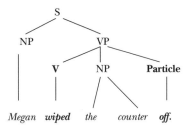

speaker by converting the meaning-related underlying structure to pronunciation-related surface structure. When the difference is in the position of constituents, the rule will have to move parts of the sentence; such rules are called movement rules (one example of which is Wh-Movement; see Section 3.4. of Chapter 1). The Particle Movement Rule that applies here can be formulated as follows:

(11) X **V Particle** NP Y → X **V** NP **Particle** Y

The formulation in (11) says that given a verb, a particle and a noun phrase in this order (possibly preceded and followed by other material, which is what X and Y stand for), the order of the particle and the noun phrase can be switched. The application of the rule is optional: if the rule is applied, we get the discontinuous order; if it is not applied, the underlying structure surfaces unchanged yielding the continuous sentence *Megan wiped off the counter.* This account thus accommodates the paradigmatic conflict of alternative orderings as well, discussed in Section 2.2.

Movement rules are needed in Transformational Generative Grammar because, in most versions of this approach, both underlying and surface structures are linearly ordered. In approaches where selection and order are separately specified, there is no need for re-ordering the particle and the object: selectionally, the particle is a sister of the verb and the linearization rules provide two options for its order relative to the object.

While employing a composite tree, such as (3), to represent a sentence that has contradictory properties amounts to legitimizing the contradiction, representing the sentence as two distinct trees is a classic case of 'splitting the entity' in order to resolve a contradiction. The concept of assuming multiple representations for sentences of paradoxical nature is similar to psychiatrists analysing psychotic patients as having multiple personalities. In both instances, the motivation for the analysis is that a single entity has contradictory properties. 'Pulling apart' a contradictory object into two parts each of which is free of contradiction is, as noted in Chapter 1, one of the conceptual tools that people employ in contending with paradoxes of any sort. It corresponds to 'splitting the entity' in terms of the viewpoint under which we look at that entity ((4vii) in Section 3.2. of Chapter 1).

In Transformational Grammar, underlying and surface structures are both within the syntactic component. A more radical 'splitting' of the paradoxical entity has also been proposed in the literature, where the conflicting representations belong to different components of the grammar. In Jerrold Sadock's *Autolexical Grammar* (1991), syntax, morphology and semantics are all separate components with tree representations constructed independently for each. It is then proposed that there are mismatches between syntactic and semantic structure but not within either of these two components of grammar. Thus, unlike in Transformational Grammar, where there are multiple syntactic representations, in Autolexical Grammar there is a single syntactic representation of a sentence. Sentences with discontinuous verb–particle constructions are assigned one tree structure in the syntactic component where the two constituents are non-adjacent, and another tree structure in the semantic component where verb and particle are adjacent. Unlike in Transformational Grammar, the difference between the two trees is shown not by directed rules that change one tree into the other, but by association lines which simply connect corresponding sections of the trees.

(12) shows an autolexical representation of the sentence *Megan wiped the counter off*, with the mismatches between meaning and syntax highlighted. In this diagram, the upper tree belongs to the syntactic component and the lower tree is in the semantic component; the dotted lines show correspondences between constituents in the two components. Note that the particle is not a separate constituent in semantics: *wiped* and *off* are two constituents in syntax but they form a single constituent in semantics (see Sadock 1987: 296–7.)

(12)

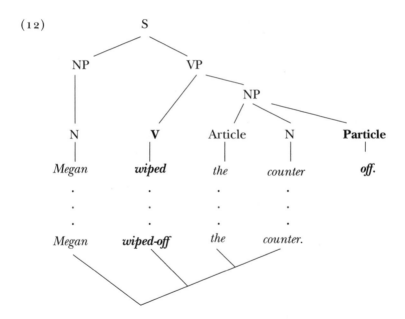

In the autolexical representations, 'discontinuity has vanished into the crack between the two representations' (ibid.: 297): one diagram is in the semantic component and the other in the syntactic component. What this means is that a contradiction that would be offending if assumed to occur within syntactic form is now viewed as simply a manifestation of the gaping abyss that is independently known to exist between meaning and syntactic form. Since meaning and form are by definition vastly different things, such mismatches are to be expected rather than being an anomaly.

2.4 SUMMARY

Let us summarize our discussion of discontinuous structures. The notion of discontinuity is based on two observations. One observation is that two words, or sequences of words, are linearly non-adjacent. The other is that these two parts of the sentence form a unit in some sense and would thus be expected to be adjacent.

At the end of Section 2.1 (in (20)), two conflicts were identified in connection with discontinuous constituents. They are restated in (1) specifically for verb–particle constructions.

(1) (a) PARADIGMATIC CONFLICT (= alternative orderings of the same constituents **in the same language**)
The verb and the particle are adjacent in some English sentences and non-adjacent in others.

(b) SYNTAGMATIC CONFLICT (= a given constituent bears one syntactic relation to one constituent and another syntactic relation to another constituent **in the same sentence**)
The particle is selectionally related to the verb but it is not adjacent to it in some English sentences.

Regarding the paradigmatic conflict, we have seen two solutions, summarized in (2).

(2) SOLUTIONS TO THE PARADIGMATIC CONFLICT (1a)
Both solutions say that what appears to be alternative orderings of the **same** constituents – verb and particle – in fact involve **different constituents**.

(a) Jacobson's solution: The two order patterns involve two different verbs.
(b) Sag's solution: Of the two order patterns, what appears as a particle is a preposition in one construction and a prepositional phrase in the other construction.

Regarding the syntagmatic conflict, we have seen three ways of dealing with the discrepancy between selectional and order relations. They are summarized in (3).

(3) SOLUTIONS TO THE SYNTAGMATIC CONFLICT (1b)
All three solutions claim that the particle participates in two different partonomic relations: when it is adjacent to the verb, it is sister to the verb, but when it is non-adjacent to the verb, it is an immediate daughter of the sentence.

The three solutions nonetheless differ in the way the two different constituent structures are represented.

(a) Solution in (3) of Section 2.2: The two partonomic configurations are jointly represented in a **single composite tree**.

(b) Solution in Transformational Grammar ((10) in Section 2.3): The two partonomic configurations are represented in **different trees, each on a different level of the syntactic component** of the grammar.

(c) Solution in Autolexical Grammar ((12) in Section 2.3): The two partonomic configurations are represented in **different trees each in a different component** of the grammar (syntactic and semantic).

While composite trees showing multi-domination reflect the contradiction just as it is, separate-tree representations relegate each of the contradictory properties to only one representation. Of the two accounts that posit separate trees, multi-level representations within a single component of the grammar represent a minimal step towards 'pulling apart' a contradictory entity. The multi-componential account, which relegates contradictory statements to different components of the grammar, is in turn a radical solution to the task of accommodating contradictory facts within a non-contradictory account.

We will see similar strategies of coping with contradictions cropping up in alternative analyses of other syntactic patterns as well. Our second example has to do with the conflict between word selection and word form selection as it arises in alternative agreement patterns.

3 Long-distance agreement

3.1 HUNGARIAN

Transitive verbs in Hungarian agree with both the subject and the direct object. Subject agreement is in person and number, direct object agreement is in definiteness and, in one instance, in person. This is illustrated in (1). (The glosses of the verb suffix first refer to the subject and second to the object. For example, S1:S2.OBJ means singular first person subject and singular second person object.)

(1) (a) *Én akar-**ok***   ***egy** filmet.*
      I   want-**S1:INDEF.OBJ a**   film
      'I want a film.'

(b) *Én akar-**om***   ***a***   *filmet.*
      I   want-**S1:DEF.OBJ the** film
      'I want the film.'

(c) *Én akar-lak* *téged.*
I want-**S1:S2 you**_S
'I want you_S.'

If the subject is first person singular, the verb takes the *-ok* suffix if the object is indefinite (as in (1a)) and it takes *-om* if the object is definite (as in (1b)). If the object is second person, the verb suffix is *-lak* (as in (1c)). (In the examples below, these suffixes will show up in phonologically conditioned allomorphic form: *-ek*, *-em* and *-lek*.)

Consider now complex sentences that contain two verbs: a main verb and an infinitive. Of the two verbs, the infinitive shows no agreement but the main verb agrees with its subject and with the direct object of the infinitive. Thus, in (2a) and (2b), the main verb 'want' agrees both with its subject 'I' and with 'film', which is the object of the infinitive; and in (2c), it agrees both with its subject 'I' and with the object of the infinitive: 'you_S'. In (3), the sentences show the same pattern for the main verb 'forget'. Note that Hungarian is a 'pro-drop language', that is, subject pronouns are optional. They have been omitted in (3).

(2) (a) *Én egy film-et* *akar-ok* *néz-ni.*
  I a film-ACC want-**S1:INDEF.OBJ** watch-INF
  'I want to watch a film.'

  (b) *Én a film-et* *akar-om* *néz-ni.*
  I the film-ACC want-**S1:DEF.OBJ** watch-INF
  'I want to watch the film.'

  (c) *Én téged* *akar-lak* *néz-ni.*
  I you_S:ACC want-**S1:S2.OBJ** watch-INF
  'I want to watch you_S.'

(3) (a) *Mindig elfelejt-ek* *egy hozzáértő-t megkérdez-ni.*
  always forget-**S1:INDEF.OBJ** a expert-ACC ask-INF
  'I always forget to ask an expert.'

  (b) *Mindig elfelejt-em* *a hozzáértő-t megkérdez-ni.*
  always forget-**S1:DEF.OBJ** the expert-ACC ask-INF
  'I always forget to ask the expert.'

  (c) *Mindig elfelejt-lek* *téged megkérdez-ni.*
  always forget-**S1:S2.OBJ** you_S:ACC ask-INF
  'I always forget to ask you_S.'

Verb–object agreement in these examples seems not at all as expected. The pattern is exceptional because the main verb appears to agree with the object of the subordinate verb. Most instances of verb agreement across languages obey a constraint: the noun phrases that control agreement on the verb are arguments of that verb. In other words, verb agreement is generally local: both controller(s) and target are constituents of the same clause.

The locality of agreement is illustrated in (4) and (5) with English examples. When two clauses are conjoined into a single sentence as in (4), the verb of the first clause will show agreement with the subject of its own clause and not with that of the other clause. This is also true when one clause is subordinate to another, as in (5) where the embedded clause is the object of the main verb.

(4) (a) ***John was cleaning*** *the shack and his sisters were looking on.*
     (b) *****John were cleaning*** *the shack and **his sisters** were looking on.*

(5) (a) ***Sam believes*** *that ladybugs bite.*
     (b) **Sam **believe** that **ladybugs** bite.*

Given that agreement is generally local, the Hungarian verb–object agreement pattern shown in (2)–(3) would be nothing out of the ordinary if – despite appearances – it could be analysed as local. Is this a possible analysis? The answer depends on whether the verb and the object that the verb agrees with are to be viewed as occurring in the same clause or in different clauses. Putting it differently, the issue is whether the sentences in these examples are mono-clausal or bi-clausal. If each sentence in the examples is to be analysed as a single clause having only a single verb, then verb agreement is local since in that case the direct object is the argument of the only verb of the sentence. But if each sentence is viewed as consisting of two clauses so that the object that the main verb agrees with belongs to the subordinate clause, there is a problem since in that case, the main verb agrees with a direct object that is not its own so that agreement is non-local.

So are these sentences mono-clausal or bi-clausal? Katalin É. Kiss, who discusses this problem in detail (1987: 224–43), cites evidence on both sides.

Here are two pieces of evidence for **bi-clausality**. The first is from selection. Each sentence in (2) and (3) contains a noun phrase that is marked for the accusative – the case of the direct object. Which verb governs this case: the main verb or the infinitive? The main verbs in (2) and (3) – 'want' and 'forget' – are transitive and thus they may be the governors of the object case. However, in (6), the main verb, translatable as 'to try', 'to strive', 'to make an effort', is intransitive and thus it cannot possibly be responsible for the accusative case.

(6) (a) *Igyeksz-**ek**   majd **egy** hozzáértőt   megkérdez-ni.*
          try-**S1.INDEF.OBJ** later an expert:ACC ask-INF
          'I will try to ask an expert.'

          but: **Igyekezek   egy hozzáértőt.*
          try-**S1.INDEF.OBJ** an expert:ACC

(b)   *Igyeksz-**em**   majd **a**   hozzáértőt   megkérdez-ni.*
      try-**S1.DEF.OBJ** later **the** expert:ACC ask-INF
      'I will try to ask the expert.'

   but: **Igyeksz-em   a   hozzáértőt.*
      try-S1.DEF.OBJ the expert:ACC

(c)   *Igyekez-**lek**   majd **téged**   megkérdez-ni.*
      try-**S1:S2.OBJ** later **you$_S$:ACC** ask-INF
      'I will try to ask you$_S$.'

   but: **Igyekezlek   téged.*
      try-S1:S2.OBJ you$_S$:ACC

Thus, the object that the verb 'to try' agrees with cannot be its own object: it cannot take objects at all. The infinitive 'to ask', however, is obligatorily transitive: it must occur with a direct object. Thus, the object noun phrase in these sentences is best analysed as the object of the subordinate verb. This suggests that the sentence consists of two clauses one headed by the main verb and the other by the infinitive.

A second argument for the object belonging with the infinitive rather than the main verb and that therefore the entire sentence is bi-clausal comes from word order. While Hungarian has fairly free word order, one of the few iron-clad rules is that the focused constituent must directly precede the verb of the clause that it belongs to. The sentence in (7) shows the object – that controls agreement on the main verb – in focus position relative to the infinitive. This suggests that it is the infinitive's own object. (The focused constituent is in all-capitals.)

(7)   *Igyekezlek   **TÉGED**   hivni fel holnap   először.*
      try:S1:S2.OBJ **you$_S$:ACC** to:call up tomorrow first
      'It is you$_S$ that I will try to call tomorrow first.'

Let us now turn to arguments on the other side: that the sentence is **mono-clausal**. Word order also provides evidence on this side. While (7) shows that the object can be in focus position relative to the infinitive, (8) shows that it can also be in focus position relative to the main verb just as if it were the main verb's own object.

(8)   ***TÉGED**   igyekezlek   felhívni   holnap   először.*
      you$_S$:ACC try:S1:S2.OBJ to:call:up tomorrow first
      'I will try to call you$_S$ tomorrow.'

A second argument for mono-clausality comes from verb inflection. Notice that of the two verbs, only one – the main verb – is inflected: the infinitive is not. Since clauses normally have inflected verbs, this argues against the infinitive occurring in an independent clause.

And, of course, the very fact that the main verb agrees with the object is also a reason for analysing the object as belonging to the main verb rather than to the infinitive. Verb agreement is a third type of evidence for the monoclausal analysis.

All in all, evidence regarding the nature of these sentences is conflicting. It is summarized in (9).

(9) (a) Indications that the object belongs to the infinitive and thus the entire sentence is bi-clausal:
- the object is selected and case-marked by the infinitive rather than by the main verb;
- the object may occur in focus position relative to the infinitive.

(b) Indications that the object belongs to the main verb and thus the entire sentence is mono-clausal:
- the object may occur in focus position relative to the main verb;
- only the main verb is inflected, the infinitive is not;
- the object controls agreement with the main verb.

So how should the Hungarian sentences be analysed: as mono-clausal with the object being the complement of the main verb, or as bi-clausal with the object as an argument of the infinitive? Considering the evidence on both sides of the matter, É. Kiss concludes (1987: 237, 239; emphasis added):

It appears that the mono-clausal and bi-clausal properties of [the constructions in (3), (6), (7) and (8)] are equally weighty; neither can be ignored or explained away. What is more, they are **simultaneously** present; consequently, the bi-clausal structure and mono-clausal structure that can be associated with [this construction] cannot represent two subsequent stages of the derivation, but must hold simultaneously . . . The different grammatical processes take place on the mono-clausal or bi-clausal side of the construction depending on whether the structural description they require is met on the bi-clausal or on the mono-clausal side.

The tree representation that she suggests is given in (10b) (a simplified version of the diagram in É. Kiss 1987: 238) for the sentence in (10a). The top side of the diagram represents the sentence as bi-clausal; the bottom side represents it as mono-clausal.

(10) (a) (Én) *szeretné-lek*   *lát-ni   téged.*
        I   would:like-S1:S2.OBJ see-INF you$_S$:ACC
        'I would like to see you$_S$.'

(b)

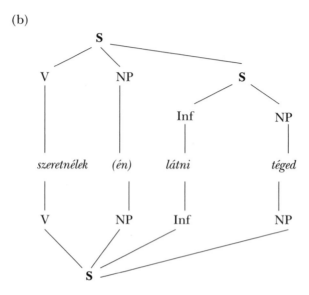

Baltin, in his analysis of English *too*-constructions (Section 2.3), encountered a problem with complex tree representations that showed two alternative mother nodes for a subordinate clause. The problem was that there was no way of forcing a syntactic rule to apply to the 'right' structure – as opposed to the other one that would yield an ungrammatical sentence. In the Hungarian case, however, there is no such problem: syntactic rules may apply to either of the two sides of the tree or to both without resulting in ungrammaticality. In particular, the rule that places the object into focus position can apply to either side: as seen above, it is grammatical for the direct object to occupy focus position relative to the main verb or relative to the infinitive. Object agreement, however, cannot but apply on the mono-clausal (lower) side since on the bi-clausal side, infinitives are proposed to form a complex predicate with the main verb so that they cannot themselves be agreement targets.

The tree is a further example of splitting a contradictory entity but the split is conceptualized somewhat differently than in the analyses of discontinuity surveyed in Section 2. In connection with the syntagmatic conflict in discontinuity, we have seen three kinds of representations of different syntactic relations among constituents: multi-domination in a single composite tree, distinct trees on different syntactic levels and distinct trees in different components of the grammar. Bifacial trees as in (10) are an additional kind, falling between composite trees and distinct trees on different syntactic levels.

Let us summarize the core conflict that the Hungarian facts pose and that calls for this complex analysis. The initial conflict is that agreement seems an exception to how agreement works in general: this agreement pattern seems 'long-distance' in that the main verb agrees with a noun phrase that is not its own object. This conflict could be resolved by considering the sentence to be mono-clausal, rather than bi-clausal, because then the object that controls agreement on the main verb would belong to that verb. However, evidence turns out to be contradictory: in some ways, the object does seem to belong to the main verb but in other ways it seems to be related to the infinitive. The resulting conflict is stated in (11).

(11) In some Hungarian sentences that include a main verb (of a particular kind), an infinitive and a direct-object noun phrase, this noun phrase is the direct object both of the infinitive and of the main verb.

Is this a contradiction? As always, it depends on the assumptions that we make. If we allow for a noun to bear the same grammatical relation – such as objecthood – to more than one constituent, there is no contradiction, only complexity. But the simpler assumption, one that much of syntactic evidence is in conformity with, is that a noun phrase can bear a grammatical relation only to a single constituent. In the light of this assumption, (11) does present a contradiction.

The dual tree proposed by É. Kiss resolves this conflict by assuming that the sentences in question have two aspects each represented as a face of the tree. One face shows the direct object as belonging to the infinitive, the other as belonging to the main verb. The conceptual tool of bifacial trees amounts to a minimal 'splitting' of a paradoxical entity to accommodate its contradictory nature.

3.2 TSEZ

There are also other languages that show 'long-distance agreement', that is, sentences where a noun phrase in one clause appears to control agreement on the verb of a different clause. The second instance comes from Tsez, a Dagestanian language of the Caucasus. Here is an example, already cited in from Section 1; it is given here with more detailed glossing (Polinsky and Comrie 1999: 117).

(1) *Eni-r*   *b-iy-xo*   *už-a*   *magalu*
    mother-DAT **CL3**-know-PRES boy-ERG bread:ABS:**CL3**
    b-ac'-ru-λi.
    CL3-eat-PASTPART-NOMINALIZER
    'The mother knows that the boy ate bread.'

Note first that Tsez is an ergative language. What this means is that unlike in English, intransitive subjects are not case-marked as transitive subjects; instead, intransitive subjects have the same case marking as the Patient arguments of transitive sentences (which would be direct objects in English). Case marking according to the so-called 'accusative system' is illustrated by actual English data in (2), contrasted with hypothetical English data in (3) mimicking the 'ergative system'.

(2) (a) ***He** hit him.*
     (b) ***He** ran.*

(3) (a) *He hit **him**.*
     (b) ****Him** ran.*

The names of the cases in the two marking systems are shown in (4) and (5).

(4) accusative case marking:
     • transitive sentence: **Nominative** Accusative
     • intransitive sentence: **Nominative**

(5) ergative case marking:
     • transitive sentence: Ergative **Absolutive**
     • intransitive sentence: **Absolutive**

Let us now consider the Tsez example of (1). In the subordinate clause, 'boy' is marked ergative, 'bread' is marked absolutive and the verb 'eat' agrees with 'bread'. In the main clause, the verb is 'know', which takes a dative experiencer – thus, 'mother' is in the dative case. A more literal translation of the sentence is 'The bread having been eaten by the boy is known to the mother.'

Notice now the agreement of the main verb. As noted in Section 1, Tsez verbs show agreement in gender. The main verb is marked for Class 3 – the gender of 'bread'. Even though what the mother knows is a proposition – that the boy ate the bread – the verb 'know' agrees not with the subordinate clause that expresses this proposition but with a daughter constituent of this clause: 'bread'. Thus, just as in the Hungarian sentences analysed in Section 3.1, the main verb bears a syntactic relation with a part of the subordinate clause rather than the entire subordinate clause. The similarities are highlighted in (6), with the agreement controllers and targets in bold and identified with subscripts C and T.

(6) (a) HUNGARIAN (see (2c) in the preceding section)
          'I **want**$_T$ to see **you**$_C$.'

     (b) TSEZ ((1))
          'The mother **knows**$_T$ that the boy ate **the bread**$_C$.'

In spite of the basic agreement pattern being the same, there are also differences between the Hungarian and the Tsez constructions.

The first difference has to do with the **agreement features**: in Hungarian, agreement is in definiteness (and person) while in Tsez, agreement is in gender (and number, not shown in the example above).

A second difference has to do with the **controller** of the agreement. As noted above, Tsez is an ergative language while Hungarian is an accusative language. Thus, while in Hungarian, the controller of main verb agreement is the subordinate object, in Tsez, the controller of main verb agreement is the absolutive noun phrase of the subordinate clause that corresponds more to the subject than to the object of accusative languages. Nonetheless, in both languages, it is the subordinate Patient that is the controller.

Two other differences pertain to the agreement **target(s)**:

- In Hungarian, only the main verb agrees with the controller while in Tsez, both the main verb and the subordinate verb do.
- In Hungarian, the main verb must agree with the subordinate object; there is no alternative agreement pattern.

In Tsez, however, there is a choice: the main verb may alternatively agree with the entire clause as a whole instead of agreeing with the subordinate Patient. This was already shown in Section 1 (example (2)) and is shown again in (7). The sentence (7a) shows agreement with the object of the subordinate clause, (7b) shows agreement with the subordinate clause itself.

(7) (a) *Eni-r*   *b-iy-xo*   *už-a*   *magalu*
     mother-DAT **CL3**-know-PRES boy-ERG bread:ABS:**CL3**
     b-ac'-ru-λi.
     CL3-eat-PASTPART-NOMINALIZER
     'The mother knows that the boy ate bread.'

(b) *Eni-r*   *r-iy-xo*   *už-a*   *magalu*
     mother-DAT **CL4**-know-PRES boy-ERG bread:ABS:**CL3**
     b-ac'-ru-λi.
     CL3-eat-PASTPART-NOMINALIZER
     'The mother knows that the boy ate bread.'

The difference between (7a) and (7b) is the agreement prefix on the main verb: in (7a), it is Class 3 in agreement with 'bread'; in (7b), it is Class 4 in agreement with the entire subordinate clause.

Thus, unlike verb agreement in Hungarian, the Tsez agreement pattern involves both a paradigmatic and a syntagmatic conflict. The paradigmatic conflict is between alternative agreement patterns in the same language. This does not arise in Hungarian where the main verb must agree with the subordinate object: it cannot, as in Tsez, agree with the entire clause. The syntagmatic conflict is one familiar from Hungarian: the pattern of 'long-distance agreement'.

Since the study to be discussed below (Polinsky and Comrie 1999) does not address the problem of why there are alternative agreement patterns in Tsez, we will have nothing to say about it. In what follows, we will reproduce only a proposal to account for the long-distance agreement option.

As was seen above, the problem of the double allegiance of the subordinate Patient in Hungarian was solved by É. Kiss by assuming that the sentence is both bi-clausal and mono-clausal at the same time with the two structures represented as two faces of a dual tree. It is tempting to propose this solution for Tsez as well; but Polinsky and Comrie reject it. This is because, apart from the fact that the main verb agrees with it, the Patient does not behave as part of the main clause: it is a staunch constituent of the subordinate clause only (Polinsky and Comrie 1999: 118–20).

This is shown by **word order**. In Hungarian, the subordinate Patient acts as part of the main clause not only in that the main verb agrees with it but also in that it can be ordered to precede the main verb as its own focus constituent. In Tsez, however, the subordinate Patient must be ordered within the subordinate clause: in (7a), 'the bread' must follow 'the boy' and precede 'eaten'.

Apart from word order, another piece of evidence for the consistent bi-clausality of the Tsez sentences comes from the distribution of **reflexive pronouns**. In this language, the antecedent of a reflexive pronoun must be an ergative noun phrase of the same clause, which we will call the subject.

Take now the sentence 'The father knows Ali$_1$ to have sent himself$_1$ a letter' where, as the subscripts show, 'himself' refers to Ali. If the sentence were bi-clausal with the subordinate clause – 'Ali to have sent himself a letter' – separate from the main clause, the sentence with the intended meaning would be grammatical: 'himself' would refer back to the subject of the subordinate clause – 'Ali'. But if the sentence were mono-clausal, the subject of the sentence would be 'the father'. 'Ali' in turn would not be a subject and therefore the reflexive pronoun could not refer to him.

In actual fact, in the Tsez equivalent of the sentence, the reflexive pronoun must refer to Ali. This shows that 'Ali' is the subject of the clause where the reflexive pronoun occurs. This in turn means that the subordinate clause is indeed a clause separate from the main clause and the entire sentence is bi-clausal.

Let us summarize the verb–agreement problem in Tsez. The syntagmatic conflict posed by the Tsez data is the same as it is in Hungarian: a verb agrees with a noun phrase that is not its own complement. This is a problem because verb agreement is generally local: verbs agree with their own complements. É. Kiss's solution for Hungarian saves the locality of agreement by proposing that the sentences in question have a dual structure: they are both mono-clausal and bi-clausal. Since verb–object agreement applies on the mono-clausal side, the agreement pattern is local, after all. For Tsez, this solution is not possible: whereas in Hungarian there is additional evidence for the subordinate Patient being a constituent of the main clause, in Tsez, there is no such evidence. How can then the conflict be solved for Tsez?

A tentative proposal by Polinsky and Comrie is that the main verb should be considered a legitimate agreement target for the Patient of the subordinate verb even though the Patient is not the main verb's complement. They propose that, rather than insisting that agreement is local only if controller and target are clause-mates, the notion of locality should be relaxed by allowing a more comprehensive definition of what is a local domain (1999: 121).

In further work (2003: especially 302–8), Maria Polinsky makes a concrete proposal regarding permissible agreement domains. She suggests that the noun phrase of the subordinate clause that controls agreement with the main verb is moved to a clause-peripheral position in the embedded clause and that this position should be allowed to qualify as falling within a local domain for agreement.

Polinsky provides independent evidence for this proposal but for our purposes, the details are not relevant. What is important here is the way the proposal attempts to resolve a conflict. On the one hand, the Tsez data show that the subordinate Patient controls agreement with the main verb even though it is not the main verb's argument. On the other hand, there is a general principle which says agreement is local in the sense that verbs only agree with their own arguments. The solution proposed is that the locality requirement should be relaxed so as to accommodate the Tsez agreement pattern. In other words, Comrie and Polinsky propose to change the definition of 'local' so that it includes what, under the old definition, counts as 'non-local'. This is an instance of eliminating a contradiction by modifying one of the two conflicting statements (discussed in Section 3.2 of Chapter 1).

Here is the summary of the conflict that arises in connection with long-distance agreement in the Hungarian and Tsez data and the alternative solutions offered by É. Kiss and by Comrie and Polinsky.

(8) (a) CONFLICT:
   (i) THE LOCALITY OF AGREEMENT IN LANGUAGES
       Verb agreement is local in that verbs must agree with their own complements.
   (ii) NON-LOCAL AGREEMENT IN HUNGARIAN AND TSEZ
       Verb agreement in Hungarian and in Tsez is not local because verbs may or must agree with a noun phrase that is not their own complement.

   (b) RESOLUTION:
       • É. Kiss for Hungarian:
         Statement (ü) – that verb agreement is not local because verbs can agree with a noun phrase that is not their own complement – is not true for Hungarian. This is because the sentences in question have two simultaneous representations, one bi-clausal and one mono-clausal. Whereas in the bi-clausal representation, the bifacial noun phrase is not a complement of the main verb, in the mono-clausal representation, it is. Since object–verb agreement applies to the mono-clausal side of the tree, the locality of agreement is upheld.

- Comrie and Polinsky for Tsez:
  Statement (i) – that verb agreement must be local in that
  verbs must agree with their own complements – should be
  changed, with locality more broadly defined so as to
  accommodate the agreement pattern in Tsez. If this is
  done, the locality of agreement in Tsez is upheld.

Both proposals attempt to cope with the contradiction between the locality
of agreement in general and the exceptions to it in Hungarian and Tsez by
showing that apparent exceptions are not real: agreement is local, after all.
In É. Kiss's proposal for Hungarian, agreement is analysed as local with
respect to one of the two faces of the tree representations of the sentence
type in question. Thus, in this proposal, the conflict between the two statements is eliminated by relegating it to the structure of the sentences in question: it is now the structural representation of the sentences that contains a
conflict by being both mono-clausal and bi-clausal. In Polinsky and Comrie's
proposal for Tsez, it is admitted that agreement in Tsez is non-local under
the existing definition; but they propose that Tsez agreement is local if the
definition of 'local' is changed so as to cover the Tsez cases.

3.3 THE LARGER PICTURE

In addition to Hungarian and Tsez, many other languages also have sentences
that pose similar conflicts: a single noun phrase seems to bear syntactic
relations to more than one verb. English is one of these languages. The examples in (1)–(4) show subordinate subjects acting as subjects and objects of
main verbs ((1), (2)), and subordinate objects acting as main subjects or
main objects ((3), (4)). Alternative expressions of the same meanings are
given in parentheses to make explicit the grammatical functions of these
noun phrases in the subordinate clause.

(1) A noun phrase is both
  - **subject** of the infinitive and
  - **subject** of the main verb:
  (a) ***John*** *seems to have passed the exam.*
      (cf. *It seems that **John** has passed the exam.*)

  (b) ***The storm*** *is likely to hit tonight.*
      (cf. *It is likely that **the storm** will hit tonight.*)

(2) A noun phrase is both
  - **subject** of the infinitive and
  - **object** of the main verb:
  (a) *I take **the problem** to have been solved.*
      (cf. *I take it that **the problem** has been solved.*)

    (b) *The doctor expects **Susan's weight** to turn out to be the problem.*
        (cf. *The doctor expects that **Susan's weight** will turn out to be the problem.*)

(3) A noun phrase is both
- **object** of the infinitive and
- **subject** of the main verb:

    (a) ***This customer** is easy to please.*
        (cf. *It is easy to please **this customer**.*)

    (b) ***The kitten** is fun to tease.*
        (cf. *It is fun to tease **the kitten**.*)

(4) A noun phrase is both
- **object** of the infinitive and
- **object** of the main verb:

    (a) *They are seeking **a secretary** to hire.*
        (cf. *They are seeking to hire **a secretary**.*)

    (b) *The dog wants **a cat** to fight.*
        (cf. *The dogs wants to fight **a cat**.*)

Some evidence for the double syntactic function of such noun phrases was presented in Section 1 of Chapter 1 in connection with the sentence *Susan expected him to succeed.* Note, for example, the occurrence possibilities of reflexive pronouns in (5).

(5) (a) *John$_i$ considers **himself**$_i$ to have been fired.*
     (b) *John$_i$ believes **Jim**$_j$ to have hurt **himself**$_j$.*

These sentences are similar in structure to those in (2). They consist of a main clause and a subordinate clause. The question is which clause do the bold noun phrases (*himself* in (5a) and *Jim* in (5b)) belong to?

The distribution of reflexive pronouns provides contradictory answers. The general rule about these pronouns in English is the same, as we saw, for Tsez: reflexives have to be clause-mates to their antecedents. In (5a), the reflexive pronoun *himself* refers to 'John', so this indicates that it is part of the main clause. In (5b), the noun phrase in the same position as *himself* in (5a) is *Jim* and thus one would assume that Jim is part of the main clause just as *himself* in (5a). But in (5b), *himself* can only refer to Jim, not John. This means that *Jim* cannot be part of the main clause since if that were the case, the general rule about antecedent and reflexive pronouns being clause-mates would be violated. In order for the clause-mate condition to be upheld, *Jim* has to be analysed as part of the subordinate clause. Thus, evidence is contradictory regarding the allegiance of the bold noun phrases in (5).

What exactly are the similarities between the English sentences in (1)–(4) and the Hungarian and Tsez examples discussed above? The Tsez examples are in some ways like the English sentences in (1): the subordinate subject functions as the subject of the main verb. This is shown in (6), with the Tsez structure mimicked by using English words in (6a).

(6) (a) Tsez: '**The bread** is known to have been eaten.'
     (b) English: ***The bread*** *seems to be gone.*

The Hungarian examples are in turn analogous to the English sentences in (4): a subordinate object functions as a main object. This is shown in (7), with the Hungarian structure mimicked by English words in (7a).

(7) (a) Hungarian: 'I would like **you** to see.' (meaning 'I would like to see you.')
     (b) English: *I would like **a book** to read.*

As was seen in Chapter 1 (Section 1), syntacticians have considered different ways of accounting for the double function of such noun phrases. In **Word Grammar**, it is simply acknowledged that a single noun phrase can be dependent on more than one head. In **Relational Grammar**, the two functions of this noun phrase are shown to hold in two different strata of the tree diagram of the sentence; and in (some versions of) **Transformational Grammar**, they are shown to hold in two different tree diagrams each representing a distinct level of syntactic representation.

In addition, there are three analyses in the literature that succeed in placing these constructions in a broader context. These will be discussed next.

The first analysis is **structural**: it underscores a common denominator to the four patterns illustrated in (1)–(4). The common denominator has to do with the grammatical function that the noun phrase has in the main clause: in all cases, it is the same grammatical function as that which the subordinate clause bears relative to the main clause. For an example, take the sentence *We found her to be out of breath* (of the type illustrated in (2) above). Here are three facts about this sentence:

- selectionally, the entire subordinate clause *she was out of breath* is the **object** of the **main verb** *found*;
- selectionally, *her* is the **subject** of the **subordinate verb** *to be out of breath*;
- by case marking, *her* is the **object** of the **main verb** *found.*

Notice the match between the grammatical function of the entire clause within the main clause (in terms of selection) and the grammatical role of *her* in the main clause (in terms of case marking): in both cases, the grammatical function is objecthood.

This pattern was recognized and formulated in Relational Grammar as the **Relational Succession Law**. As was seen in Chapter 1 (Section 1), in this framework noun phrases change their grammatical function in the course of a syntactic derivation. In our examples, the noun phrase in question starts out as an argument of the subordinate clause and then is advanced to becoming an argument of the main clause. In this process, called ascension, the ascending noun phrase inherits the grammatical function of the subordinate clause that it comes from. The principle is given in (8) (NP is taken to dominate the subordinate clause); (9) illustrates it for all four sentence types cited in (1)–(4). Note that the pre-ascension versions of the sentences may or may not be grammatical in English.

> (8) 'An ascendee assumes within the clause . . . into which is ascends the grammatical relation of its host NP (the NP . . . out of which it ascends).'
>
> (Perlmutter and Postal 1983: 35)

(9) (a) Before ascension: the subordinate clause is **subject** of the main clause.
Example: ***That he won the case*** *appears.*
After ascension: the subject of the subordinate clause becomes the **subject** of the main clause.
Example: ***He*** *appears to have won the case.*

(b) Before ascension: the subordinate clause is **object** of the main clause.
Example: *We found **that she was out of breath**.*
After ascension: the subject of the subordinate clause becomes the **object** of the main clause.
Example: *We found **her** to be out of breath.*

(c) Before ascension: the subordinate clause is **subject** of the main clause.
Example: ***To beat this flu*** *is tough.*
After ascension: the object of the subordinate clause becomes the **subject** of the main clause.
Example: ***This flu*** *is tough to beat.*

(d) Before ascension: the subordinate clause is **object** of the main clause.
Example: '*Jim wants **that he read a good book**.*'
After ascension: the object of the subordinate clause becomes the **object** of the main clause.
Example: *Jim wants **a good book** to read.*

Thus, these four seemingly disparate constructions all obey a single generalization captured by the Relational Succession Law.

The second analysis that places these sentences into a broader context is **functional**: it interprets the Relational Succession Law within the domain of general human conceptualization. In his analysis within the framework of Cognitive Grammar, Ronald Langacker (1995a) recognizes this pattern as an instance of a very widespread phenomenon called **metonymy**. Metonymy is a figure of speech where a concept is referred to not directly by the word that conveys it but by a word that refers to something associated with that concept. Often, the operant relationship is partonomy: a part may be used for the whole. In rhetorical tradition, this subtype of metonymy is called 'pars pro toto' ('part for whole' in Latin). In (10a–c), reference to persons is by mentioning a body part. In (10d) and (10e), an object – a car, a house – is referred to by mentioning a relevant structural part of these objects.

(10) (a) *Give me a **hand**.*
      (b) *It was a meeting of great **minds**.*
      (c) *Move your **rear end**.*
      (d) *So you got new **wheels**.*
      (e) *They just wanted a **roof** over their heads.*

Examples of metonymic patterns are common outside language as well, such as when a lock of hair of an ancestor is preserved in the family as a reminder or when the embalmed hand of a saint is revered by the faithful.

In pars-pro-toto constructions as in (10), the part is used in exactly the same grammatical function as the whole would be. This is parallel to the noun phrases discussed in this section: a part of the subordinate clause is used in the same grammatical function as that which the whole clause has, with the overall meaning being the same as when the subordinate clause is the actual argument of the main clause. These constructions are therefore instances of the part-pro-toto pattern.

But how do these constructions arise in the course of **historical evolution**? In his study of a similar construction in another Caucasian language, Godoberi, Martin Haspelmath (1999: 147–8) points out that these strange patterns are the result of a well-known diachronic process called grammaticalization. This third account once again provides a broader vista for the existence of the constructions discussed in this section.

Grammaticalization involves the re-analysis of meaningful constructions into merely formal ones devoid of the original semantic content. They involve the reduction of both meaning and form. An example is the English expression *going to*. It originally referred to actual locomotion, but now it is used to express simple future even if no movement is involved, with its form often reduced to *gonna* (e.g. *I am going to (or gonna) continue in my present job*).

Another example of grammaticalization is the process whereby definite articles arise from demonstratives in the course of history. Thus, in English, certain instances of the English demonstrative *that* have become bleached of their original spatial meaning and reduced in form to today's *the*. A similar process gave rise to the definite article in Spanish, French and Italian all having evolved from *ille, illa, illud* – the three gender forms of Latin 'that'.

One of the changes that happen in the course of grammaticalization is for a constituent to reduce its broad semantically based scope to a narrower one in its formal expression (see Lehmann 1995: 143–7). If we assume that the sentences showing long-distance agreement are historically derived from sentences that contain two distinct clauses, the process of the main verb losing its scope over the entire subordinate clause and limiting it to one noun phrase of that clause is an instance of scope narrowing. Thus, it is an instance of the multiply documented general historical process of grammaticalization.

4 Conclusions

In his introduction to the paper on Tsez agreement by Maria Polinsky and Bernard Comrie discussed above, Greville Corbett writes: '[Polinsky and Comrie] show how certain (main) verbs can agree with a noun phrase in a lower clause . . . This is a domain which many would have considered **impossible**, because of locality, and the existence of such an agreement pattern is a challenge to many existing theories of agreement' (Corbett 1999: 194; emphasis added).

This is an apt characterization of what are ultimate problems in scientific analysis: a phenomenon occurs even though it seems completely beyond the realm of possibilities. It holds for long-distance agreement, as well as for the other syntactic pattern discussed in this chapter: discontinous order. In both cases, constituents show unique, possibly even 'unheard-of' behaviour, one that runs counter to expectation.

Both discontinuity and long-distance agreement have to do with 'distance': discontinuity involves linear distance whereas long-distance agreement involves syntactic distance: being or not being clause-mates. In discontinuous constructions, constituents that are otherwise related are, surprisingly, dissembled in linear order; in long-distance agreement, constituents that are not otherwise related are, surprisingly, linked by agreement. Discontinous constructions thus present us with an unexpected lack of adjacency between related constituents; long-distance agreement presents us with an unexpected agreement relation between unrelated constituents.

We have seen various attempts to solve these conflicts. In the case of discontinuous verbs and particles, the proposals addressing the syntagmatic conflict between the various syntactic relations in the same sentence involved either accepting the conflict or 'pulling apart' the paradoxical entity to various degrees so that, of the conflicting properties, each property holds only for one part of that entity or it holds for that entity when viewed from one of several angles. In the case of long-distance agreement, the two solutions discussed amounted to showing that the exceptional cases were not in fact exceptional either because the sentences had two faces and agreement applied to the face where it was local, or because the locality condition was proposed to be relaxed. Each of these solutions bears out one of the limited set of ways in which, as was seen in Chapter 1 (Section 3.2), conflicts can in principle be resolved.

In the analyses surveyed, we have seen various degrees of separation of the conflicting properties in a sentence. A summary of the options is given in (1). 'A' and 'B' stand for contradictory properties; a V-shape, standing or inverted, symbolizes a constituent-structure tree. Each rectangle defines a component of the grammar (such as semantic or syntactic).

(1) (a) **Composite tree**
Conflicting sentence properties represented on the same side of a single diagram (see Section 2.2)

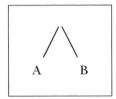

(b) **Bi-facial tree**
Conflicting sentence properties represented on different sides of a single diagram (see Section 3.1)

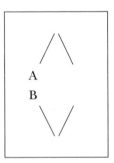

(c) **Multiple trees in a single component**
Conflicting sentence properties represented in different diagrams within the same component of grammar (see Section 2.2)

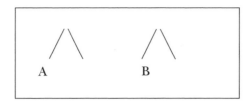

(d) **Multiple trees in different components**
Conflicting sentence properties represented in different
diagrams in different components of the grammar
(see Section 2.2)

 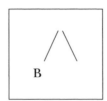

The legitimacy of the splits depends on their independent justification.
Composite trees (1a), bifacial trees (1b), and multiple trees in a single component (1c) are in need of extensive justification. The syntax–semantics split
(1d), however, rests on firm grounds since meaning and syntactic form are
obviously distinct entities. This approach reduces contradictions within syntax
to contradictions between two domains – form and meaning – that are known
to be multiply contradictory and thus indeed best viewed as distinct entities.

Notes

2.1   What is discontinuous order?

- For additional evidence for the unithood of discontinuous
  elements, see McCawley 1982b: 98–9.
- Two excellent collections of studies on discontinuity and the ways
  different theories have dealt with it are Huck and Ojeda 1987;
  and Bunt and van Horck 1996.
- For a collection of recent studies on verb–particle constructions,
  see Dehé *et al.* 2002.

3.2   Tsez
For other examples of apparent long-distance agreement and how to
re-intepret them as local, rather than long-distance, see Polinsky 2003.

3.3   The larger picture
On grammaticalization, see for example Heine *et al.* 1991; Traugott and
Heine 1991.

Exercises

1. As discussed in the chapter, Breton has topicalization constructions and the topicalized words must form a phrase.

   (a) Identify similar topicalization constructions in English.
   (b) What constituents can be topicalized in English? Can verbs be topicalized as in Breton?
   (c) Is it true for English, as it is for Breton, that the topicalized material must form a single phrase?

2. Find examples of English sentences with constituents alternatively ordered as adjacent and non-adjacent. Which of the alternative orders would be expected based on selectional and other syntactic relations between the constituents?

3. In examples (1)–(4) of Section 3.3, four patterns were shown where a noun phrase appears to have a syntactic function both in the subordinate clause and in the main clause. Some evidence for the double function of that noun phrase in pattern (2) – a noun phrase being the subject of the subordinate clause and the object of the main clause – was presented in that section and in Section 1 of Chapter 1. Find similar evidence for the double functioning of the bold noun phrases in the other three construction types.

4. How does agreement work in English? What can be controller and target, and what are the agreement features?

5. Consider the data from the six languages in the Appendix. Apart from English, which of the languages show agreement? What are the controllers, targets and agreement features?

Chapter Three

Alternative Analyses of Symbolic Correspondence Relations: Co-ordination

[C]ontradictions are of the greatest importance in the history of thought – precisely as important as is criticism. For criticism invariably consists in pointing out some contradiction; either a contradiction within the theory criticized, or a contradiction between the theory and another theory which we have some reason to accept, or a contradiction between the theory and certain facts – or more precisely, between the theory and certain statements of facts. . . . Without contradictions, without criticism, there would be no rational motive for changing our theories: there would be no intellectual progress.

(Popper 1962: 316)

1 Preliminaries

In the preceding chapter, alternative analyses of conflicts within syntactic form were discussed. In this chapter and the next, we will turn to conflicts between syntactic form and meaning.

Symbolic objects – traffic signs, hand gestures, rituals or sentences – convey content through form. One of the ways in which the form of a symbolic object can closely trace its meaning is if each segment of the form corresponds to a segment of the meaning and each segment of meaning corresponds to a bit of form. This strict, one-to-one relationship between components of form and components of meaning is called **compositionality**.

Compositionality holds, for example, for the hand signals that the conductor gives to his orchestra. The direction in which the baton is pointed indicates the instruments for which the message is meant and the size and shape of the gesture conveys the dynamics intended. In this case, all of form relates to meaning and no meaning is left to be inferred: the gesture is compositional. A symbol that falls short of compositionality is a stop sign: there is nothing in the design of the sign that indicates that it is meant for vehicles only, not for pedestrians.

Sentences of human languages vary in whether they are compositional or not. Take the simple sentence *The weather is stormy.* Its meaning is a present-tense predicate – 'is stormy'; the semantic argument that it is stated of is 'the weather'. The predicate, its tense and the subject are all overtly expressed in the form of the sentence. Thus, the sentence is compositional.

Contrast this example with the following:

(1) (a) *Go home!*
     (b) *John went home and fixed dinner.*
     (c) *John is a better cook than Sue.*

In each sentence, there is a meaning element that has no corresponding expression. The sentence in (1a) is understood as having a 'you'-subject; yet, the word *you* is not present (cf. the discussion in Chapter 1, Section 3.1.). In (1b), the predicate 'fixed dinner' has no overtly expressed subject: we know that it is John only by inference. In the second part of (1c) in turn, a subject is given – 'Sue' – but it lacks an expression of the predicate 'is a cook'.

These sentences exemplify one of three basic non-compositional patterns: 'more meaning than form'. In this respect, they are like stop signs where no part of the form indicates that the message is for vehicles only. The opposite kind of violation of compositionality is also amply exemplified from both inside and outside language. Consider a clock. The circular layout of the hours of the day and the two hands convey the message: they tell you what time it is. But other aspects of its form – such as colour and shape – are add-ons: they do not correspond to any part of the meaning. Here, there is 'more form than meaning'.

The sentences in (2) show the same kind of departure from compositionality.

(2) (a) *There is a mouse in the cabinet.*
     (b) *It is snowing.*
     (c) *My children do not like cakes.*

In each sentence, there is a bit of form that is empty of meaning. These are: *there, it* and *do*. The meaninglessness of *there* is proven by the fact that the same message can be conveyed even if *there* is omitted, as in *A mouse is in the cabinet*. And the meaninglessness of all three words is shown by the fact that when these sentences are translated into other languages, equivalents of these words may not be part of the sentences; yet the meaning is intact. Here are the Russian equivalents:

(3) (a) *Myš   v   garderobe.*
         mouse in cabinet

     (b) *Sneg id'ot.*
         snow goes

     (c) *Moi d'eti   n'e jed'at torta.*
         my children no eat   cake

We have so far seen two ways in which symbols may fall short of compositionality, which we labelled as 'more meaning than form' and 'more form than meaning'. A third way in which symbols may fall short of compositionality has to do with relationship among meaning elements and the relationship among the corresponding form elements. A picture intending to represent a chicken that does not include the head is an example of 'more meaning than form'; one that shows two heads exemplifies 'more form than meaning'. Both of these fail what might be called **selectional compositionality**, since these mismatches have to do with the selection of meaning elements and form elements. But what is wrong with a picture of a chicken that shows the legs coming out of the head? All meaning elements – the body parts – are represented and there are no extra bits of form; but the form components do not faithfully reflect the arrangement of the parts. This picture complies with selectional compositionality but fails **relational compositionality**.

Such non-congruent arrangements of meaning parts and form parts also occur in syntax, as shown in (4).

(4) (a) *The detective looked the address up.*
     (b) *The girl came to my office who was carrying a suitcase.*
     (c) *The fact bothered Mary that John was leaving.*

The construction represented in (4a) is familiar from Chapter 2, Section 2.2: verb and particle are separated even though they form a single semantic unit. In (4b), the semantic unity of head and relative clause is disrupted and so is the semantic unity of head and complement clause in (4c).

Such mismatches between meaning and syntactic form have been central problems in syntactic theorizing. Various aspects of this problem will be discussed in this chapter and the next along with alternative solutions. In this chapter, we will see how compositionality fares in one particular syntactic pattern: co-ordination.

In Section 2, co-ordinate constructions will be introduced along with the ways in which they may satisfy or deviate from compositionality. In Section 3, two of the possible types of deviations will be focused on along with their alternative analyses. Section 4 presents some conclusions.

2 Compositionality in co-ordinate constructions

The highlighted parts in (1) offer examples of co-ordinate constructions.

   (1) (a) ***The sparrow and the seagull*** *are common in Wisconsin.*
        (b) ***The sparrow, the seagull and the Canadian goose*** *are common in Wisconsin.*

As these examples show, the syntactic composition of co-ordinate constructions varies in how many parts they include: two in (1a) and three in (1b). The examples in (2) and (3) show other syntactic differences among them: what the parts are, whether the parts are or are not connected by a linking element, and if they are, what that linking element is.

   (2) TYPE OF PARTS: NOUN PHRASE, VERB PHRASE, ADJECTIVAL PHRASE, PREPOSITIONAL PHRASE, CLAUSE
      (a) *Ralph liked **the tomato soup and the roasted turkey**.*
      (b) *Ralph **liked the tomato soup but disliked the turkey**.*
      (c) *The **well-spiced and well-cooked** turkey was a real treat.*
      (d) *This pumpkin pie should be served **on a silver platter and with a silver spatula**.*
      (e) ***The tomato soup was served first and then Jill brought in the turkey**.*

   (3) LINKING ELEMENT
      (a) *Peter voted for Bush, ____ Paul for Gore **and** Pat passed.*
      (b) *Peter voted for Bush **but** Jill disagreed with him.*
      (c) ***Either** most voters opted for Bush **or** the talliers goofed.*

What defines all these constructions as instances of the same type: co-ordination? In each, there are two or more like parts joined into a larger unit of the same kind. The parts are called **conjuncts**; the linking element is called **connective** (or conjunction), and the entire expression is termed **co-ordinate construction**. Conjuncts of the same co-ordinate construction will be termed **co-conjuncts**. The verbs 'co-ordinate' and 'conjoin' will be used synonymously,

Under what conditions are co-ordinate constructions compositional and under what conditions do they violate compositionality? Since, as seen above, compositionality has to do with a piece-by-piece match between meaning and form, to answer these questions we first need to describe the meaning of these constructions.

Accounts of meanings are called semantic representations. They consist of **propositions**. Each proposition consists of a **predicate** and a set of **arguments**. Propositions roughly correspond to sentences, predicates correspond to verbs and arguments are noun phrases. For example, in *Peter showed the ladybug to his friend*, the predicate is 'showed' and the arguments are 'Peter', 'the ladybug' and 'his friend'. Both arguments and predicates bear semantic functions. The function of a predicate is its modality: whether it is asserted (as in a main clause) or presupposed (as in a relative clause) or questioned. In the example above, the predicate 'showed' is asserted. For arguments, function equals semantic participant role: the role that the referent of an argument plays in the event described by the predicate. In the sentence above, the three arguments have different participant roles: 'Peter' is the doer, which we will call Agent; 'the ladybug' is the undergoer, or Patient; and 'his friend' is the Recipient.

While this is only a sketchy characterization of semantic representations, it is sufficient for us to formulate some requirements that well-formed meaning representations of co-ordinate constructions must meet.

(4) (a) Semantic co-ordinate constructions must be semantic constituents.
    (b) Semantic conjuncts must be semantic constituents.
    (c) Semantic co-conjuncts must be of the same semantic type.
    (d) Semantic co-ordinate constructions must be of the same semantic type as their co-conjuncts.

The statements in (4a) and (4b) say that the entire co-ordinate construction and each conjunct within it must be a semantic constituent: a complete argument or a complete predicate or a complete proposition. That in (4c) says that semantic co-conjuncts have to be of the same semantic type:

- **Two semantic constituents** may be conjoined if they agree in their term type, such as if both are predicates, or both are arguments, or both are propositions; but not if one is argument and the other a predicate, or one is a predicate and the other a proposition, and so on.
- **Two predicates** may be conjoined if they agree in their modality, such as if both are asserted, or both are presupposed, or both are interrogative; but not if one is asserted and the other is presupposed and so on.
- **Two arguments** may be conjoined if they agree in their participant role, such as if both are Agents, or both Patients, or both Recipients; but not if one is an Agent and the other is a Patient and so on.

And finally, (4d) says the entire co-ordinate structure has to be of the same semantic type as each co-conjunct. For example, if the co-conjuncts are Agents, the entire construction has to be an Agent.

Let us see how these requirements hold for a specific example. In (5) is shown the semantic representation of the sentence *The sparrow and the seagull are common in Wisconsin*, with the co-ordinate structure highlighted. ('Theme' is the label for the semantic participant role designating a participant of a happening or state, rather than of an action.)

(5) ((ASSERTION, PRESENT, COMMON), (**(THEME (THEME, SPARROW, GENERIC), (THEME, SEAGULL, GENERIC) (AND))**), (LOCATION, WISCONSIN))

As (4a) requires, the entire semantic co-ordinate construction ('the sparrow and the seagull') is a semantic argument of the predicate 'be common'. Each of the two conjuncts ('the sparrow' and 'the seagull') is a semantic constituent (cf. (4b)) and they are of the same type: both are Themes (see (4c)), sharing this participant rule with the entire co-ordinate structure (see (4d)).

The discussion so far had to do with the meaning of co-ordinate constructions; let us now turn to their syntax. What would it look like for the syntax of co-ordinate constructions to be compositional – that is, to mirror their semantic structure as described in (4)? As seen in Section 1, compositionality may hold between constituents of meaning and form and between the relationships of the constituents on the two levels. The first kind – selectional compositionality – means that for each meaning constituent, there is a syntactic constituent and for each syntactic constituent, there is a meaning constituent. Thus, for selectionally compositional co-ordinate constructions, the following has to be true:

(6) (a) For each semantic conjunct, there is a syntactic conjunct.
    (b) For each syntactic conjunct, there is a semantic conjunct.

Relational compositionality in turn requires that for each semantic relation, there be a corresponding syntactic relation and vice versa. Thus, relationally compositional co-ordinate constructions have to duplicate the semantic relations among semantic conjuncts as described in (4): semantic constituency must be paralleled by syntactic constituency and semantic sameness relations among constituents must be paralleled by syntactic sameness. The four characteristics of relationally compositional co-ordinate constructions are listed in (7).

(7) (a) Syntactic co-ordinate constructions are syntactic constituents.
    (b) Syntactic conjuncts are syntactic constituents.
    (c) Syntactic co-conjuncts are of the same syntactic type.
    (d) Syntactic co-ordinate constructions are of the same syntactic type as their co-conjuncts.

In the balance of this chapter, we will test two of these predictions: the partonomic requirement in (7b), that syntactic conjuncts must be syntactic constituents; and the taxonomic requirement in (7c), that syntactic co-conjuncts must be of the same syntactic type. (Points (7a) and (7d) will be taken up in exercise 3 at the end of the chapter.) As we will see, co-ordinate structures do not always fulfil these expectations. The resulting mismatches between meaning and syntactic form have been addressed in various ways in the literature.

3 Non-compositionality in co-ordinate constructions and its alternative analyses

3.1 CONJUNCTS THAT ARE NOT CONSTITUENTS

3.1.1 The problem

In an obvious sense, conjuncts are syntactic constituents by definition. A set of words is analysed as a single constituent if and only if they serve to facilitate the formulation of a generalization. Since conjuncts of co-ordinate structures are obviously conjoined, they serve as terms in the description of co-ordinate constructions and thus they are constituents in this limited sense.

But the interesting question is this: is the syntactic constituenthood of conjuncts motivated outside co-ordination so that they are constituents for purposes of other syntactic patterns as well? It is in this sense that the constituency of conjuncts has been a much-debated issue in the literature. Many examples of non-constituent co-ordination have been found and several solutions proposed. By 'non-constituent conjunct' we will mean conjuncts whose constituency is not borne out by any syntactic pattern outside co-ordination.

To highlight the issue, let us first take an example where conjuncts are multiply motivated constituents. Consider (1).

(1) ***Two hikers and three dogs*** *disappeared in the storm.*

There is evidence that *two hikers* and *three dogs* are each a multiply motivated syntactic constituent. First, note that their internal composition – the selection and order of the word classes they consist of – is phrasal. If in sentences such as *Two cookies are missing, two cookies* is a phrase, then so are *two hikers* and *three dogs* because they all contain a numeral followed by a noun.

Second, the conjuncts in (1) are phrases by their external syntax as well. Take the two rules in (2).

(2) (a) In English, the direct object noun phrase must stand after the verb.
     (b) In English passive sentences, the agentive noun phrase must occur with the preposition *by*.

As shown in (3), the conjuncts in (1) are indeed noun phrases for purposes of these two rules: they serve as direct objects in (3a) and (3b) and they form *by*-phrases in (3c) and (3d).

(3)　(a)　*The rescue squad spotted **two hikers**.*
　　(b)　*The policeman picked **three dogs**.*
　　(c)　*The mountain was climbed by **two hikers**.*
　　(d)　*The wolf was scared away by **three dogs**.*

However, not all conjuncts pass these constituency tests. Consider the sentences in (4). Some of the conjuncts in (4) are multiply motivated syntactic constituents but others are not.

(4)　(a)　**The cook prepared the salad** *and* **the busboy, the dressing.**
　　(b)　**Jack was born in Chicago** *and* **his sister, in Bloomington.**
　　(c)　**Peter wrote** *and* **his brother edited the book.**
　　(d)　**I met** *and* **my brother drove home our cousin.**
　　(e)　*John saw* **Mary in Chicago** *and* **Harry in Sheboygan.**

The examples in (5) list the instances where the second conjunct is a non-constituent; (6) lists the cases where the first conjunct is a non-constituent; and (7) shows that in (4e), neither conjunct is a constituent for purposes of other patterns.

(5)　In (4a): CONST: *the cook prepared the salad*
　　　　　　　NON-CONST: the busboy, the dressing

　　　In (4b): CONST: *Jack was born in Chicago*
　　　　　　　NON-CONST: his sister, in Indiana

(6)　In (4c): **NON-CONST: Peter wrote**
　　　　　　　CONST: *his brother edited the book*

　　　In (4d): **NON-CONST: I met**
　　　　　　　CONST: *my brother drove home our cousin*

(7)　In (4e): **NON-CONST: Mary in Chicago**
　　　　　　　NON-CONST: Harry in Sheboygan

Evidence for the non-constituency of the bolded units is manifold. From the point of view of internal structure, two juxtaposed noun phrases as in *the busboy, the dressing* do not match any independently attested phrasal structure, nor does subject & verb as in *I met*. Furthermore, these structures also fall short of being constituents from the point of view of their external syntax or distribution. For example, phrases generally have corresponding pro-forms (pronoun-phrases such as *he* or *it*, or 'pro-verbs' such as *do so*); but there is no pro-form available to fill the position of any of the bolded material in (5), (6) and (7). The sentences in (8) and (9) show how the sequence verb & direct object has an available pro-form to replace it, but the sequence subject & transitive verb lacks such a pro-form.

> (8) (a) *John **saw Mary** in Chicago and Bill **saw Mary** in Sheboygan.*
>   (b) *John **saw Mary** in Chicago and Bill **did so** in Sheboygan.*

> (9) (a) ***John saw** Mary in Chicago and **John saw** Jill in Sheboygan.*
>   (b) *****John saw** Mary in Chicago and **PRO-FORM** Jill in Sheboygan.*

The problem is summarized in (10).

> (10) EXPECTATION
>   Compositionality requires that, just as every semantic conjunct is a semantic constituent, every syntactic conjunct be a syntactic constituent.
>   OBSERVATION
>   In actual fact, some syntactic conjuncts are syntactic constituents, others are not.

A comment by Simon Dik highlights the problem. He notes that both sentences in (11) are well-formed:

> (11) (a) *John **washed the dishes** and **cleaned the sink**.*
>   (b) ***John washed** and **Mary dried** the dishes.*

If we insisted that conjuncts be constituents, we would have to view the verb and the object as making up a constituent in (11a) and the subject and the verb as forming a constituent in (11b). Such an analysis would result in a complex partonomic structure: the two phrases would overlap in the verb. In other words, the verb would be a part of two distinct wholes at the same time. Dik remarks (1997: 196):

> Since no theory of grammar claims (indeed, can claim) that subject + predicate **and** predicate + object form unified constituents at the same time, the hypothesis that only constituents can be co-ordinated cannot be upheld without very powerful additional assumptions.

Let us now see what the powerful assumptions are that syntacticians have adopted in their accounts of non-constituent co-ordination. We will discuss two approaches: Noam Chomsky's Transformational Generative Grammar as formulated in the 1960s and 1970s, and David Pesetsky's Dual Structure theory of 1995. As we will see, both accounts acknowledge that non-constituent conjuncts are just what they seem to be; but both propose that these constructions also have another, somewhat hidden 'personality' where non-constituents are regular, multiply motivated constituents. With respect to this other 'personality' the tight fit between meaning and syntactic form required by compositionality does hold. Both proposals split the controversial object into two parts and relegate exceptionality to only one of the two.

3.1.2 Constituents on one level, not on another

According a version of Generative Transformational analysis as practised in the 1960s and 1970s, non-constituent conjuncts in surface structure are actually constituents in underlying structure. For example:

(1) (a) Surface Structure:
  *John sat on the chair and **Peter, on the sofa**.*
 (b) Underlying Structure:
  *John sat on the chair and **Peter sat on the sofa**.*

(2) (a) Surface Structure:
  ***John wrote** and Bill edited the book.*
 (b) Underlying Structure:
  ***John wrote the book** and Bill edited the book.*

The descriptive apparatus involves two rules: a Co-ordination Rule and a Deletion by Identity Rule. **The Co-ordination Rule** joins together well-formed sentences yielding the constructions in (1b) and (2b). Underlying and surface structure are in a 'derivational relationship', which means that they are linked by various rules that change underlying structures into surface structures (see the discussion in Chapter 1, Sections 3.3 and 3.4.). The rule applying to the underlying structures to yield surface structures in (1) and (2) is the **Deletion by Identity Rule**. This rule optionally erases one of two identical parts in conjoined sentences according to certain directionality constraints. In (1a), it eliminates the second occurrence of *sat*; in (2a), it deletes the first occurrence of *the book*. Underlying constituent conjuncts may thus surface as non-constituents: a noun phrase & prepositional phrase in (1a) and a subject & verb in (2a).

Notice that in light of this analysis, there is no reason to expect surface conjuncts to be constituents. Conjuncts do have to be constituents for the Co-ordination Rule; but since this rule applies in underlying structure, the conjuncts that surface do not have to be constituents. Surface constructions are not inputs to the Co-ordination Rule; they are its outputs. The inputs of the Co-ordination Rule are full sentences, which are multiply motivated constituents.

Surface structure may thus be compared to a building ravaged by fire. The charred ruins of a house may not look much like a house at all but they are not an 'exception' to what houses look like as long as they are understood to have been 'derived' from a well-formed building.

The Transformational Analysis is convincing only to the extent that the descriptive apparatus that it utilizes has independent justification. Thus, the theoretical construct of underlying structure and the Deletion by Identity rule need to be independently motivated: if they were posited only to explain away non-constituent conjuncts, the account would be circular.

Much of the vast literature on Transformational Generative Grammar of the 1960s and 1970s indeed focuses on shoring up the assumptions of underlying structures and transformations, including Deletion by Identity – and with considerable success.

To start with the utility of underlying structure outside co-ordinate structures: it can be documented with respect to wh-questions (see Chapter 1, Section 3.4). Consider the sentences in (3) and (4).

(3) (a) *Jill met a friend last night.*
     (b) **Jill married an idea last night.*

(4) (a) *Who did Jill meet last night?*
     (b) **What did Jill marry last night?*

In (3) it is shown that in statements, the verb *meet* requires a human for its direct object. In (4) it is shown that in wh-questions, the verb *meet* requires a human interrogative pronoun. The two observations can be collapsed into a single generalization if we assume that the question pronoun is the direct object of the verb. As noted in Chapter 1, in this version of the transformational framework, grammatical functions and linear relations are inseparable. This means that the direct-object question pronoun occurs post-verbally in underlying structure just as other direct objects do, before a transformation moves it into sentence-initial position. This account eliminates the need for a special selection rule for the question pronoun by subsuming this pattern under the more general one that applies to *meet* and its direct object regardless of whether the direct object is a full noun phrase or a question pronoun. To the extent that this account makes crucial use of underlying structures, it supports the general concept of this level of representation.

The Deletion by Identity transformation can be similarly shown to be a useful device outside co-ordinate constructions. Consider the following sentences:

(5) (a) *Peter promised Paul to pay back the loan.*
     (b) *Peter persuaded Paul to pay back the loan.*

Even though the two sentences do not appear distinct in syntactic form, they greatly differ in interpretation: in (5a), the understood subject of *pay back the loan* is 'Peter' while in (5b), it is 'Paul'. A way of accounting for this is by assuming distinct underlying structures for the two sentences. The Deletion by Identity rule then collapses them into identical surface structures. The underlying structures can be paraphrased as follows:

(6) (a)   *Peter promised Paul [**Peter** pay back the loan]ₛ.*
     (b)   *Peter persuaded Paul [**Paul** pay back the loan]ₛ.*

In (6a), there are two occurrences of *Peter*; in (6b), in turn, *Paul* is mentioned twice. Thus, in (6a), Deletion by Identity applies to *Peter* in the second clause; in (6b), it applies to *Paul.* Since this account crucially relies on the assumption of both an underlying structure and the rule of Deletion by Identity, it provides motivation for both.

   In sum: according to this version of the transformational approach, non-constituent conjuncts are acknowledged to be non-constituents in surface structure but they are derived from well-formed constituents in underlying structure. Since the Co-ordination Rule applies in underlying structure, the generalization that only constituents can serve as conjuncts is upheld. The relational compositionality of co-ordinate constructions thus holds on that level: syntactic conjuncts are syntactic constituents paralleling the semantic constituent status of the corresponding semantic conjuncts.

3.1.3 *Constituents in one structure, not in another*

The second solution for non-constituent co-ordination to be discussed here is offered by David Pesetsky (1995: especially 227–91). According to the transformational solution, non-constituent conjuncts are indeed non-constituents in surface structure; what 'redeems' them is that they are transformationally derived from constituents. Pesetsky's proposal is somewhat different. He, too, claims that sentences have two distinct syntactic representations, but, unlike in the transformational version, these are simultaneously available and both serve as inputs for syntactic rules. He claims that what appear to be non-constituent conjuncts are non-constituents in one of the two representations, called Layered Structure, but are constituents in the other, called Cascade Structure.

   Here is an example of the two constituent structure diagrams Pesetsky posits. What is shown in (1) and (2) is the verb phrase of the sentence *Bill [gave the book to them in the garden on Tuesday]*ᵥₚ (see Pesetsky 1995: 229, 233). For easier understanding, some of Pesetsky's category labels that do not play a role in the argument are replaced by more traditional ones; tense is not shown. The boxes around some of the nodes will be explained below.

(1) Layered Structure

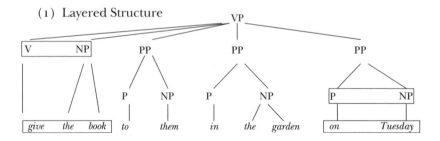

(2) Cascade Structure

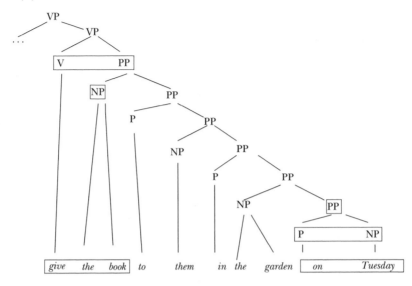

There are two relevant differences between Layered Structure and Cascade Structure. First, whereas in Layered Structure, nodes may have multiple branches, in Cascade Structure, only binary branching is allowed. The second difference has to do with how the relationship between selector and selectee is represented. In Layered Structure, there is only one configuration allowed to hold for selector and selectee: the selectee must be a sister to the selector. In Cascade Structure, however, selectees have a choice: a selectee may either be sister to the selector, as in Layered Structure, or it may be a daughter of the selector's sister – that is, a niece, rather than a sister, of the selector. In the two diagrams in (1) and (2), selector and selectee are boxed.

For the phrase *on Tuesday*, the sisterhood-constraint on selectors and selectees holds in both structures: *on* is the selector and it is sister to its selectee: *Tuesday*. Now consider *give* as selector of *the book*. In the Layered Structure of (1), the selectee – the *book* – is sister to the selector: *give*. In the cascading tree of (2), this is not so: *the book* is not sister to *give*; the sister of *give* is a prepositional phrase that *the book* is a daughter of. But the broader constraint on selectors and selectees still holds: *give* (the selector) is an aunt to the selectee (*the book*).

Why are two distinct constituent structures necessary?

The traditionally recognized constituents in Layered Structure are borne out, for example, by the alternative positioning of chunks of sentences, which in Pesetsky's framework is accounted for by movement rules. Thus, for example, *in the garden* and *on Tuesday* can occur in either order. While this fact is accounted for by Layered Structure, where the two phrases are separate sister constituents, it is not allowed by Cascade Structure, where they are not: *on Tuesday* is embedded in *in the garden* and thus no node can call up *in the garden* without also bringing *on Tuesday* with it. If we apply the movement rule to Cascade Structure, the generalization according to which movement rules move constituents fails; but the generalization holds if the rule is applied to Layered Structure.

Similarly, assuming that the replacement by pro-forms – such as *there* for *in the garden* and *then* for *on Tuesday* – must apply to constituents, Layered Structure provides the required constituency.

Thus, alternative ordering and pro-form replacement justify positing the Layered Structure; but what is the utility of Cascade Structure? As seen above, Cascade Structure would provide an exception to the generalization that the terms of movement and pro-verb replacement are constituents; but it supports another generalization that would in turn fail in the light of Layered Structure: that co-ordinate conjuncts are constituents. Consider (3) (see Pesetsky 1995: 175, 176):

(3) *Sue gave the book **to them in the garden on Tuesday** and **to us in the café on Wednesday**.*

The two conjuncts in this sentence are not constituents in Layered Structure, but, as indicated by (2), each forms a single prepositional phrase constituent in Cascade Structure. Other seemingly non-constituent conjuncts, such as *John saw **Mary in Chicago** and **Harry in Sheboygan***, are also represented as constituents in Cascade Structure.

This so far just shows that it is possible to design a constituent structure representation for sentences where what would be non-constituent conjuncts in Layered Structure are shown as constituents. But if the only justification for creating Cascade Structure is to account for non-constituent co-ordination, the endeavour is ad hoc. Cascade Structure is acceptable only if, like Layered Structure, it is supported by multiple evidence.

Pesetsky provides several arguments for the need for Cascade Structure independently of coordination. We will take up only one of these, having to do with the distribution of reflexive pronouns (such as *themselves*) and reciprocal pronouns (such as *each other*) (Pesetsky 1995: 172–5).

As discussed earlier (Chapter 2, Sections 2.3, 3.2, 3.3), the normal pattern is that these pronouns can be used only if their antecedents c-command the pronouns. Here is a definition of the c-command relation:

(4) Node A c-commands node B if the first node dominating A also dominates B (and A does not dominate B).

In other words, A c-commands B if A is either a sister or an aunt, great-aunt or great-great-aunt and so on to B. Thus, a node c-commands nodes 'sideways' and 'downwards at an angle'. C-command is a purely partonomic relation: linear precedence relations between commander and commandee are irrelevant.

For example, in (5), NP_1 c-commands all other nodes except for S; VP c-commands only NP_1; V c-commands NP_2, Art and N; NP_2 c-commands V; and Art and N c-command each other.

(5)

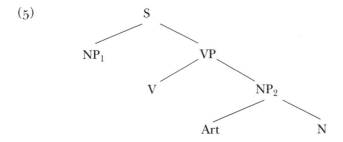

A bit of data that illustrates the force of the c-command constraint on the distribution of reflexive and reciprocal pronouns is given in (6):

(6) (a) *His cousin likes himself.*
     (b) *His cousin's friend likes himself.*

In (6a), *his cousin* (NP_1 in (5)) c-commands *himself* (NP_2 in (5)) and the sentence is grammatical. The sentence in (6b) is grammatical on the reading where *himself* refers to *his cousin's friend*; it is, however, ungrammatical if *himself* is intended to refer to *his cousin*. This is because *his cousin's friend* (NP_1 in (5)) does c-command the reflexive pronoun (NP_2 in (5)) but *his cousin* does not because it is part of the NP_1, which does not c-command *himself*.

There is, however, an exception to the generalization according to which only c-commanding antecedents can license reflexive and reciprocal pronouns. Consider (7), (8) and (9) (the (b)-sentences are adapted from Pesetsky 1995: 161). Antecedents and pronouns are in bold; subscripts indicate their co-reference relations; capitalized words form the difference between the (a) and (b) sentences.

(7) (a) *Sue told **each employee**₁ about **his own**₁ pay cheque.*
     (b) *Sue spoke TO **each employee**₁ about **his own**₁ paycheque.*

(8) (a) *Sue introduced to Mary **each employee**₁ in **his own**₁ house.*
     (b) *Sue spoke to Mary ABOUT **each employee**₁ in **his own**₁ house.*

(9) (a) *Gidon Kremer visited **every Baltic republic**₁ on **its**₁ independence day.*
     (b) *Gidon Kremer performed IN **every Baltic republic**₁ on **its**₁ independence day.*

The partonomic difference between antecedent–pronoun relations in the (a) and (b) sentences is shown in (10) on the example of (7). The node immediately dominating the antecedent is boxed to make clear how that node also dominates the pronoun in (10a) but not in (10b).

(10) (a)

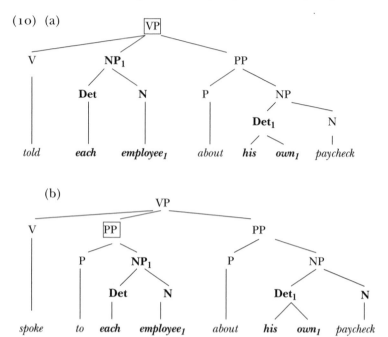

In (10a), co-reference between antecedent and pronoun is correctly predicted by the c-command requirement: the antecedent noun phrase *each employee* is an aunt of the pronoun *his own*. However, the grammaticality of the (b) sentence is not predicted by (10b) because here, the antecedent (*each employee*) is part of a prepositional phrase. The prepositional phrase as a whole does c-command the pronoun *his own* but the antecedent noun phrase itself does not since it is immediately dominated by the prepositional phrase node that does not dominate the pronoun as it ought to for c-command to hold.

However, while Layered Structure predicts the grammaticality of (10a) but wrongly predicts ungrammaticality for (10b), Cascade Structure predicts the grammaticality of both (10a) and (10b). The relevant parts of the cascading trees for the VPs in (7a) and (7b) are given in (11). In both cases, the antecedent is immediately dominated by a PP node (boxed) that also dominates the pronoun, just as the c-command requirement requires.

This argument provides justification for Cascade Structure independently of evidence from co-ordination.

In sum, in Pesetsky's account, what appear to be non-constituent conjuncts are shown to be constituents for some but not for all syntactic purposes. Relational compositionality for co-ordinate constructions is vitiated in Layered Structure but observed in Cascade Structure.

(11) (a)

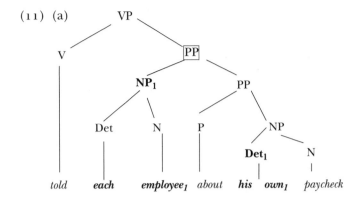

(b)

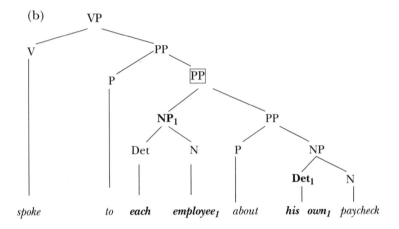

3.1.4 Summary

Here is the argument of this section. The statements in (1) re-iterate the problem formulated in Section 3.3.1; (2) wraps up the two alternative solutions.

(1) EXPECTATION:
Compositionality requires that just as every semantic conjunct is a semantic constituent, every syntactic conjunct be a syntactic constituent.
OBSERVATION:
In actual fact, some syntactic conjuncts are syntactic constituents, others are not.

(2) ALTERNATIVE SOLUTIONS
  (a) Transformational Generative Grammar:
      Some conjuncts are non-constituents in surface structure but
      they are constituents in underlying structure. Since it is the
      underlying structure that serves as the input to the Co-
      ordination Rule, the requirement that the rule should apply
      to constituents is met and thus the compositionality
      requirement is satisfied.

  (b) Dual Structure hypothesis:
      Some conjuncts are non-constituents in Layered Structure
      but they are constituents in Cascade Structure. Since it is
      Cascade Structure that serves as the input to the Co-
      ordination Rule, the requirement that the rule should apply
      to constituents is met and thus the compositionality
      requirement is satisfied.

The two accounts seem to be saying almost the same thing: they both
posit two representations one of which shows non-constituent conjuncts
to be non-constituents and the other showing them to be constituents.
But the claims are not identical. In the transformational analysis, the two
structures are derivationally related: each present at a different stage of
the analysis, whereas in Pesetsky's framework, both are simultaneously
available. In the transformational framework, surface structure is input
to no syntactic rule: it simply represents how the sentence is pronounced.
In Pesetsky's framework, however, both structures are inputs to some
syntactic rules.

Both solutions employ the familiar 'splitting the paradoxical entity'
approach to conflict resolution discussed in Section 3.2 of Chapter 1 that we
have seen employed in other solutions to syntactic conflicts as well (see Chapter
2). In both approaches, the problematic sentences are viewed as Janus-faced:
exceptionality in one representation is rendered regular in the other.

As warned by Simon Dik (see Section 1), both solutions do indeed
invoke 'very powerful additional assumptions' in accounting for non-
constituent conjuncts. For Transformational Grammar, these assumptions
are different levels of syntactic analysis and transformations to connect
them; for the Dual Structure analysis, they are co-existing constituent
structures. Nonetheless, in both approaches, the descriptive apparatus
employed to account for non-constituent co-ordination has some independent motivation.

This section discussed one requirement for compositionality in co-
ordinate structures mentioned in Section 1: that syntactic conjuncts be syntactic constituents. In the next section, we turn to a second requirement: that
co-conjuncts be of the same syntactic type. As in the present section, first
some data will be presented where this prediction does not appear fulfilled

(Section 3.2.1), followed by two alternative approaches to accommodating these cases (Sections 3.2.2 and 3.2.3) and by a summary (Section 3.2.4).

3.2 CO-CONJUNCTS THAT ARE NOT OF THE SAME SYNTACTIC TYPE

3.2.1 *The problem*

There is much evidence to show that syntactic co-constituents are generally tokens of the same type. The sentences in (1) and (2) illustrate the point. In (1) it is shown that, while both a noun and an adjective can be predicates by themselves, and so can the conjunction of two nouns or two adjectives, a noun and an adjective cannot be combined to form a conjoined predicate.

(1) (a) *Jill is **a teacher and a mother**.*
    (b) *Jill is **kind and pretty**.*
    (c) **Jill is **a teacher and kind**.*

In (2) it is shown that while two nouns can be conjoined and so can two clauses, a noun and a clause cannot.

(2) (a) ***Paul and Bill*** *impressed me.*
    (b) ***That Paul challenged the best player and that he defeated his opponent*** *impressed me.*
    (c) ****Paul and that he defeated his opponent*** *impressed me.*

However, co-conjuncts do not have to be of the same type in all respects. Differences between co-conjuncts belong to two large classes: those that do not matter for conjoinability and those that do.

Two examples of conjunct properties of the first kind are provided in (3). They show that lexical identity between the heads of co-conjuncts is not required. In these sentences, the conjuncts are prepositional phrases involving different prepositions.

(3) (a) *Take aspirin **for pain and against insomnia**.*
    (b) *Bill walked **with a cane and without any help**.*

While the lexical identity of heads – in this case, of prepositions – is not a condition on co-ordination, complete syntactic categorial identity is not a requirement, either. This is shown in (4)–(11).

(4) CO-CONJUNCTS ARE NOUN PHRASES CONTAINING
DIFFERENT TYPES OF NOUNS
(a) SINGULAR AND PLURAL NOUN
The teacher and the children *went to the park.*

(b) MASCULINE AND FEMININE NOUN
German:
Der   **Mond und die**   **Sonne** *sind fern.*
the(MASC) moon and the(FEM) sun   are far
'The moon and the sun are far.'

(c) PROPER NOUN AND COMMON NOUN
Peter and his brother *are good friends.*

(5) CO-CONJUNCTS ARE DIFFERENT TYPES OF PRONOUNS
  (a) PERSONAL PRONOUNS OF DIFFERENT PERSONS
  You and she *were the winners.*

  (b) QUESTION PRONOUNS OF DIFFERENT CASES
  When and how *did you first meet your husband?*

(6) CO-CONJUNCTS ARE A NOUN AND A PRONOUN
She and Peter *have bought a house.*

(7) CO-CONJUNCTS ARE AN ADJECTIVAL PHRASE AND A
PREPOSITIONAL PHRASE
He felt **quite happy and at ease** *in his new surroundings* (Dik 1968: 28).

(8) CO-CONJUNCTS ARE AN ADVERB AND A PREPOSITIONAL
PHRASE
Do it **carefully and within an hour.**

(9) CO-CONJUNCTS ARE A PREPOSITIONAL PHRASE AND AN
INFINITIVE
Take aspirin **for pain and to ward off insomnia.**

The examples presented in (3)–(9) illustrate that some differences between conjuncts do not present an obstacle for their co-ordination. Let us now analyse co-ordinate constructions where differences between conjuncts do matter, as we have already seen to be the case in (1) and (2). Some of these differences merely constrain the linear order of the co-conjuncts rendering them irreversible. Other differences, however, bar their co-occurrence regardless of their order.

Here are examples of irreversible co-ordinate structures: co-conjuncts that are grammatical only in one of their two possible linear orderings. In (10) it is shown that the conjunct containing a pronoun referring to an antecedent in the other conjunct must be second.

(10) (a) *the man$_1$ and his$_1$ tractor*
     (b) **his$_1$ tractor and the man$_1$*

In (11) it is shown that if a verb has a prepositional complement conjoined with a clausal one, the prepositional complement has to come first.

(11) (a) *I am surprised* **at the news and that nobody called me about the accident.**

(b) **I am surprised* **that nobody called me about the the accident and at the news.**

In (12) is shown that if, in a pair of conjoined pronouns following the preposition *between*, only one of the pronouns takes the case governed by the preposition (a pattern common in colloquial English), that pronoun must be adjacent to the preposition.

(12) (a) *Just between* **you and I,** *Sue has been fired.*

(b) **Just between* **I and you,** *Sue has been fired.*

In (13) is shown that if of a pair of subject conjuncts, the preposed verb agrees in number with only one of the conjuncts (as it does in colloquial English), this conjunct must be adjacent to the verb.

(13) (a) *There was* **the man and all the dogs from the kennel.**

(b) **There was* **all the dogs from the kennel and the man.**

In (14) is shown that if two propositions that share a subject are conjoined and the shared subject is expressed only once, it must be expressed in the first conjunct.

(14) (a) **Bill washed the dishes and hand-dried the glasses.**

(b) ***Washed the dishes and Bill hand-dried the glasses.**

However, as shown in (15), if the two propositions share a direct object and this object is expressed only once, it must be expressed in the second conjunct.

(15) (a) *Bill* **washed** *and Pat* **put away** *the dishes.*

(b) **Bill* **washed the dishes** *and Pat* **put away.**

In these examples, co-ordination of the two phrases is not barred: only one of their orderings is. Let us now consider cases where the very conjoinability of two phrases is excluded regardless of the order in which the conjuncts appear. Some examples were given in the beginning of this Section: (1c) shows that a predicate noun and a predicate adjective cannot be conjoined (**a teacher and kind*) and (2c) shows that a noun subject and a clause subject cannot, either (**Paul and that he defeated his opponent*). More examples are given in (16)–(19).

(16) CO-CONJUNCTS ARE A DIRECT OBJECT AND AN INDIRECT OBJECT

(a) **Mary lent* **money and to her brother.**

(b) **Mary lent* **to her brother and money.**

(17) CO-CONJUNCTS ARE A PLACE ADVERBIAL AND A TIME ADVERBIAL
    (a) **Mary lived **in Germany and two years ago**.*
    (b) **Mary lived **two years ago and in Germany**.*

(18) CO-CONJUNCTS ARE AN INFINITIVE AND A CLAUSE
    (a) **It's odd **for John to be busy and that Helen is idle now**.*
    (b) **It is odd **that Helen is idle now and for John to be busy**.*

(19) CO-CONJUNCTS ARE A PARTICIPLE AND A CLAUSE
    (a) **Bobby is the man **defeated by Billie Jean and who beat Margaret**.*
    (b) **Bobby is the man **who beat Margaret and defeated by Billie Jean**.*

What can we conclude from these examples regarding how similar co-conjuncts have to be? Since, as seen in Section 1, semantically, 'same type' for co-conjuncts meant having the same semantic function – that is, the same modality or same participant role – a plausible hypothesis is that in syntax, too, it is functional identity that is required for conjoinability. Syntactic function is the syntactic counterpart of semantic modality and semantic participant role: it refers to distinctions such as statement and question and distinctions such as subject and direct object, direct object and indirect object, and place adverbial and time adverbial.

This assumption goes some way towards explaining the data that we have seen. On the one hand, it explains why gender and number differences among nouns and the difference between proper and common noun, or noun and pronoun do not bar conjoinability (see (4), (5) and (6) above). On the other hand, it explains why direct and indirect objects, and place and time adverbials cannot be conjoined (see (16) and (17) above).

However, a definition of 'same type' on the basis of same syntactic function leaves hosts of data unaccounted for. We will focus on two classes of problems.

First, as seen above in (10)–(15), there are co-conjuncts that are of the same syntactic function and while their conjunction is indeed grammatical, this is so only if they occur in one particular linear order. This shows that shared syntactic function may be necessary but it is not sufficient to guarantee grammaticality.

Second, there is evidence to show that identity of grammatical function is not even necessary for conjoinability. Consider (5b) again: **When and how did you first meet your husband?** *When* is a time adverbial and *how* is a manner adverbial and therefore, if shared grammatical function is a condition on conjoinability, these two constituents should not be conjoinable. Yet, the construction is grammatical.

Let us summarize the problems.

(20) COMPOSITIONALITY:
    (a) Compositionality predicts that, just as semantic co-conjuncts have the same semantic semantic function, syntactic co-conjuncts should have the same syntactic function.

For noun phrase co-ordination, this means that all noun phrases of the same grammatical function – two subjects, two objects, two time adverbials and so on – should be conjoinable but noun phrases that differ in grammatical function – say, a subject and an object, or a time adverbial and a place adverbial – should not.

(b) Compositionality suggests – but does not strictly predict – that syntactic conjuncts should be freely orderable because of their like semantic and syntactic function.

OBSERVATIONS IN CONFLICT WITH COMPOSITIONALITY:

(A) Some constituents are not of the same grammatical function; yet, they can be both selected and freely ordered as co-conjuncts (Section 3.2.3).

(B) Some co-conjuncts are of the same grammatical function but they can be co-conjuncts only in one of their orders (Section 3.2.2).

In what follows, we will see two approaches to accounting for the problematic data. In Section 3.2.2, we start with (B) above, taking up irreversible co-conjuncts, which present cases of unexpected ungrammaticality. In Section 3.2.3, we go on to (A) above and discuss cases where noun phrases that differ in grammatical function are nonetheless conjoinable – that is, cases of unexpected grammaticality.

3.2.2 *Co-conjuncts that differ in linear position*

If two constituents are conjoinable at all, we would expect them to be conjoinable regardless of their linear order relative to each other. This is because conjoinability requires the co-conjuncts to be of the same type. If they have to be ordered in one particular way, this would suggest that, for purposes of the rule that orders conjuncts, they have to be tagged as different.

However, as some of the examples in Section 3.2.1 (those in (10)–(15)) already illustrated, the expectation of freely orderable co-conjuncts is not always met: some co-ordinate structures are irreversible. Janne Bondi Johannessen (1998) shows that asymmetry between conjuncts may show up under either of two conditions: when co-ordinate structures are at the receiving end of a selectional pattern or when they are at the assigning end.

Let us consider the first of these two patterns, where co-ordinate structures are selectees – such as governees. That asymmetry is shown in case assignment: conjuncts can differ in their case – is shown in (1). ((1a) is repeated from (12) in Section 3.2.1.)

(1) (a) *Just between* **you and I**, *Sue has been fired.*
    *Just between **I and you**, *Sue has been fired.*

(b) ***She and him*** *will drive to the movies.*
****Him and she*** *will drive to the movies.*
(Johannessen 1998: 16)

In (1a), the preposition *between* governs the oblique case but only the first pronoun has that case: *I* is in the nominative. In (1b), the main verb governs the nominative for the subject; yet, only *she* is in the nominative case, *him* has the oblique form.

Similar instances occur in other languages as well, such as in Italian (Johannessen 1998: 17):

(2) **Io   e   te**   *andremo insieme   a   Roma.*
I:NOM and YOU_{SG}:ACC go   together to Rome
'You and I go together to Rome.'

*Te   e   io   *andremo insieme   a   Roma.*
YOU_{SG}:ACC and I:NOM go   together to Rome

Co-ordinate structures can act asymmetrically also when they are selectors, rather than selectees – for example, if they are agreement controllers. This was shown in (13) in Section 3.2.1, repeated below along with a Latin example (ibid.: 30).

(3) (a) *There **was the man** and all the dogs from the kennel.*
** There **was·all the dogs** from the kennel and the man.*

(b) *Popul-i*   ***provinci-ae**-que*   *liberat-**ae***   *sunt.*
people-PL:MSC **province-PL:FEM**-and freed-**PL:FEM** are
'The people and the provinces are liberated.'

Provinci-ae   **popul-i-que*   *liberat-**ae***   *sunt.*
province-PL:FEM **people-PL:MSC**-and freed-**PL:FEM** are

In the English example (3a), the verb is the target of agreement in number; the agreement controller is a co-ordinate subject. If the verb shows agreement with only one of the two conjuncts, that conjunct has to be adjacent to the verb. In other words, the singular verb is possible only if the singular conjunct is adjacent to it but not if the plural conjunct is. The Latin example in (3b) is similar. The verb agrees with the subject in number and gender; the subject is a co-ordinate construction. The conjunct that the verb shows agreement with must be adjacent to it.

Irreversible co-conjuncts show that shared grammatical function does not guarantee grammaticality. They also violate compositionality: the conjuncts have the same semantic function and thus they should count equally for purposes of co-ordination; yet, they do not.

How can this conflict between semantically 'balanced' and syntactically 'unbalanced' co-ordination be resolved? Johannessen gives full credit to the syntactic asymmetry of co-ordinate constructions by proposing that asymmetry is the rule in co-ordination rather than the exception. In fact, she claims that all co-ordinate structures are asymmetrical in syntax. In (4a) is shown the traditionally assumed symmetric structure of co-ordinate constructions such as *the man and the dog*; in (4b) is shown the traditionally assumed asymmetric structure of subordinate constructions such as *the man with the dog*; and in (4c) is shown the asymmetric structure proposed for co-ordination by Johannessen (see ibid.: 109). The node labels used by Johannessen have been replaced by traditional labels since the differences are not relevant for our purposes. Co stands for conjunctive (Johannessen's term for conjunction); CoP stands for conjunctive phrase – in this analysis, the head of the conjunct that is associated with the conjunction is the conjunction. Conjuncts are boxed.

(4) (a) Symmetric Structure for Co-ordination:

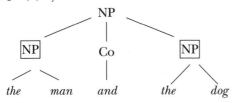

(b) Asymmetric Structure for Subordination:

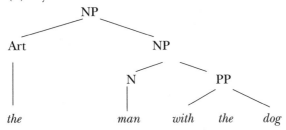

(c) Asymmetric Structure for Co-ordination:

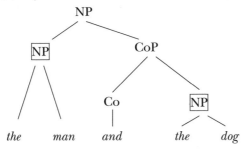

The asymmetrical structure assigned by Johannessen to co-ordination in (4c) is more like (4b) than (4a). In (4c), the first conjunct is the first immediate constituent of the phrasal node. The second conjunct, which is sister to the first conjunct in (4a), is now only a niece to the first conjunct. Thus, the first conjunct in (4c) has the same constituent structure position as the article in (4b) and the second conjunct has the same position as the prepositional phrase complement in (4b).

What is the justification for assigning asymmetrical syntactic structure to co-ordinate constructions? First, it accounts for irreversible co-ordinations. Since one of the two conjuncts is higher in the structure and thus in a privileged position, that conjunct is expected to serve as a selector in agreement and the selectee in government. The other conjunct, because of its subordinate position in the tree, may not participate in these selectional patterns.

Second, if co-ordinate constructions are assigned symmetrical structure, as in (4a), they are an exception to all – or almost all – other syntactic constructions, which tend to be asymmetrical. In Johannessen's account, all co-ordinate constructions are assigned asymmetric structure and thus they are brought into line with other syntactic constructions.

A third argument in favour of the asymmetric syntactic structure of co-ordinate constructions is a typological correlation. Johannessen (1998: 54–60) notes two things. First, regarding irreversible co-ordination, languages differ in whether it is the first or second conjunct that behaves as expected – that is, that shows the expected case or that controls agreement. Second, she also notes that the two kinds of languages differ in their basic ordering of verb and object. For example, in English or Czech, both VO languages, the first conjunct behaves as expected with the second showing exceptional behaviour, while in Japanese and Hopi, both OV, the second conjunct is regular and the first exceptional. This is explained if we view both verb-and-object constructions and co-ordinate constructions as consisting of a head and a complement. In verb-and-object constructions, the verb is the head and the object is the complement; in co-ordinate constructions, the conjunct that acts as expected is the head and the other is the complement. Thus, a single linearization rule ordering heads and complements relative to each other will account both for the order of verb and object and for the order of 'regular' and 'irregular' conjuncts in a language.

But if all co-ordinate constructions have the asymmetrical structure of (4c), how can syntactically symmetric co-ordinations be accounted for? They are now the unusual, or marked, construction and, accordingly, Johannessen makes special provisions for them (ibid.: 139–40).

However, while assigning asymmetrical syntactic structure to co-ordinate constructions is in line with the syntactic asymmetry of some co-ordinate constructions, it appears to open up a wide gap between meaning and form. The semantic structure of co-ordination is symmetrical, with the co-conjuncts being sisters, whereas their syntactic structure is now represented as asymmetrical, with one co-conjunct as aunt to the other rather than its sister. Johannessen's answer to this problem is quite radical: she suggests that co-ordinate structures may be asymmetrical in their semantic representation as well (ibid.: 237–51).

In sum, Johannessen accounts for irreversible co-ordinations by representing the conjuncts as having different partonomic positions: rather than being sisters, one conjunct is an aunt to the other. While this structure would appear to be at odds with semantic structure, in her account compositionality is restored by proposing, albeit tentatively, that the semantic structure of coordinate constructions may also be asymmetrical. If so, the conflict between semantic and syntactic structure is solved by modifying one of the two propositions that are in conflict. In the light of compositionality, there is a conflict between symmetric semantics and asymmetric syntax; the conflict is resolved if semantics, too, is asymmetrical.

3.2.3 *Co-conjuncts that differ in grammatical function*

As noted in Section 1 of this chapter, co-conjuncts in semantic representation must share the same semantic function. If we assume that syntactic co-conjuncts closely mirror this fact, it would follow that syntactic co-conjuncts must share the same syntactic function. As we have already seen, this assumption does indeed explain the grammaticality of many coordinate constructions and the ungrammaticality of others, such as in (1) and (2).

(1) (a) *I subscribed to Time magazine for my nephew and for his friend.*
    (b) **I subscribed to Time magazine for my nephew and for two years.*

(2) (a) *Billy completed his studies in Bloomington and in Chicago.*
    (b) **Billy completed his studies in Bloomington and with honours.*

In (1) is shown that two benefactive phrases can be conjoined but a benefactive and a temporal phrase cannot. In (2) is shown that two locative phrases can be conjoined but a locative and a manner phrase cannot.

But the condition that syntactic co-conjuncts should share the same function does not always hold. Consider the conversational interchange in (3) involving three speakers: A, B and C.

(3) (a) A: ***Where and how*** *did Billy complete his studies?*
    (b) B: *Billy completed his studies in Bloomington and with honours.*
    (c) C: *No; Billy did complete his studies but **not in Bloomington and not with honours.***

While in (2b), the locative phrase *in Bloomington* and the manner phrase *with honours* were seen as unconjoinable, in each of the three sentences of (3), a locative and a manner phrase are successfully conjoined. A similar example was seen before in Section 3.2.1 in (5): *Where and how did you first meet your husband?*

This conflict would be resolved if the locative and manner phrases in (3) could somehow be shown to be of the same syntactic function in spite of their categorial difference. This idea has in fact been explored in the literature (e.g. Matthews 1981: 214–15; Schachter 1977: 91). Commenting on the examples in (4):

(4)   (a)   **John met Mary **on a blind date and in 1968**.*
      (b)   ***How and when** did John meet Mary?*

Schachter (1997: 91) writes:

> As /(4a)/ shows, it is not in general possible to conjoin an expression of circumstance (such as *on a blind date*) with an expression of time (such as *in 1968*). Yet /(4b)/ shows that *how* and *when*, the interrogative counterparts, are in fact conjoinable. Evidently the function that *how* and *when* share, that of requesting information, takes priority over the function that distinguishes them, and the requirement of functional similarity is satisfied.

In other words, Schachter suggests that interrogative function is more important in determining whether conjuncts are or are not of the same type than syntactic function, such as being manner adverbial or time adverbial or place adverbial. If we assume that interrogative function has priority over syntactic function, the grammaticality of co-conjuncts such as *how* and *when*, or *where* and *how* is in line with the requirement that syntactic conjuncts should be of the same syntactic type. And, if we similarly assume that interrogative function is also a semantic property of arguments so that arguments are semantically conjoinable if they share interrogative function even if their participant roles are different, compositionality is satisfied.

As (3) shows, adverbials of different syntactic functions are conjoinable not only in questions, as in (3a), but also in their answers, as in (3b), as well as when they are contrastively negated, as in (3c). This shows that the function that takes priority over syntactic function and semantic participate roles must be broader than interrogation. Notice that the three constructions – question, answer and negation – have a single property in common: focus, or emphasis. This property, called discourse function, provides a common semantic denominator for otherwise distinct phrases and overrides syntactic categorial differences among co-conjuncts.

In sum: by adopting discourse function as a syntactic and semantic factor and assuming that discourse function overrides syntactic function and semantic participant role, examples of co-ordinations where constituents are successfully co-ordinated in spite of their differing semantic participant roles and syntactic functions are accounted for and compositionality is satisfied.

3.2.4   Summary

Here is a summary of the requirements set by compositionality, the facts that conflict with them and the solutions to the conflicts that have been discussed above.

COMPOSITIONALITY:
(a) Compositionality predicts that, just as semantic co-conjuncts have the same semantic function, syntactic co-conjuncts should have the same syntactic function.

   For noun phrase co-ordination, this means that all noun phrases of the same grammatical function – two subjects, two objects, two time adverbials and so on – should be conjoinable but noun phrases that differ in grammatical function – say, a subject and an object, or a time adverbial and a place adverbial – should not.

(b) Compositionality suggests – but does not strictly predict – that syntactic conjuncts should be freely orderable because of their like semantic and syntactic function.

OBSERVATIONS IN CONFLICT WITH COMPOSITIONALITY:
(A) Some constituents are not of the same grammatical function; yet, they can be both selected and freely ordered as co-conjuncts (Section 3.2.3).

(B) Some co-conjuncts are of the same grammatical function but they can be co-conjuncts in only one of their orders (Section 3.2.2).

SOLUTIONS:
Re (B): Johannessen's solution: It is not true that semantic co-conjuncts are symmetric. The fact that they are asymmetric brings asymmetric syntactic conjuncts in line with compositionality.

Re (A): Schachter's solution: Co-conjuncts that appear to differ in syntactic function are alike in discourse function. Since shared discourse function also renders semantic constituents conjoinable, compositionality is not violated.

   Johannessen and Schachter address different issues about co-ordination and thus their solutions are not alternatives. What is nonetheless common to them is that both are dealing with a mismatch between meaning and syntactic form and both resort to the same type of solution to this conflict. They both propose a different view of semantic co-ordination in the light of evidence about syntactic co-ordination. Prompted by evidence about irreversible co-conjuncts, Johannessen suggests that semantic co-conjuncts may not be sisters. Prompted by evidence of syntactic co-conjuncts differing in syntactic function, Schachter proposes that semantic co-conjuncts may differ in participant role as long as they have the same discourse role.

4 Conclusions

Chapter 3 analysed mismatches between the meaning and syntactic form of co-ordinate constructions. As stated in Section 3.1, given certain assumptions about their meaning, if syntactic co-ordinations are to be compositional, conjuncts have to be syntactic constituents and they have to be of the same type. However, neither requirement is complied with by all co-ordinate constructions: there are exceptions to both. The main conflicts that we saw were these two:

- Semantic constituents that are co-ordinated in semantic representation are not always syntactic constituents when syntactically co-ordinated.
- Co-conjuncts may not be of the same semantic and syntactic type.

The four solutions that we have surveyed represent two lines of argument. One approach is to take the conflicted object – syntactic form – and split it so that, while one part of it remains in conflict with meaning, the other is in harmony with it. In Transformational Grammar, the two representations of form were Underlying Structure and Surface Structure; in the Dual Structure analysis, they are Layered Structure and Cascade Structure.

These two analyses responded to the partonomic discrepancy between meaning and form in co-ordinate constructions: the difference between semantic conjuncts being constituents but some syntactic conjuncts not being constituents. The two structures posited by each account – Underlying and Surface, Layered and Cascade – may be considered either as parts of a single object or as a single object viewed from alternative angles.

The other argument responds to the taxonomic discrepancy between the syntactic co-conjuncts: that co-conjuncts may not be of the same type. Johannessen's answer is to propose that the meanings of co-ordinate structures may be as asymmetrical as their form is. Schachter in turn maintains that both semantic and syntactic co-ordination are symmetrical. He enriches both syntactic form and semantic representation with discourse role that overrides categorial differences both in semantics and in syntax.

Notes

1   Preliminaries
On compositionality, see for example Janssen 1997.

2   Compositionality in co-ordinate constructions and
3   Non-compositionality in co-ordinate constructions and its alternative analyses
These sections are based on the existing literature on co-ordination, especially Dik 1968; 1997; Stockwell *et al.* 1973: 294–418; Schachter 1977;

Matthews 1981: 195–219; Pesetsky 1995; Johannessen 1998. Many of the examples cited in the chapter come from these sources even if they are not individually referenced.

Exercises

1. In Section 3.1.1, it was pointed out that the assumption that conjuncts are constituents necessitates positing overlapping constituents (see example (11)). The following examples also support this point. Draw constituent structure trees for them and establish where the overlaps are.

1.	(a)	*her elder and younger brother*
	(b)	*her elder brother and sister*
2.	(a)	*three white and grey sparrows*
	(b)	*three white seagulls and sparrows*
3.	(a)	*want to open and clean the room*
	(b)	*want to open the room and the cabinet*

2. Here is a TV commercial for aspirin: 'Take it for pain. Take it for life.' Consider the following co-ordinate structures formed out of the two sentences:

   (a) *Take it for pain and take it for life.*
   (b) *Take it for pain and for life.*
   (c) *Take it for pain and life.*

How do they differ in grammaticality? What might be the explanation for the differences?

3. In this chapter, only two of the four relational compositionality require-ments for co-ordinate constructions, listed in (7) of Section 2, were consid-ered: those that pertained to the partonomic and taxonomic relations between conjuncts. The two that have not been taken up have to do with the relationship between the conjuncts and the entire co-ordinate construction:

   (i)   Syntactic co-ordinate constructions must be syntactic
         constituents.
   (ii) Syntactic co-ordinate constructions must be of the same
         syntactic type as their co-conjuncts.

Is there evidence to support them or to disprove them?

4. The following co-ordinate structures are ungrammatical or at least awkward. Why?

   (i)   (a) **John ate **with his mother and with good appetite***
              (Schachter 1977: 89).

(b) **I subscribed to Time magazine **for my nephew and for two years.***

(ii) (a) **John **probably and unwillingly** went to bed* (Schachter 1977: 89).
(b) *?Man offers friend **hope and liver**.*
(*The Milwaukee Journal Sentinel*, 30 December 2000)

5. Chapter 2 discussed some patterns of constituent order and verb agreement as examples of conflicts within syntactic form. Could those cases also be analysed as involving a conflict between syntactic form and meaning?

Chapter Four

Alternative Analyses of Symbolic Correspondence Relations: Grammatical Functions

> Role, function, and category are independent dimensions of linguistic substance. Within the constraints on their correspondences, mismatches are possible.
>
> (Bresnan 2001: 22)

1 Preliminaries

The discussion of co-ordinate structures in Chapter 3 showed one kind of mismatch between meaning and syntactic form: lack of **compositionality**. For co-ordinate structures, compositionality requires that semantic conjuncts should be expressed as syntactic constituents; and that syntactic conjuncts be of the same type. Sentences like ***The president hired and the manager trained*** *the new secretary* lack compositionality (at least on the face of it) because they violate the first requirement mentioned above: the conjunct *the president hired* is not a syntactic constituent. Other co-ordinate structures – such as *Where and when should I meet you?* – seem to fail the test of compositionality because they fall short of fulfilling the second requirement: even though each of the syntactic conjuncts they include – *where, when* – are semantic constituents, they do not meet the criterion of being of the same participant role.

Other construction types that we discussed earlier also violate compositionality. In Chapter 2, examples of discontinuous order and long-distance agreement were analysed as constructions with conflicted form; but they also involve a conflict between form and meaning. In discontinuous verb–particle constructions – as in *Bill will* **check** *the problem* **out** (Section 2 of Chapter 2) – the form conflict is between selection and linear order: the verb selects the particle even though it is not adjacent to it. But this construction also violates compositionality. Discontinuous verb and particle order constructions are compositional from the point of view of selection: each semantic component has a corresponding counterpart in syntactic structure. But they are not compositional from the point of view of the relationship between constituents: the semantic tie between verb and particle – *check* and *out* – is not paralleled by linear adjacency.

In long-distance agreement (Section 3 of Chapter 2), it is word selection and word form selection that are at odds: the subordinate object is selected by the subordinate verb, yet, it controls agreement on the main verb. But in addition to this conflict in syntactic form, long-distance agreement also defaults on compositionality: when agreement does not happen along the lines of syntactic selection, a link is formed between two constituents that are not only formally but also semantically unrelated. Thus, both long-distance agreement and discontinuous verb–particle constructions are **relationally non-compositional**.

Two other constructions discussed earlier also deviate from compositionality. In Chapter 1 (Section 3.4), we analysed a conflict in the form of interrogative structures such as *Where does Jim work?* The problem was that the wh-word was syntactically selected by the verb but was not adjacent to it. This is paralleled by a conflict between syntactic form and meaning: the wh-word is selected by the non-adjacent verb not only syntactically but also semantically. Thus, (non-subject) wh-questions are another instance of discontinuous order and, just as non-adjacent verb–particle constructions and long-distance agreement, they are relationally non-compositional.

A similar argument applies to English imperatives (e.g. *Speak louder!*). As discussed in Sections 3.1 and 3.3 of Chapter 1, they involve a conflict in form: the verb syntactically selects a YOU-subject but this subject is not present in syntactic structure. However, imperatives also involve a conflict between syntactic form and meaning. The verb does not only syntactically

select a YOU-subject but selects it semantically as well. Thus, these imperative sentences are **selectionally non-compositional**.

Compositionality is one of the ways in which the meaning and the form
of a symbol can be congruent; but it isn't the only one. The compositionality requirement has to do with meaning-form relations within individual
symbols: it requires that every meaning component of a symbol should have
a corresponding form component and every form component should have
a symbolically equivalent meaning component. It stipulates a one-to-one
relationship between bits of meaning and bits of form within individual
symbols.

There is also another way for form to trace meaning closely. Meaning and
form are in close correspondence if the one-to-one relationship holds not
only **within symbols** but also **across symbols**. By this requirement, there
should not be two or more symbols in the system that have the same form
but different meanings; or two or more symbols that have the same meanings but different form. In other words, neither synonymy nor ambiguity is
allowed. This constraint is called **isomorphism**. Systems that are free of
ambiguity and synonymy are called isomorphic.

The diagrams in (1) and (2) show compositionality and isomorphism and
their violations. Each box delimits a symbol. In (1), F_1, F_2, F_3 stand for form
components, M_1, M_2, M_3 stand for meaning components. In (2), F_1, F_2,
F_3 stand for the entire forms of symbols, M_1, M_2, M_3 stand for entire meanings. In (1)(B), (a) and (b) are violations of selectional compositionality;
(c) depicts a violation of relational compositionality.

(1) (A) compositionality

$$
\begin{array}{|ccc}
\hline
F_1 & F_2 & F_3 \ \ldots \\
| & | & | \\
M_1 & M_2 & M_3 \ \ldots \\
\hline
\end{array}
$$

  (B) violations of compositionality:
    (a) more form components than meaning components:

$$
\begin{array}{|ccc}
\hline
F_1 & F_2 & \mathbf{F_3} \ \ldots \\
| & | & | \\
M_1 & M_2 & \mathbf{0} \ \ldots \\
\hline
\end{array}
$$

    (b) more meaning components than form components:

$$
\begin{array}{|ccc}
\hline
F_1 & F_2 & \mathbf{0} \ \ldots \\
| & | & | \\
M_1 & M_2 & \mathbf{M_3} \ \ldots \\
\hline
\end{array}
$$

(c) lack of matching relations between form components and meaning components:

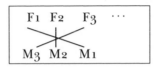

(2) (A) isomorphism

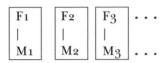

(B) violations of isomorphism
(a) ambiguity

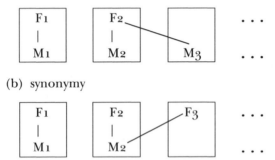

(b) synonymy

The difference between compositionality and isomorphism may be illustrated on road signs. A road sign is compositional if each meaning element is represented by a component of the design and there are no meaningless form components. A parking sign which says 'Two-hour parking M–F 7am–7pm' is not compositional because part of the intended message – that outside these hours and over the weekend there is unlimited parking – is left to be inferred rather than explicitly stated. An example of the reverse type of violation of compositionality is the same parking sign that also includes the picture of, say, a lizard – an idle form element that does not contribute to the expression of the sign's meaning.

Here are examples of isomorphism and its violations for road signs. A system of road signs is isomorphic if for every message there is only one sign and each sign conveys only a single message. A road sign system that includes synonymous signs for 'Stop!', such as the well-known red shield with the word STOP and a flashing red light, is not isomorphic because the same meaning has more than one alternative expression – an example of synonymy. The system of hand signals used by drivers lacks isomorphism for the opposite reason: the gesture of the driver sticking his arm out of the car window is ambiguous: it may mean 'Slow down', or 'I am about to turn'.

Let us now consider isomorphism in syntax. As pointed out above, a number of constructions discussed in the preceding chapters violate compositionality. Note now that some of them also violate isomorphism. Take first verb–particle constructions. As shown in (3), the two constructions – verb and particle adjacent and non-adjacent – are synonymous: a violation of isomorphism.

(3) (a) *Bill emptied out the apartment.*
    (b) *Bill emptied the apartment out.*

The same is true for co-ordinate structures: as shown in (4), the same meaning is conveyed whether the construction is elliptical or complete. Thus, these alternative expressions are another instance of synonymy.

(4) (a) *Bill is moving to Chicago and his brother is moving to New York.*
    (b) *Bill is moving to Chicago and his brother, to New York.*

And, as was seen in Section 3.2. of Chapter 2, Tsez verb agreement also offers a choice of forms: the main verb may agree either with a noun phrase of the subordinate clause or with the entire clause, with the meaning remaining the same.

Violations of compositionality create a syntagmatic conflict: a mismatch between meaning and form within a single sentence. Violations of isomorphism are instances of paradigmatic conflict: a mismatch between meaning and form across sentences.

Of the two constraints on symbol systems where form is to be closely tailored to meaning – compositionality and isomorphism – the rest of this chapter will focus on violations of the latter. Of the two possible deviations from isomorphism – ambiguity and synonymy – the construction types that will be discussed are instances of synonymy, whether real or apparent.

2 Semantic participant roles and grammatical functions

2.1 ACTIVE AND PASSIVE SENTENCES

Consider the following data.

(1) (a) *The wind swept away the bushes.*
    (b) *The bushes were swept away by the wind.*

(2) (a) *The singer performed three songs.*
    (b) *Three songs were performed by the singer.*

(3) (a) *The squirrel ate the acorns.*
    (b) *The acorns were eaten by the squirrel.*

The (a) and (b) sentences have different forms yet they convey the same message: they are synonymous. Let us see what the sentences in (1) mean. They include a semantic predicate: the action 'swept away'. This action involves two arguments (i.e., two participants of the action): the wind and the bushes. The roles that the two arguments play in the action are not the same: the wind is the active participant while the bushes undergo the act. As already discussed in Chapter 3 (Section 2), the active participant is called **Agent**, the undergoer is **Patient**. The (a) sentences, where the Agent is the subject, are called **active** sentences, the (b) sentences, where it is the Patient that functions as subject, are called **passives**.

Agent and Patient are **semantic participant roles**; Subject and (Direct) Object are **grammatical functions**. **Subject** in English is a cover term for the class of noun phrases that exhibit the following characteristics:

- they precede the verb
- they control agreement on the present-tense verb in number and person (e.g. *he goes, they go*)
- if the subject is a pronoun that has distinct nominative and accusative forms, it occurs in the nominative (e.g. *he* and not *him*)
- they have no preposition

(Direct) Object in turn is a cover term for a class of noun phrases in English with the following properties:

- they follow the verb
- they do not control agreement on the verb
- if the object is a pronoun that has distinct nominative and accusative forms, it occurs in the accusative form (e.g. *him* and not *he*)
- they have no preposition

The synonymy of active and passive sentences is due to the lack of one-to-one correspondence between semantic roles and semantic functions: Agents may be alternatively expressed as subjects or *by*-phrases and Patients may be objects or subjects. This is shown in (4).

(4) semantic participant roles: grammatical functions:

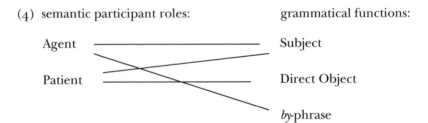

Agent   Subject

Patient   Direct Object

                                              by-phrase

Active and passive pairs are not the only constructions that exhibit a lack of one-to-one correspondence between semantic participant roles and grammatical relations. Another such construction type will be discussed next.

2.2 DOUBLE-OBJECT AND OBJECT–DATIVE SENTENCES

The active–passive dichotomy seen above applies to sentences that include two participants: Agent and Patient. Let us now consider sentences with three participants: in addition to Agent and Patient, there is a Recipient – a person who receives the result of the act. As the following examples show, there are again alternative ways of expressing such predications.

(1) (a) *The clerk sent a letter to the customer.*
    (b) *The clerk sent the customer a letter.*

(2) (a) *I brought roses to my cousin.*
    (b) *I brought my cousin roses.*

(3) (a) *Jill told the news to her father.*
    (b) *Jill told her father the news.*

While in active and passive sentences, the source of synonymy is the alternative expressions of Agent and Patient, in these examples, it is the Patient and the Recipient that are variably lined up with grammatical functions. In the (a)-sentences, the Patient is the object and the Recipient is a prepositional phrase. In the (b)-sentences, it is the Recipient that is the object.

The object function of the Recipient in the (b)-sentences is shown by the fact that the Recipient follows the verb, does not control verb agreement and, if pronominal, it takes the accusative case. The Patient in the (b)-sentences is also somewhat like an object. For example, it has no preposition and it follows the verb. However, it does not immediately follow the verb.

We will call the constructions in (a) **object–dative sentences** and those in (b) **double-object sentences** (in the literature, the latter are also termed di-transitive sentences). The cover term that will be used for both is **Patient–Recipient sentences**, since both constructions include these two semantic participant roles. In double-object sentences, the first verb complement will be termed **Object-1** and the second, **Object-2**. Here is a synopsis of the terminology:

(4)

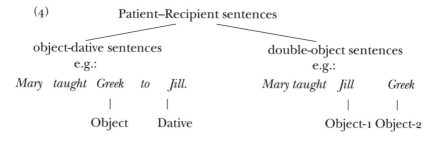

The many-to-one relations among semantic participant roles and grammatical functions in Patient–Recipient sentence pairs are shown in (5). Patients may be alternatively expressed as Object-1 or Object-2. Recipients may be expressed as Dative or Object.

(5) semantic participant roles: grammatical functions:

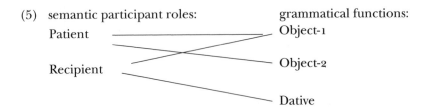

Patient ——————————————— Object-1

Recipient ——————————————— Object-2

Dative

For the rest of this chapter, we will focus on the two expressions of Patient–Recipient sentences (but in Section 5 we will return to actives and passives). The question is: why is there more than one form for the single meaning of Patient–Recipient sentences? Why is there no one-to-one correspondence between semantic participant roles and grammatical relations? The problem may be cast as a conflict between the facts and the isomorphism requirement:

A. ISOMORPHISM
Isomorphism requires a one-to-one relation between sentence form and sentence meaning: each sentence form should have a single meaning (no ambiguity) and each sentential meaning should be expressed by a single form (no synonymy).

B. PATIENT–RECIPIENT SENTENCES
(a) FORM:
The verb–complement structure of some Patient–Recipient sentences may appear in two different forms: object-dative (NP_1 *to*-NP_2) and double-object (NP_2 NP_1).
(b) MEANING:
The two constructions have the same meaning.

C. THE CONFLICT
The two forms of Patient–Recipient sentences are synonymous. The isomorphism requirement, however, bans synonymy.

D. POSSIBLE RESOLUTIONS OF THE CONFLICT
The conflict can be resolved by showing that the syntactic and semantic characterizations of these sentences as given in B. are incorrect . . .
(a) . . . either because what appear to be two different forms are actually the same form,

(b) . . . or because what appears to be a single meaning is
actually two different meanings.

This topic has a very large literature; we will discuss only a sample of the
available accounts. They fall into two groups. Some of them revise the
claim that there are two distinct forms involved: they propose that, in some
sense of the word, the alternative constructions have a single form ((D(a)
above). The other approach takes on the other pole of the opposition: that
the two constructions express one meaning ((D(b) above). They argue
that the meanings are not quite the same: there are actually two meanings
involved.

Both approaches end up restoring isomorphism (at least to an extent)
either by showing that the one meaning corresponds to one form rather
than to two forms, or by arguing that the two forms correspond to two meanings rather than to one.

3 Analysing Patient–Recipient sentences by unifying the two forms

3.1 SYNTACTIC CHARACTERISTICS OF PATIENTS AND RECIPIENTS

In this section, we will consider proposals that attempt to reduce the formal
differences between object–dative and double-object sentences. Before
looking at these accounts, let us see just how different the syntactic form of
the two constructions is.

For an example, consider the following pair of sentences:

(1) (a) object–dative construction:
The zoo keeper showed the baby chimp to the visitors.
(b) double-object construction:
The zoo keeper showed the visitors the baby chimp.

First, we review the basic facts discussed in Section 2.2. Apart from the Agent
(*the zoo keeper*), which is the subject in both sentences, the two semantic arguments are the Patient (*the baby chimp*) and the Recipient (*the visitors*). Each
of these arguments has alternative expressions in the two sentences: the
Patient is Object-1 in (1a) but Object-2 in (1b); the Recipient is Dative (*to*
& NP) in (1a) and Object in (1b).

Let us now see in more detail how the alternative forms of each participant differ. We will first compare the two expressions of the Recipient and
then the two expressions of the Patient.

3.1.1 *Dative Recipients and Object Recipients*

Recipients are alternatively expressed in different syntactic forms. Exactly
how do the two alternative expressions differ?

First of all, the two expressions of the Recipient in object–dative and double-object sentences have some things in common that differentiate both from the subject:

(1) Similarities between Dative Recipients and Object Recipients:
    (a) They both follow the verb.
    (b) Neither controls verb agreement.
    (c) If pronouns, they are both in the accusative case.

But there are also differences between them:

(2) Differences between Dative Recipients and Object Recipients:
    (a) They differ in case marking: the Dative Recipient has a preposition, the Object Recipient does not.
    (b) The Object Recipient directly follows the verb while the Dative Recipient follows it only indirectly, with the Patient intervening.

The characteristics that differentiate the Object Recipient from the Dative Recipient are not unique to the Object Recipient: they are shared by the Patient when it is expressed as Object-1.

(3) Similarities between Object Recipients and Object-1 Patients:
    (a) Both are bare noun phrases.
    (b) Both directly follow the verb.
    (c) Both may be subjects of passive sentences, as shown in (i) and (ii).

    (i) Object Recipient passivized:
      *The zoo keeper showed **the visitors** the baby chimp.*
      ***The visitors** were shown the baby chimp by the zoo keeper.*

    (ii) Object-1 Patient passivized:
      *The zoo keeper showed **the baby chimp** to the visitors.*
      ***The baby chimp** was shown to the visitors by the zoo keeper.*

Whether the ability to be a passive subject is a characteristic of Object Recipients only or whether it is shared with Dative Recipients cannot be decided. It will be assumed here that it is a shared property of Recipients regardless of their expression.

However, while Object Recipients and Object-1 Patients share some of their characteristics, they do not share all of their syntax. Here are five of their differences (see Siewierska 1991: 96–7) all showing that Object 1 Patients 'can do more' than Object Recipients.

(4) Differences between Object Recipients and Object-1 Patients:
- (a) Object-1 Patients can be the subject of *it is easy* sentences but the Object Recipients cannot, as shown in (iii) and (iv).

  (iii) *It is easy to tell **stories** to this girl.*
  __Stories__ are easy to tell to this girl.

  (iv) *It is easy to tell **this girl** stories.*
  ****This girl** is easy to tell stories.*

- (b) Object-1 Patients can occur in *of-*phrases of gerundive nominals; Object Recipients cannot, as shown in (v) and (vi).

  (v) *John taught **Greek** to Jill.*
  *The teaching **of Greek** to Jill was interesting.*

  (vi) *John taught **Jill** Greek.*
  The teaching **of Jill Greek was interesting.*

- (c) A long, syntactically complex Object-1 Patient can be placed at the end of the sentence; but a similarly long and complex Object Recipient cannot, as shown in (vii) and (viii).

  (vii) *Fred sent **several brochures with all the accommodation details** to his clients.*
  *Fred sent to his clients **several brochures with all the accommodation details**.*

  (viii) *Fred sent **his new South-East Asian clients** the brochures.*
  Fred sent brochures **his new South-East Asian clients.*

- (d) Object-1 Patients can be relativized (i.e. replaced by a relative pronoun) but Object Recipients cannot, as shown in (ix) and (x).

  (ix) *You taught **the rules** to the girl.*
  *The rules **which** you taught to the girl were new.*

  (x) *You taught **the girl** the rules.*
  The girl **who(m) you taught the rules was my niece.*

- (e) The Object-1 Patient can be questioned; the Object Recipient cannot, as shown in (xi) and (xii).

  (xi) *You taught **the rules** to the girl.*
  __What__ did you teach to the girl?

(xii) *You taught **the girl** the rules.*
   Who *did you teach the rules?*

Here is a summary of the similarities and differences among Dative Recipients, Object Recipients and Object-1 Patients in terms of ten morphological and syntactic characteristics:

> Agr = controlling verb agreement
> VX_ = following the verb whether directly or indirectly
> V_   = following the verb directly
> Prep = having a preposition
> Pass = being passivizable
> *easy* = being able to be the subject of an *easy*-construction
> *of* = being able to occur as the *of*-complement of a gerundive
> end = having an alternative position at the end of the sentence
> rel = being relativizable
> qu   = being able to be questioned
> +   = the characteristic is present
> −   = the characteristic is absent
> NA   = the characteristic is not applicable

	Agr	VX_	V_	Prep	Pass	*easy*	*of*	end	rel	qu
DatRec	−	+	−	+	+	−	−	NA	+	+
ObjRec	−	+	+	−	+	−	−	−	−	−
Obj-1 Pat	−	+	+	−	+	+	+	+	+	+

This chart reveals the following:

(a) Dative Recipients and Object Recipients have no positively stated characteristic in common that is not also shared by Object-1 Patients.

(b) Object Recipients and Object-1 Patients have two uniquely shared characteristics: immediately post-verb position, and no preposition

(c) Object Recipients and Object-1 Patients nonetheless differ in the last five properties on the chart.

These observations flesh out the point made in Section 2.2 about the relations between semantic participant roles and grammatical functions in Patient–Recipient sentences: the relations are indeed many-to-one. On the one hand, the same semantic participant role of Recipient is expressed in two alternative ways that differ in form ((a) above). On the other hand, Recipients and Patients, although they differ in semantic participant role, can be expressed in ways that are somewhat alike ((b) above) while also somewhat different ((c) above).

After this survey of the alternative expressions of the Recipient in object–dative and double-object sentences, let us examine the alternative expressions of the Patient in the two constructions.

3.1.2 *Object-1 Patients and Object-2 Patients*

Our focus is on the form of noun phrases such as *the news* in (1a), dubbed 'Object-1 Patient', and in (1b), dubbed 'Object-2 Patient'.

    (1) (a) *Sue told **the news** to Sheila.*
          (b) *Sue told Sheila **the news**.*

Given that the two phrases have the same participant role – they are both Patients – we would expect their formal characteristics also to be the same. And they do indeed share some form properties.

    (2) Shared characteristics of Object-1 Patients and Object-2 Patients:
          (a) They both follow the verb.
          (b) They both lack prepositions.
          (c) Neither controls verb agreement.
          (d) Both can be questioned, as shown in (i) and (ii).

              (i) *Sue told **the news** to Sheila.*
                  ***What** did Sue tell to Sheila?*

             (ii) *Sue told Sheila **the news**.*
                  ***What** did Sue tell Sheila?*

          (e) Both can be relativized, as shown in (iii) and (iv).

            (iii) *Sue told **the story** to Sheila.*
                 *The story **which** Sue told to Sheila was sad.*

            (iv) *Sue told Sheila **the story**.*
                 *The story **which** Sue told Sheila was sad.*

On the other side, there are also some differences between the two expressions of the Patient.

    (3) Differing characteristics of Object-1 Patients and Object-2 Patients:
          (a) Object-1 Patients may be passivized; Object-2 Patients may not, as shown in (v) and (vi).

             (v) *Sue told **the story** to Sheila.*
                *****The story** was told to Sheila by Sue.*

    (vi) *Sue told Sheila **the story**.*
      ** **The story** was told Sheila by Sue.*

  (b) Object-1 Patients can occur as subjects of *easy*-constructions but Object-2 Patients cannot, as shown in (vii) and (viii).

    (vii) *Sue told **the story** to Sheila.*
        ***The story** is easy to tell to Sheila.*

    (viii) *Sue told Sheila **the story**.*
        ** **The story** is easy to tell Sheila.*

  (c) Object-1 Patients can occur as *of*-complements of gerundives; Object-2 Patients cannot, as shown in (ix) and (x).

    (ix) *Sue told **the story** to Sheila.*
      *the telling of **the story** to Sheila*

    (x) *Sue told Sheila **the story**.*
      ** the telling of **the story** Sheila*

  (d) Object-1 Patients can be relativized; Object-2 Patients cannot, as shown in (xi) and (xii).

    (xi) *Sue told **the story** to Sheila.*
      *the story **which** Sue told to Sheila*

    (xii) *Sue told Sheila **the story**.*
      ** the story **which** Sue told Sheila*

Here is a comparative chart. Abbreviations are as in the chart at the end of Section 3.1.1.

	prep	Agr	VX_	qu	V_	Pass	*easy*	*of*	rel	end
Obj-1 Pat	−	−	+	+	+	+	+	+	+	−
Obj-2 Pat	−	−	+	+	−	−	−	−	−	NA

The comparison of the two expressions of Patients once again bears out the lack of one-to-one correspondence between semantic participant role and syntactic form: Patients can be expressed by two kinds of phrases that are somewhat alike in form but different in other ways.

3.2 A RELATIONAL GRAMMAR ACCOUNT

Our question, stated in Section 2.2, is this: why are the same semantic participant roles expressed alternatively by different grammatical functions? Relational Grammar answers this question by saying that even though the alternative forms are indeed different on one level of syntactic representation, they are the same on another syntactic level. This approach thus chips away at the claim that the two forms are different. It splits form representations into two levels and relegates the difference between the two forms to only one of the two levels.

Relational Grammar was introduced in Chapter 1 (Section 1) and Chapter 2 (Section 3.3). The analyses of the alternative forms of Patient–Recipient sentences in this framework are sketched in (1) and (2) (see Perlmutter and Postal 1983: 93). This framework uses the symbol '1' for Subject, '2' for Direct Object and '3' for Indirect Object. 'Chomeur' – a French word meaning 'unemployed' – labels a noun phrase that is neither Subject nor Direct nor Indirect Object.

(1) Object–dative constructions, e.g. *John sent the letter to Mary.*

single level: Predicate	1	3	2
sent	*John*	*Mary*	*the letter*

(2) Double-object constructions, e.g. *John sent Mary the letter.*

first level:	Predicate	1	3	2
second level:	Predicate	1	2	chomeur
	sent	*John*	*Mary*	*the letter*

In this account, double-object sentences thus have a more complex structure than object–dative constructions. The two representations are the same on the first level; but double-object sentences have an additional level in their structure. This second level differs from the first in the grammatical role assignment of Patient and Recipient. On level one, the Patient is Direct Object and the Recipient is Indirect Object just as in object–dative sentences. On the second level, the Recipient is the Direct Object and the Patient is a chomeur: it bears none of the three grammatical relations of Subject, Direct Object and Indirect Object.

What connects the two levels in (2) are rules of advancement and demotion. Two constraints play a crucial role in deriving the second level from the first:

- The rule of Advancement from 3 to 2 turns the Indirect Object into Direct Object.
- The Relational Annihilation Principle says that when a noun phrase (in this case, the Indirect Object) abandons its grammatical function and assumes the grammatical function of another noun phrase in the sentence (in this case, of the Direct Object), this latter noun phrase ceases to bear that grammatical function (i.e., it is demoted to a chomeur) (see Johnson 1977: 155).

The Relational Annihilation Principle amounts to a constraint that a single level of representation cannot have more than one noun phrase having the same grammatical function.

The Relational Grammar account of Patient–Recipient sentences thus softens the one-meaning-two-forms conflict by proposing that the two forms are different only on the surface level but they are the same on the underlying level. The same idea of assuming two levels of form, one of which shows one-to-one correspondence between semantic participant roles and grammatical functions, is fundamental to an account of Transformational Generative Grammar as well, to which we will turn next.

3.3 TRANSFORMATIONAL GENERATIVE GRAMMAR ACCOUNTS

3.3.1 *Dative Movement*

As already mentioned in the preceding chapters, in Transformational Generative Grammar the various levels of syntactic representation are envisaged not as levels of a single tree diagram as in Relational Grammar but as separate diagrams. As in Relational Grammar, rules mediate between the structures by changing one representation that is more meaning-like to one that is closer to how the sentences are actually pronounced.

In the so-called Extended Standard Theory of generative grammar, the transformational rule that does the job of Relational Grammar's 'Advancement from 3 to 2' rule is Dative Movement given in (1) (also known as Indirect Object Inversion Transformation; Jacobs and Rosenbaum 1968: 143–8).

(1) NP V NP$_1$ *to*-NP$_2$ → NP V NP$_2$ NP$_1$

In prose: given a noun phrase, a verb, and two noun phrases in this order with the second preceded by *to*, this second noun phrase may be moved immediately after the verb while losing its preposition.

As in Relational Grammar, the two versions of Patient–Recipient sentences have the same structure on the underlying level. This same structure has an Object Patient and a Dative Recipient, as in *John gave the book to Jill*. Since both Advancement from 3 to 2 and Dative Movement are optional, the rule may not apply and in that case the underlying structure surfaces unchanged; or if it does apply, the alternative form *John gave Jill a book* is produced.

Both the Relational Grammar account and the Dative Movement analysis include the following claims:

(2) • Semantic participant roles are in a one-to-one relation with grammatical functions.
  • Semantic participant roles are not in a one-to-one relation with grammatical functions.

In its unqualified form, this is a paradox: a contradiction that violates the consistency requirement of scientific accounts. In both approaches, the conflict is resolved by assuming that form is not one thing: there is underlying form and there is superficial form. With this qualification, the paradox can be re-cast so that it no longer poses a contradiction:

(3) • Semantic participant roles are in a one-to-one relation with grammatical functions on the underlying level of form.
   • Semantic participant roles are not in a one-to-one relation with grammatical functions on the surface level of form.

The claims in (3) are more complicated than those in (2) because (3) makes reference to two kinds of form. However, it has the advantage of not being contradictory: the contradiction has been reduced to complexity.

In more recent versions of Transformational Generative Grammar, Dative Movement has been merged into another, more general rule. This will be shown next.

3.3.2 NP-Movement

One difference between Relational Grammar and Transformational Grammar has to do with the status of the grammatical functions Subject, Object and Indirect Object. Relational Grammar does not attempt to define these notions: they are assumed to be 'primitives' – that is, concepts that have intuitive content but cannot be explicated in terms of other notions. Thus, in the sentence representations of Relational Grammar, the predicate and the various noun phrases are not differentiated in terms of their hierarchical position in the tree: they are all immediate constituents of the sentence node. Similarly, their ordering does not reflect their actual order in sentences: by convention, the predicate is shown first followed by the noun phrases. Given that across languages, noun phrases bearing the same grammatical function differ in their configurational (i.e., partonomic and linear) characteristics, Relational Grammar's way of representing Subject, Object and Indirect Object makes these concepts neutral to such differences and thus cross-linguistically applicable.

Transformational Grammar's view of grammatical functions is different. Grammatical functions are not primitives: they are identified by their position in a constituent structure tree both by their partonomic position and by their linear ordering. For example, in Noam Chomsky's seminal work *Aspects of the Theory of Syntax*, the subject in English is a noun phrase preceding the verb and immediately dominated by the sentence node and the direct object is a noun phrase following the verb and immediately dominated by the verb phrase node (Chomsky 1965: 68–9).

It is under this latter assumption – that the various formal properties of subjects, objects and indirect objects are related to their partonomic and linear properties – that Richard Larson approaches the analysis of Patient–Recipient sentences (Larson 1988).

When we looked at the syntactic properties of the verb complements in Section 3.1, our goal was to assess the differences among alternative expressions of the same participant roles: Patient and Recipient. Larson's focus is not the same since the framework that he is working in is syntax-centred. Thus, what he compares are the syntactic characteristics of the verb complements that occur in these sentences regardless of semantic participant roles.

Larson acknowledges the synonymy of object–dative and double-object constructions and aims at reducing the differences between the forms of the two constructions (ibid.: 350–1). In surveying the similarities and differences between the verb complements in the two sentence types, he makes two observations. We will use the sentences in (1) to illustrate them.

(1) (a) *Fred gave Sue the pencil.*
    (b) *Fred gave the pencil to Sue.*

His first observation is that there are formal differences between *Sue* and *the pencil* in (1a). More generally, the Object Recipient and the Object-2 Patient of double-object sentences have different syntactic properties.

For example, the Object Recipient can be an antecedent to a reflexive pronoun but not vice versa (ibid.: 336):

(2) (a) *I showed Mary **herself**.*
    (b) **I showed **herself** Mary.*

Also, a negator may be incorporated in the Object Recipient but not in the Object-2 Patient (ibid.: 337):

(3) (a) *I showed **no** one anything.*
    (b) **I showed anyone **nothing**.*

Larson's second observation is that this asymmetric relationship between *Sue* and *the pencil* in a double-object construction like (1a) is paralleled by the same asymmetric relationship between *the pencil* and *to Sue* in object–dative constructions, such as (1b). The Object Recipient is in some ways like the Object-1 Patient (as we have also seen above (Section 3.1.1)), and the Dative Recipient is in some ways like the Object-2 Patient. This is shown by comparing reflexivization in object–dative sentences as in (4) with reflexivization in double-object constructions, as in (2) above.

(4) (a) *I showed Mary **to herself**.*
    (b) **I showed **herself** to Mary.*

The parallelism is also evident if we compare negative placement in object–dative sentences, as in (5), with negative placement in double-object sentences, as (3) above.

(5) (a) *I showed **nothing** to anybody.*
     (b) **I showed anything to **nobody.***

Both observations are puzzling. First, why should the Object-2 constituent in double-object sentences have different syntactic properties from Object-1? They are both bare noun phrases and, except for linear order, there is no obvious difference between them in their position in constituent structure. And, second, why would the Object-2 phrase in double-object constructions be similar to the Dative Recipient in object–dative sentences? The task for Larson is to design a constituent structure for double-object sentences where Object-1 and Object-2 differ in their position in constituent structure in the same way as Object and Dative do in object–dative sentences. If this could be achieved, the same asymmetric behaviour that holds between the two verb complements of double-object constructions and between the two verb complements in object–dative constructions would be reflected by the same asymmetric constituent structure representation for the two constructions.

Here is the account that Larson suggests. As in Relational Grammar and in the Dative Movement analysis, there is a single underlying structure proposed for object–dative and double-object sentences. The sketch of the verb phrase portion of this structure as exemplified by the sentences in (1) is given in (6) (see ibid.: 342) (V' is a verb-phrase-like constituent).

(6)

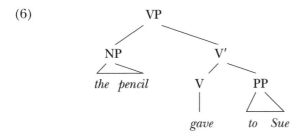

Sentences that are direct reflections of the assumed underlying structure – such as *Fred the pencil gave to Sue* – are ungrammatical. To turn them into a grammatical surface form, a rule of Verb Raising is assumed that transforms the verb phrase into *gave the pencil to Sue.*

(7)

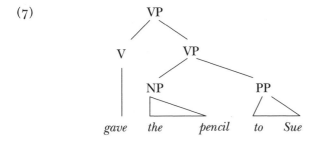

This structure receives support by some facts of co-ordination, such as those in (8) (see ibid.: 345).

(8) (a) *Fred gave **the pencil to Sue** and **the pen to Sally**.*
    (b) *I gave **five dollars to Maxwell** and **three dollars to Chris**.*

If we assume – as is generally done and as we did in Chapter 3 – that conjuncts must be constituents, *the pencil to Sue*, *the pen to Sally*, *five dollars to Maxwell* and *three dollars to Chris* should all be represented as constituents. And this is just what the structure in (7) achieves.

Verb Raising derives one of the two constructions from the underlying structure in (6): object–dative sentences such as *Fred gave the pencil to Sue*. How do we get the double-object version: *Fred gave Sue the pencil?* Similarly to Dative Movement, a rule moves the Dative Recipient of the underlying structure – *to Sue* – to the position of the object – *the pencil* – which in turn moves to the end of the sentence. The Dative Recipient loses its preposition in the process. The resulting verb phrase structure is *Sue gave the pencil*, to which Verb Raising applies as it did in the derivation of the object–dative construction, yielding *gave Sue the pencil*.

Larson's rule moving *to Mary* does the job of the Extended Standard Theory's Dative Movement by inverting the two complements and eliminating the Recipient's preposition. Is there any difference at all between the two rules? The difference is that whereas Dative Movement is specific to Patient–Recipient sentences, Larson's movement rule has some independent motivation from outside these constructions. He points out that the proposed derivation is similar to how passives are derived in this framework.

The underlying structure of passive sentences is illustrated in skeletal form for *The pencil was purchased by Fred* (see Haegeman 1994: 306). IP stands for Inflectional Phrase, which roughly corresponds to Sentence. I' is the predicative part of the sentence that excludes the subject; I stands for Inflection and it accommodates tense; e indicates that the subject noun phrase is an empty, lexically unfilled node.

(9)

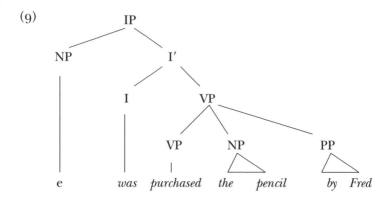

The surface form of the passive sentence is produced by a rule that moves *the pencil* to the empty subject position.

How is the derivation of passives similar to the derivation of double-object constructions? Compare the underlying structure of passives in (9) with the underlying structure of verb phrase of Patient–Recipient sentences repeated from (6).

(10)

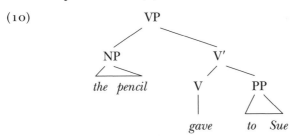

In (10), the verb and the Dative Recipient – *gave to Sue* – make up what Larson calls a 'small predicate'. The Object Patient – *the pencil* – is in subject position relative to this predicate. Thus, when *to Sue* is raised from its position in (10) to the place of this subject: *the pencil*, the process is comparable to the raising of *the pencil* from its position in (9) to subject position.

Larson thus posits a single rule (dubbed NP-Movement) to operate in the derivation of passives and double-object constructions. In passives, the direct object is moved up to become the subject of the entire sentence. In double-object constructions, the indirect object is moved up to become the subject of the verb phrase. In both cases, an object has been moved to a subject position, and the other noun phrase is expressed as an adjunct. In passives, the adjunct is the by-phrase; in double-object constructions, it is the Object-2 Patient (Larson 1988: 352).

This analysis accounts for Larson's two initial observations. First, the differences between Object-1 Recipients and Object-2 Patients in double-object sentences are accounted for by the fact that they have different positions in constituent structure: Object-2 Patients are lower than Object-1 Recipients. The particular difference in constituent structure between the two explains the differences between them regarding reflexivization and negative placement. This is because Larson assumes that antecedents of reflexives must c-command the reflexives and that, similarly, the negative element must c-command the negative polarity item such as *anybody* or *anything*.

As discussed in Chapter 3 (Section 3.1.3; see also Chapter 2, Section 2.3) the c-command relation is defined as follows: constituent A c-commands constituent B if the first branching node over A dominates B (and A does not dominate B).

If the Object Recipient and the Object-2 Patient were represented as sisters, either would c-command the other and thus the ungrammaticality of **I showed herself Mary* ((2) above) and **I showed anyone nothing* ((3)

above) would not be accounted for. In the structure proposed by Larsen, however, once the Dative Recipient has been moved from its underlying position to become the object, it is higher than the Object-2 Patient and it c-commands the latter. The two nodes in c-command relation are shown in bold in (10). (t stands for 'trace' marking the position from which the verb has been raised.) The structure thus correctly predicts that *I showed Mary herself* is grammatical but *I showed herself Mary* is not.

(11)

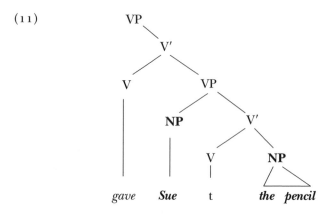

Second, this analysis also accounts for Larson's second observation: the syntactic likeness between Object-2 Patients and Dative Recipients. They now both have the same constituent structure position and are both c-commanded by the other complement of the verb. This is clear from a comparison of (11) – the double-object construction – and (12): the object–dative constructions. In (12), the nodes in c-command relation are once again in bold.

(12)

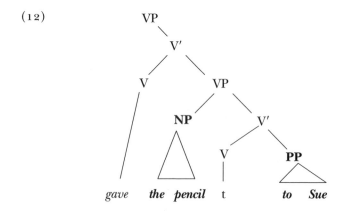

The similarity between his account and that of Relational Grammar is recognized by Larson. In both, there is an advancement-type rule that puts the Dative Recipient into direct object position. The connection between this rule and that of the passive is also shared by the two accounts. In

Larson's analysis, there is a single rule that yields both passives and double-object constructions. In Relational Grammar, as we saw earlier, the rule that derives double-object constructions is 3-to-2 Advancement: the advancement of an Indirect Object to a Direct Object. For the derivation of passive sentences from active ones, Relational Grammar employs a similar advancement rule: one that advances 2 to 1 – that is, Direct Objects to Subjects. Thus, in both accounts, it is the same rule or rule type that is instrumental in deriving passives and double-object constructions.

As Larson says (1988: 354), his account gives a 'structural interpretation of the standard Relational Grammar analysis': while advancement rules in Relational Grammar are stated in terms of structurally uninterpreted grammatical function labels, NP-Movement is stated in terms of constituent structure and linear order.

3.4 A Lexicase account

Stanley Starosta's Lexicase framework has something in common with the Relational Grammar analysis and the transformational accounts of Patient–Recipient sentences. He, too, posits a derivational relationship between object–dative and double-object constructions (Starosta 1988: 32–3, 171; 1996: 241). However, while in the other two frameworks the rules apply to sentences, in Starosta's approach they apply to lexical items: verbs in the lexicon.

He posits two distinct classes of verb: those that occur in the object–dative construction (e.g., *give, bring, send, serve, teach, donate* and *cook*), and those that can also occur in the double–object construction (such as *give, bring, send, serve* and *teach*). The lexical entries for the second class of verbs have the contextual specification +[___NP NP] – that is, that the verb may occur preceding two noun phrases. Members of the first class are specified as +[___NP PP] – that is, these verbs can occur preceding a noun phrase and a prepositional phrase. There is a lexical derivation rule that derives the +[___NP NP] verbs from the +[___NP PP] verbs. Starosta suggests that the speaker can move items from one class to the other by analogy and is able to understand new examples.

Thus, in this analysis, too, double-object constructions are derived from object–dative constructions: the basic lexical frame for the two is the same.

4 Analysing Patient–Recipient sentences by splitting their meaning

4.1 Semantic characteristics of Patients and Recipients

The central problem of the two expressions of Patient–Recipient constructions that we are addressing is that they create a paradigmatic conflict by violating isomorphism: the same meaning is expressed in two alternative ways. The solutions that we have seen so far took issue with one of the two poles of the opposition: form. Relational Grammar, Transformational Grammar and

Lexicase are all derivational accounts: they propose that the different surface forms are underlain by another level where these forms are the same. Taking form on that level, isomorphism is upheld: one meaning, one form.

As indicated before (Section 2.2), there is another type of account that explores the opposite approach. Accounts of this type propose that the seemingly identical meanings of the object–dative and double-object constructions are not in fact the same. If the meanings are not the same, isomorphism is once again complied with: two forms, two meanings.

Meaning differences between the two constructions have been noted by a number of linguists. Nomi Erteschik-Shir claims that the two differ by which verb complement is interpreted as being semantically dominant (1979: 443, 449). A phrase is semantically dominant if the speaker intends to draw the hearer's attention to its meaning.

The position of the dominant phrase is sentence-final. Thus, in double-object sentences, such as *John gave Mary the book*, attention is drawn to Object-2 (the Patient: *the book*) rather than Object-1 (the Recipient: *Mary*). In object–dative sentences in turn, such as *John gave the book to Mary*, the focus of attention is on the dative phrase (the Recipient: *Mary*) as opposed to the object (the Patient: *the book*). Thus, the two constructions differ in whether the focus of attention is on the Patient or on the Recipient.

This proposal is supported by the ungrammaticality of the double-object sentences in (1)–(2) (ibid.: 449)

(1) (a) *John gave it to Mary.*
   (b) **John gave Mary it.*

(2) (a) *Who did John give the book to?*
   (b) **Who did John give the book?*

Erteschik-Shir explains the ungrammaticality of both (1b) and (2b) by an inherent conflict: in each sentence, a pronoun is forced to be both dominant and non-dominant. In (1b), the anaphoric pronoun *it* is an Object-2 and thus its position requires it to be semantically dominant; but pronouns, being brief anaphoric references to a noun phrase mentioned elsewhere, resist being put in the limelight.

In (2b), the problem with the pronoun *who* is the reverse. By position, it should be non-dominant (since the Object-2 noun phrase *book* is in dominant position); but given that it is a question pronoun, it is inherently predestined to be focused. Thus, it is because a single constituent cannot be both dominant and not dominant that the two sentences (1b) and (2b) are ungrammatical.

Another fact explained by the variable dominance hypothesis has to do with the contexts in which the following sentences are used.

(3) (a) *Pass me the salt please.*
   (b) *Pass the salt to me please.*

The sentence in (3a) is the more natural version if somebody is asking for the salt because the salt is in the semantically dominant position. The sentence in (3b) would in turn be used if *to me* were to be understood contrastively, in opposition to another person to whom the salt might be passed.

A similar meaning difference between the two constructions is proposed by Talmy Givón (1979, 1984b: 153–7). Consider his examples:

(4) Question: *Who did John give the book?*
    Answer: (a) *He gave the book to Mary.*
            (b) *?He gave Mary the book.*

(5) Question: *What did John give to Mary?*
    Answer: (a) *He gave Mary the book.*
            (b) *?He gave the book to Mary.*

When it is the Recipient that is asked about as in (4), the more natural answer has the Recipient in focus position at the end of the sentence. But when the question is about the Patient, as in (5), it is the Patient that preferentially occupies the sentence-final focus position.

Three syntactic frameworks that base their analyses on the insight that the meanings of object–dative and double-object sentences are somewhat different are Functional Grammar, Construction Grammar and Cognitive Grammar. They will be discussed in turn.

4.2 A Functional Grammar account .

Simon Dik's Functional Grammar gives explicit recognition to the fact that the meaning of a sentence is not exclusively made up by the semantics of the predicates and the semantic roles of their participants. An additional meaning component is what Dik calls perspective.

Perspective defines the interpretation of a state of affairs. As Anna Siewierska puts it (1991: 76), 'perspective refers to the presentation or viewing of situations and events through the eyes, literally or figuratively, of one of a range of potential parties'. The chosen perspective is reflected in the choice of grammatical functions for the expression of a given semantic participant role. The primary perspective is that of the subject; the bearer of the secondary perspective is the direct object.

It follows then that active and passive sentences are analysed as not fully synonymous. In the two constructions, different participants are assigned the subject function and they therefore describe the same state of affairs from alternative angles. In (1a), the act of hitting is represented from the Agent *Jeff*'s perspective while in (1b), it is viewed from the Patient *the child*'s angle (ibid.: 79).

(1) (a) *Jeff hit the child.*
    (b) *The child was hit by Jeff.*

If different grammatical functions correspond to different perspectives, this means that object–dative and double-object sentences must also differ in perspective since they differ in what grammatical functions express the semantic participant roles involved. Unlike in active-passive sentences, the subject – the bearer of the primary perspective – remains invariant in (2a) and (2b): it is the carrier of the secondary perspective that varies. In (2a), the object expresses the Patient and thus in this sentence, the secondary perspective is that of the Patient. In (2b), the object expresses the Recipient and therefore the secondary perspective is that of the Recipient (ibid.: 79).

(2) (a) *Charles gave the rose to Anna.*
    (b) *Charles gave Anna the rose.*

Here is Dik's account of Patient–Recipient sentences (1978: 99–115) illustrated in (2). Note that in Functional Grammar, the label 'Goal' is used for what we have called Patient. 0 shows that Functional Grammar does not attribute syntactic function to Dative Recipients and to Object-2 Patients.

Semantic participant roles in both (a) and (b):
Charles: Agent
the rose: Goal
Anna: Recipient

Assignment of grammatical functions:
in (a): *Charles*: Agent, Subject
        the rose: Goal, Object
        Anna: Recipient, 0

in (b): *Charles*: Agent, Subject
        the rose: Goal, 0
        Anna: Recipient, Object

This framework suggests certain syntactic similarities among the four arguments in the two constructions.

- Based on shared semantic participant roles:
  - Patients – whether Object-1 or Object-2 – should have some formal characteristics in common since they are both Patients.
  - Recipients – whether Dative or Object-1 – should have some formal characteristics in common since they are both Recipients.
- Based on shared grammatical function:
  - Object Patients and Object-1 Recipients should have some formal characteristics in common since they are both Objects.

- Object-2 Patients and Dative Recipients should have some
  formal characteristics in common since they both lack
  grammatical function.

That some such similarities do hold was seen in Section 3.1. The remaining challenge is to explain why particular formal similarities hold between semantically related arguments and certain others correlate with shared grammatical functions.

As Dik points out, his Functional Grammar framework is akin to Relational Grammar (ibid.: 112–26). Here is a comparison of representations of the nominal constituents of the two sentence types in the two frameworks (see ibid.: 114). The grammatical role labels are in bold.

(3) (a) *John gave the book to Peter.*

> Relational Grammar:
> **Subject, Direct Object, Indirect Object**

> Functional Grammar:
> Agent-**Subject**, Goal-**Object**, Recipient-0

(b) *John gave Peter the book.*

> Relational Grammar:
> first level: **Subject, Indirect Object, Direct Object**
> second level: **Subject, Direct Object**, Chomeur

> Functional Grammar:
> Agent-**Subject**, Recipient-**Object**, Goal-0

In both frameworks, the concept Subject and Object are primitives: atomic notions not definable by anything else. The main difference between the two accounts is that Relational Grammar represents the differences between the two versions of Patient–Recipient sentences as form-related, syntactic variation while Functional Grammar links the different grammatical functions to an aspect of meaning: variation in perspective.

4.3 A CONSTRUCTION GRAMMAR ACCOUNT

Adele Goldberg's Construction Grammar adopts isomorphism as one of its cornerstones. Following a long tradition, Goldberg proposes that 'if two constructions are syntactically distinct, they must be semantically or pragmatically distinct' (Goldberg 1995: 67).

This principle sets a clear agenda for the analysis of object–dative and double-object constructions: since they have two distinct syntactic forms – a point that is not disputed in this framework – they must have different meanings. However, it is also clear that the two constructions are synonymous in the sense that, given a situation in the world, if one of the two descriptions holds true for that situation, the other must be true, too. In other words, it cannot be that *Bill taught Greek to Belinda* correctly describes a situation that *Bill taught Belinda Greek* does not correctly describe.

Given the anti-synonymy principle and the fact that the two sentences differ in form but have the same truth value, it must be that they are different in some other component of meaning: pragmatics. This is in fact Goldberg's claim.

Pragmatics, in her view, has to do with 'particulars of information structure, including topic and focus' (ibid.: 67). The notion is akin to Erteschik-Shir's and Givón's dominance and Dik's perspective. In her analysis of Patient–Recipient sentences (pp. 89–95), Goldberg in fact cites and adopts Erteschik-Shir's insight: in double-object sentences, the Recipient is topical and the Patient is in focused, while in object–dative sentences, the Recipient is focused and the Patient is topical.

She notes the formal similarity between Patient–Recipient structures such as *Joe gave a bottle to Jim*, and 'cause-motion constructions' such as *Joe kicked the bottle into the yard*: both include a bare noun phrase complement and a prepositional phrase. She suggests that this similarity comes from the fact that the former is a metaphorical extension of the latter (pp. 93–5): both involve a transfer of the possession of an object (pp. 48–52).

This explains the difference in grammaticality between members of the following pairs of double-object and object–dative sentences.

(1) (a) *She gave him a kick.*
    (b) **She gave a kick to him.*

(2) (a) *She threw him a parting glance.*
    (b) **She threw a parting glance to him.*

The object–dative (b) sentences are ungrammatical because the pragmatics of the cause-motion event scheme is less suited to these predicates. In these sentences, the action's object – *a kick* or *a parting glance* – is intended to be focused on rather than the Recipient. Thus, when the object is placed into the non-focused position immediately following the verb, the sentence becomes conflicted.

4.4 A Cognitive Grammar account

According to Ronald Langacker's Cognitive Grammar framework (see Section 3.3. of Chapter 2), when the speaker selects a construction for describing a situation, he cannot help but select a particular image of that situation as well. Different constructions – whether available in the same language or in different languages – reflect different images. 'The symbolic resources of a language generally provide an array of alternative images for describing a given scene' (Langacker 1991: 276).

What does this view entail for the analysis of the alternative expressions of Patient–Recipient sentences? Consider Langacker's examples:

(1) (a) *Bill sent a walrus to Joyce.*
    (b) *Bill sent Joyce a walrus.*

In Cognitive Grammar, as in Construction Grammar, there is no underlying structure where two formally different sentences could be shown to have one and the same form. Thus, neither of the two sentences in (1) is syntactically derived from another. The two distinct syntactic structures are claimed to have two distinct meanings (pp. 276–7).

The semantic contrast has to do with the varying salience attributed to components of the situation described. In (1a), the preposition *to* points at the path followed by the walrus and thus highlights this path. In (1b), *to* is not present; instead, the juxtaposition of Recipient and Patient iconically depicts the possessor–possessee relationship between the two. The sentence in (1b) thus focuses on the result of the act of transfer while the transfer itself is more salient in (1a). There are thus two different images suggested by the two constructions.

Langacker points out that this analysis explains the varying felicity of members of certain pairs of sentences. These are his examples (p. 277):

(2) (a) *I sent a walrus to Antarctica.*
    (b) *?I sent Antarctica a walrus.*

(3) (a) *?I gave a new coat of paint to the fence.*
    (b) *I gave the fence a new coat of paint.*

The sentence in (2b) is infelicitous because it paints a possessor–possessee image for Antarctica and a walrus which, however, is difficult to conceptualize. The sentence in (3b) is in turn strange because it highlights a path along which the paint travels to the fence which, again, is not easy to picture.

As in Erteschik-Shir's and Goldberg's analyses, the infelicity of sentences is explained by a conflict within the sentences. In Erteschik-Shir's examples, the conflict has to do with the inherent pragmatic content of the pronouns *it* and *who* as against the pragmatic connotation of the positions in which they are placed. In Goldberg's examples, the conflict is between focal content and topical position. In Langacker's examples, the conflict is between the image of a situation suggested by the syntactic structure as opposed to the way we normally think of that situation.

In sum: the analyses presented above – Functional Grammar, Construction Grammar and Cognitive Grammar – restore isomorphism for object–dative and double-object sentences by showing that the two formally distinct constructions' meanings are not the same. The two meanings are alike in terms of truth conditions but not in terms of terms of perspective, emphasis or conceptual image.

These approaches thus take the opposite tack from the accounts discussed in Section 3. Relational Grammar, Transformational Grammar and

Lexicase identify a common denominator beneath the two different forms and thus bring this shared form in line with the one meaning. The approaches seen in this section pinpoint a component of meaning with respect to which the two constructions differ, with the result that the two distinct forms are shown to correspond to two somewhat different meanings. Either way, isomorphism is upheld.

5 A cross-linguistic outlook

5.1 Direct-object and primary-object languages

In the preceding sections, we discussed the ways in which semantic participant roles are linked to grammatical functions in English object–dative and double-object sentences. Let us now see how other languages express sentences that involve Patient and Recipient.

English is not the only language that has both constructions available. Here are parallel examples from Indonesian (Dryer 1986: 811; originally from Sandra Chung). (TRANS stands for a transitivizing prefix.)

(1) (a) *Saja mem-bawa   surat itu kepada Ali.*
         I   TRANS-bring letter the to   Ali
         'I brought the letter to Ali.'

     (b) *Saja mem-bawa-kan   Ali surat itu.*
         I   TRANS-bring-*kan* Ali letter the
         'I brought Ali the letter.'

The differences between the two sentences largely parallel the differences between their English equivalents: the presence versus absence of a preposition on the Recipient and the alternative word order. Where Indonesian departs from the English pattern is that in Indonesian, the verb codes the double-object construction by having a special suffix -*kan*.

Given that in English and Indonesian, there are two (near-)synonymous expressions of the same meaning, one might expect that there are also languages where only one or only the other is available. This is indeed the case. German, for example, has only the object–dative construction without the double-object alternative. As (2c) shows, in German, the Recipient cannot function as a direct object; only the Patient can.

(2) (a) *Ich lese das   Buch.*
         I   read **the.ACC book**
         'I read the book.'

     (b) *Ich gab   das   Buch dem   Jungen.*
         I   gave **the.ACC book** the.DAT boy
         'I gave the book to the boy.'

    (c) **Ich gab* **den**   ***Jungen*** *das*   *Buch.*
        I   gave **the.ACC boy**   the.ACC book

Conversely, there are languages where it is the Recipient that must be expressed as a direct object. Huichol is an example (Comrie 1982: 99, 107). In Huichol, the likeness between the Recipient in Patient–Recipient sentences and the direct object in transitive sentences is not shown by identical case marking since the language does not mark case. What does show that the Recipient is treated like a direct object is verb agreement. In both (3a) and (3b), the verb agrees with the subject; in addition, it also agrees with another argument. In (3a), this other agreement controller is the Patient but in (3b), it is the Recipient rather than the Patient. Agreement with the Patient – 'the chickens' – would be ungrammatical.

  (3) (a) *Nee eekie **ne-meci**-zeiya.*
          I   you **I-you**-see
          'I see you.'

      (b) *Nee waakanaari **ne-meci**-tikiiti eeki.*
          I   chickens **I-you**-give   you
          'I gave you the chickens.'

Thus, in English and Indonesian, there is a many-to-many relation between the semantic participant roles of Patient and Recipient and the grammatical function Object:

  (4) semantic participant roles: grammatical relations:

      Patient ⟍   ╱ Direct Object

      Recipient ╱   ⟍ non-Direct-Object

Huichol has less complex relations between the two:

  (5) semantic participant roles: grammatical relations:

      Patient ⟍   ╱ Direct Object

      Recipient ╱   ⟍ non-Direct-Object

German has an even simpler system: Patient and Direct Object, and Recipient and non-Direct-Object are in a one-to-one relation:

  (6) semantic participant roles: grammatical relations:
      Patient ———————————— Direct Object

      Recipient ———————————— non-Direct-Object

The English, Indonesian, German and Huichol evidence shows that cross-linguistically, there are two ways in which Patients and Recipients are classed relative to the objects of transitive sentences. The two ways are shown in (7) (P =Patient, R= Recipient)(see Dryer 1986: 814). In (7a), the Patient of three-argument sentences is lumped together with the Patient of two-argument sentences. In (7b), it is the Recipient of three-argument sentences that is lumped together with the Patient of two-argument sentences.

(7) (a) direct object   (b) primary object
       alignment: alignment:

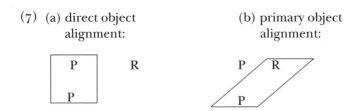

Dryer's terminology is employed in the headings of (7). The object category of (7a), which lumps together the Patient of object–dative sentences and the Patient of transitive sentences, is called the Direct Object; the Recipient of object–dative sentences is called the Indirect Object. The object category of (7b), which lumps together the Recipient of double-object sentences and the Patient of transitive sentences, is the Primary Object; the Patient of double-object sentences is the Secondary Object. Languages with Direct Objects (e.g. German) may be called direct-object languages; languages with Primary Objects (e.g. Huichol) may be called primary-object languages. English and Indonesian are both.

Dryer further claims that the alignment of Patients and Recipients in (7b) is the cross-linguistically more frequent one and thus the (7a) pattern should be derived from (7b), rather than in reverse, as is done in Relational Grammar and Transformational Grammar. In these two frameworks, as we have seen, the rule that relates the two patterns applies to object–dative constructions and promotes the indirect (dative) object to direct object while demoting the direct object, thus deriving the double-object construction. Dryer's rule (dubbed the Anti-Dative Rule, in contrast with Dative Movement) takes off from the double-object construction and, to get the object–dative construction, it promotes the Object-2 Patient to Object while demoting the Recipient to a prepositional direct object.

As we have seen, the two truth-value-wise synonymous constructions may both occur within a single language – as in English or Indonesian – or a language may have one or the other. In English and Indonesian, they create a language-internal violation of isomorphism. Huichol and German do not violate isomorphism in these constructions; but the existence of alternative constructions across languages for the expression of the same meaning constitutes a cross-linguistic violation of isomorphism.

5.2 ACCUSATIVE AND ERGATIVE LANGUAGES

In discussing the differing cross-linguistic manifestations of Patient–Recipient sentences, Dryer (1986) calls attention to a parallelism that holds between the two alignment patterns of Patients and Recipients as seen in (7) and the two alignment patterns of Patients and Agents in active and passive sentences. Consider (1).

(1) (a) *Fred has eaten the pie.*
    (b) *The pie has been eaten by Fred.*

As pointed out in Section 2.1, active and passive sentences, just like object–dative and double-object constructions, represent a departure from isomorphism. In active and passive sentences, the participant roles involved are Agent and Patient and the grammatical functions are Subject and Prepositional Phrase. This is the line-up of semantic roles and grammatical functions in active and passive sentences:

(2)   semantic roles: grammatical functions:

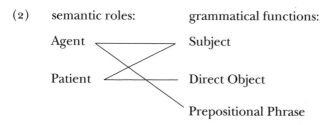

The active and passive alignment patterns between semantic participant roles and grammatical functions are shown in (3).

(3)   active alignment: passive alignment:

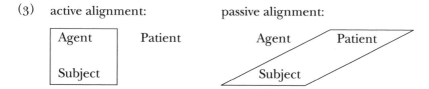

In active sentences, Agents have the same properties as intransitive subjects; Patients are different since they are expressed as direct objects. In passive sentences, it is Patients that are endowed with intransitive subject properties and Agents are different. This is illustrated in (4).

(4) active sentence:
        He is chasing them.
    passive sentence:
        They are being chased by him.
    intransitive sentence:
        They are running.

In (4), the Patient of the transitive sentence – *they* – is aligned with the subject of the intransitive sentence in case, linear position and verb agreement.

Regarding the expression of Patient–Recipient sentences, we saw that languages fall into three types: those that have both the object–dative and the double-object construction (e.g. English and Indonesian), those that have the object–dative construction but no double-object alternative ('direct-object languages', e.g. German), and those that have the double-object construction but not the object-dative alternative ('primary-object languages', e.g. Huichol). The same is true for actives and passives: the alternative grammatical function assignments of their arguments may both be available in a single language or only one of them may be. In other words, while English has both, there are languages that have the English active-type alignment and not the passive-like alignment; and there are languages that have only – or which strongly favour – the passive-like alignment.

An example of the former is Kirghiz. In this language, there is no passive equivalent for a sentence like (5) (Saltanat Mambaeva, personal communication).

(5) *Sen jangi nan jep jatasing.*
you$_S$ fresh bread eat you$_S$:eat
'You$_S$ are eating fresh bread.'

As the Chantyal and Hungarian data in the appendix show, these two languages also lack passives.

For an example of the latter – a language that has the passive-like alignment between Patient and intransitive subject – consider Walmatjari (Merrifield *et al.* 1987: problem 214).

(6) (a) *Kunyarr pa pinya nganpayi-rlu.*
dog it hit man-CASE
'The man hit the dog.'

(b) *Kunyarr pa laparni.*
dog it ran
'The dog ran.'

Here, the intransitive subject of (6b) is coded like the object of the transitive sentence of (6): 'dog' of (6a) and 'dog' of (6b) are aligned by having zero case marking and by preceding the verb. The Agent of (6a), however, has a distinct case suffix. The following English sentence structures mimic Walmatjari in terms of case marking and word order.

(7) (a) *He hits them.* ('He is hitting them.')
(b) *Run them.* ('They are running.')

OR

(c) *Them hits he.* ('He is hitting them.')
(d) *Them run.* ('They are running.')

In (7 a–b) and in (7 c–d), the Patient and the intransitive subject have the same case and the same linear position as opposed to the Agent of the transitive construction.

The Walmatjari-type alignment of transitive and intransitive sentence arguments is called **ergative** alignment, as opposed to the English type, called **accusative** alignment. The two types were introduced in Chapter 2 (Section 3.2) because Tsez, discussed there, is another ergative language. In (8) are shown the schemata for both patterns. A stands for the agentive argument of transitive sentences, P stands for patient; S stands for the single argument of intransitive verbs.

(8) (a) accusative alignment: (b) ergative alignment:

          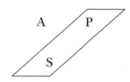

A comparison of (8) with (3) shows the parallelism between the 'active' and 'accusative' alignment among semantic participant roles, and between their 'passive' and the 'ergative' alignment. As in the case of the alignment patterns between Patients and Recipients, some languages – such as English – have both patterns, others (such as Kirghiz and Walmatjari) have only one or the other.

Let us summarize.

(a) PATIENT–RECIPIENT SENTENCES
Patients and Recipients may be aligned with transitive objects in two ways: either the Patient or the Recipient is like the Object of transitive sentences. Languages differ in their alignment patterns. All three of the possible types occur either jointly in a single language or separately.

	Patient = Object	Recipient = Object	EXAMPLE:
Type I	+	−	German
Type II	−	+	Huichol
Type III	+	+	English, Indonesian

(b) AGENT–PATIENT SENTENCES
Agents and Patients may be aligned with intransitive subjects in two ways: either the Agent or the Patient is like the Subject of intransitive

sentences. Languages differ in their alignment patterns. All three of the possible types occur either jointly in a single language or separately.

	Agent = Subject	Patient = Subject	EXAMPLE:
Type I	+	−	Kirghiz
Type II	−	+	Walmatjari
Type III	+	+	English, German

Lack of isomorphism between meaning and syntactic form is striking when it occurs within a single language; but it is also a puzzle when it occurs across languages. Given a particular meaning, what are the limits on the range of available constructions in human languages? Why do languages differ in the syntactic construction they opt for in order to express a meaning?

This question will be the focus of Section 2 of Chapter 5 for one kind of syntactic variation: word order.

6 Conclusions

In his study of Patient–Recipient sentences, Richard Larson notes that double-object constructions are a puzzle: the two objects have different syntactic characteristics even though they appear to have the same position in constituent structure. Symmetrical positions would predict symmetrical syntactic behaviour; '[t]his is what we expect, but it is not what we see' (Larson 1988: 339). This is a concise characterization of what it is like when a fact calls for an explanation. In all such instances, the problem is that fact and expectation diverge: there is a gap between the two.

In considering the ways in which grammatical functions – subject, direct object and indirect object – correspond to semantic participant roles, we identified various gaps of this sort. The one this chapter focused on concerned the object–dative and double-object constructions of Patient–Recipient sentences in English. The conflict and its possible resolutions are repeated below from Section 2.2.

A. ISOMORPHISM
Isomorphism requires a one-to-one relation between sentence form and sentence meaning: each sentence form should have a single meaning (no ambiguity) and each sentential meaning should be expressed by a single form (no synonymy).

B. PATIENT–RECIPIENT SENTENCES

(a) FORM:
The verb–complement structure of some Patient–Recipient sentences may appear in two different forms: object-dative (NP$_1$ *to*-NP$_2$) and double-object (NP$_2$ NP$_1$).

(b) MEANING:
The two constructions have the same meaning.

C. THE CONFLICT
The two forms of Patient–Recipient sentences are synonymous. The isomorphism requirement, however, bans synonymy.

D. POSSIBLE RESOLUTIONS OF THE CONFLICT
The conflict can be resolved by showing that the syntactic and semantic characterizations of these sentences as given in B. are incorrect . . .

(a) . . . either because what appear to be two different forms are actually the same form,
(b) . . . or because what appears to be a single meaning is actually two different meanings.

Six solutions to this conflict have been surveyed. They all opt for one of the logically available range of ways of dealing with conflicts in general: splitting the problematic entity into two parts – or viewing them from different angles – so that the contradiction is restricted to only one of the two parts or only to one view. The six accounts fall into two classes, each saving isomorphism in some way.

Relational Grammar, Transformational Grammar and Lexicase go with the solution described in (D(a)) above: they re-assess the **form side** of the conflict. Rather than representing two distinct forms conveying the same meaning, they differentiate two levels of form for the double-object construction so that on one level, its form is the same as that of the object–dative construction. Thus, isomorphism holds on that underlying level of form. This is shown in (1). (UF = underlying form; SF = surface form.)

(1) (a) no isomorphism   (b) partially restored isomorphism

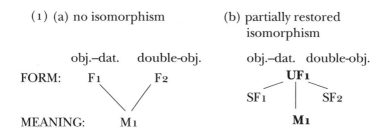

Functional Grammar, Construction Grammar and Cognitive Grammar opt for the second possible solution described in (D(b)) above: they re-analyse the **meaning side** of the conflict. Taking the fine scalpel of a surgeon to the semantics of the two constructions, they identify two kinds of meaning: truth-conditional and pragmatic, the latter including differences in focus, perspective or conceptual image. They find that the meanings of the two constructions are the same with respect to truth-conditional meaning but they are distinct from the point of view of pragmatic meaning. This is shown in (2). (TM = truth-conditional meaning, PM = pragmatic meaning.)

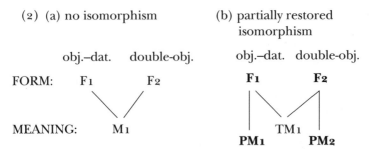

(2) (a) no isomorphism   (b) partially restored isomorphism

As we looked at languages outside English, we noted, following Dryer, that languages differ in how Patients and Recipients are aligned with transitive objects and that languages similarly differ in how Agents and Patients are aligned with intransitive subjects.

Notes

1   Preliminaries
The term isomorphism is taken from Haiman 1985a.

2.2   Double-object and object–dative sentences
For a detailed analysis of Patient–Recipient constructions, see Green 1974.

3.2   A Relational Grammar account

- For other principles associated with the account of Patient–Recipient sentences (the Re-ranking Law and the Nuclear Chaining Constraint) see Johnson 1977. On the Relational Grammar view of Patient–Recipient sentences, see also Blake 1990: 3–6, 55–8. For a concise description of the Relational Grammar framework, see Aissen 1991.
- On the analysis of double-object constructions in Functional Grammar, see also Dik 1997, Part 1: 282–4, Part 2: 370.

4.2   A Functional Grammar account
For Functional Grammar analyses of Patient–Recipient constructions, see Siewierska 1991: 93–104; Dik 1997, part 1: 250–4, part 2: 370.

4.4   A Cognitive Grammar account
Cognitive Grammar, as well as Construction Grammar and Transformational Generative Grammar, will be discussed in more detail in Chapter 6.

5   A cross-linguistic outlook

The Huichol sentence (3a) is a conjecture based on Comrie's data; in (3b), it is not clear how the past tense is expressed.

Exercises

1. Synonymy pairs similar to object–dative and double-object constructions are the following:

(i)   (a)   *Bill smeared paint on the table.*
      (b)   *Bill smeared the table with paint.*

(ii) (a)   *Bill loaded cement on the truck.*
      (b)   *Bill loaded the truck with cement.*

(iii) (a)   *Bill planted tulips in the garden.*
      (b)   *Bill planted the garden with tulips.*

(iv) (a)   *Bill squeezed toothpaste out of the tube.*
      (b)   *Bill squeezed the tube.*

What is the structural similarity between these sentences and Patient–Recipient constructions? Is there a meaning difference between members of each pair of sentences?

2. Functional Grammar, Construction Grammar and Cognitive Grammar all claim that, just as object–dative and double-object sentences differ in pragmatic meaning, so do active and passive sentences. Collect examples from written texts or live conversations of actives and passives along with the context in which they occur. Is there indeed some kind of a meaning difference between the two constructions? If so, what is it?

3. Is there a difference in pragmatic meaning between alternative expressions of verb–particle constructions, with the two continuous or discontinuous?

4. In Section 5, English sentences were re-formulated so as to show ergative case marking and word order. Take the Walmatjari data in (13). What would these sentences look like if Walmatjari were an accusative-style language, rather than ergative? Adjust both case marking and word order.

5. Here are some sentences from Samoan (Langacker 1972: 174). Is the case marking system accusative-style or ergative-style?

(a)   *E sogi e le tama le ufi i le to'i.*
      'The boy cuts the yam with the axe.'

(b) *Sa sogi e le teine le ufi.*
'The girl cut the yam.'

(c) *Sa fa'pa'u e ioane le to'i.*
'John dropped the axe.'

(d) *Sa pa'u le ufi.*
'The yam fell.'

(e) *E pa'u le to'i.*
'The axe falls.'

6. Here are some derived words in English involving the suffixes -*er* and -*ee*. They both form nouns out of verbs.

DERIVED FROM TRANSITIVE VERBS:	DERIVED FROM INTRANSITIVE VERBS:
(a) writ-er	runn-er
read-er	speak-er
winn-er	lectur-er
(b) nomin-ee	retir-ee
employ-ee	refer-ee
detain-ee	

(a) State word-formation rules for each suffix indicating whether the derived words refer to the subjects or objects of the actions expressed by the verbs.

(b) Are the rules accusative-style or ergative-style? A rule is accusative-style if it lumps together intransitive subjects and subjects of transitive verbs. A rule is ergative-style if it lumps together intransitive subjects and objects of transitive verbs.

7. Chantyal is an ergative language. In the Chantyal sentences in the Appendix, the ergative case suffix is indicated in the glosses. How is the absolutive marked?

Chapter Five

Alternative Analyses of Syntactic Variation and Change

Three umpires were discussing their roles in the game of baseball. The first umpire asserted, 'I calls 'em the way I sees 'em.' The next umpire, with even more confidence and a more metaphysical turn of mind, said, 'I calls 'em the way they *are!*' But the third umpire, displaying a familiarity with twentieth-century physics, concluded the discussion with 'They ain't *nothin'* until I calls 'em!'

(Gregory 1988: 195)

1 Preliminaries

Variation and change are paradoxical notions: they are laden with conflicts. How is it that the order of words is different in German and Quechua even though they are both human languages? And how is it that the word order in contemporary English is different from that of English of a thousand years ago – even though both are English? The paradox of variation and change is the paradox of taxonomy. The basic question is how can things that are the same also be different; or, equivalently, how can different things nonetheless be regarded as the same.

We will first take up variation in constituent order across languages and discuss different proposals for accounting for it. Second, for an instance of change, we will look at change in the language of a single individual and survey alternative accounts of the second-language acquisition of relative clauses.

Here is a preview. There are certain constituent order patterns that regularly cluster in languages. Thus, most OV languages have postpositions and genitive & noun order, most VO languages have prepositions and noun & genitive order; and all known languages that have both OV and adjective-noun order have genitive & noun order. In Section 2, several additional correlations among word order patterns will be cited from the literature and the question raised of why constituents of apparently different kinds show consistent ordering across languages. We will see three alternative attempts to bring the different pairs of constituents to a common denominator so that their ordering follows from a single principle.

Just like historical change, the target-induced change in language acquisition is gradual. Here lies the conflict: once the learner is exposed to the target language and is trying to speak it, why is acquisition not instantaneous? Why is there not an immediate match between what the learner hears and what he produces so that his production is neither more nor less than the model? As we will see, earlier and later stages of acquisition do not differ at random: there are recurrent patterns in acquisitional sequence and in the kinds of errors that learners make. Section 3 will demonstrate this for relative-clause acquisition and assess three possible sources of the patterns.

2 Alternative analyses of word order variation across languages

2.1 THE PROBLEM

Linear order involves an asymmetric relationship between two constituents: A precedes B. Thus, to formulate linear order rules, we need to assign distinct labels to the two constituents so that the rules can separately refer to what precedes and what follows. The task of a theory of word order is therefore to find the right properties that determine this linear asymmetry between constituents.

One possibility is to state the difference between the two words on the lexical level. Consider (1):

(1) *The president* **hired Peter**.

In order to get the right order in the phrase *hired Peter*, we could formulate the following rule:

(2) Given *hired* and *Peter*, *hired* must precede *Peter*.

But this statement applies only to these particular words and thus fails the most basic requirement that syntactic rules must meet: that of generality.

To be sure, there are instances where word order rules must make reference to individual lexical items. In English, for example, there is one adposition – *ago* – that is an exception to the normal preposed order: it obligatorily follows the noun phrase it pertains to (*two days ago*, **ago two days*). Another example of lexeme-level ordering comes from numerals: in some languages, the numeral 'one' is ordered differently from the rest. In Basque, Hebrew and Maltese, numerals precede the noun but 'one' follows. In the north-western Caucasian languages of Adyghe and Kabardian, it is the other way around: 'one' precedes the noun and the other numerals follow (Hurford 2003: 575). In these languages, the rule that orders 'one' must specifically mention this word.

However, such lexeme-based rules are a last resort. Normally, linearization rules can be formulated for classes of words, phrases or clauses. These classes serve as common denominators to words that are ordered alike. Thus, the order of *hired* and *Peter* in (1) is covered by the rule in (3).

(3) In English, given a verb and a direct object, the verb must precede the direct object.

The statement in (3) is more general than that in (2): it orders any verb with respect to any direct object in English. But, since we are aiming at maximal generality, it would be even better to formulate rules that order pairs of several different syntactic categories by one single stroke. Additional order patterns of English are exemplified in (4) and (5).

(4) *We bought cherries* **in Door County**.
(5) *I like* **the cherries that we bought in Door County**.

These sentences are instances of the following rules:

(6) In English, given an adposition and a noun phrase, the adposition must precede the noun.
(7) In English, given a noun and a relative clause, the noun must precede the relative clause.

We have so far noted three order patterns of English, given in (8).

(8) Verb and Object
Adposition and Noun Phrase
Noun and Relative Clause

Rather than having an individual rule for each – (3), (6) and (7) – is there a way to replace them with a single, more general rule that accounts for all three order patterns in (8)? This would be possible if we could find a common denominator for the terms that precede – verb, adposition and noun – and a common denominator for the terms that follow – object, noun phrase and relative clause.

The need for finding such common denominators becomes more pronounced if we consider cross-linguistic evidence. It turns out that in many languages, verb, adposition and noun are ordered the same way relative to their co-constituents: object, noun phrase and relative clause. Either verb, adposition and noun phrase all precede their co-constituents in a language or they all follow them.

A large-scale cross-linguistic study involving 625 languages of different language families and different geographic areas carried out by Matthew Dryer further broadens the picture. Dryer found additional pairs of constituents whose ordering patterns tend to cluster across languages. Here are seven of Dryer's 17 correlation pairs including the three in (8) (Dryer 1992: 108):

(9) Verb and Object
Verb and Adpositional Phrase
Verb and Manner Adverb
Noun and Relative Clause
Noun and Genitive
Adposition and Noun Phrase
Question Particle and Sentence

Data from Easter Island and Japanese illustrate the two cross-linguistically frequent orderings of these constituents. Since in these languages, objects are adpositional phrases, the order of the verb relative to object and to adpositional phrase is illustrated by the same example.

(10)

EASTER ISLAND	JAPANESE
Verb & Adpositional Object	**Adpositional Object & Verb**
to'o i te moni	*okane o toru*
take ACC the money	money ACC take

'take the money'

Verb & Manner Adverb	**Manner Adverb & Verb**
hapi riva	*yoku benkyoosuru*
learn well	well study

'study well'

Noun & Relative Clause	**Relative Clause & Noun**
te poki noho oruga	*sono booto ni tomatteiru*
the boy stay upon	the boat on staying
o te miro	*otokonoko*
GEN the boat	boy

'the boy who stays on the boat'

Noun & Genitive	**Genitive & Noun**
te hoi o te tagata	*sono otoko no uma*
the horse GEN the man	the man GEN horse

'the man's horse'

Adposition & Noun Phrase	**Noun Phrase & Adposition**
i te money	*okane o*
ACC the money	money ACC

'the money (ACC)'

Question Particle & Sent.	**Sent. & Question Particle**
hoki he moni tokorua	*okane ga arimasu-ka*
Q is money your	money SBJ be(polite)-Q

'Do you have money?'

Irish shows the same orders as Easter Island; Turkish is like Japanese. English in turn illustrates that the clusterings of order patterns shown above are not without exceptions. English is in some ways similar to Easter Island: it has V & O, prepositions and the relative clause follows the noun phrase. However, genitives and manner adverbs show both orders: both *the money of the man* and *the man's money* are grammatical and so are *ran quickly* and *quickly ran*. Since English has no question particles, the sixth pattern does not apply.

The cross-linguistic validity of these statistical correlations underscores the question stated above. If the preceding constituents across the pairs are as different as their labels show them to be, we would not expect them to show uniform ordering across languages. If they do show such consistency of order, this must be because they are alike in some way. The question in (11) formulates the problem; the statement in (12) schematizes the hoped-for solution.

(11) CONFLICT
     Why should constituents of **different** types show the **same** ordering across languages?

(12) RESOLUTION
     Constituents that show the **same** ordering across languages are, in some sense, of the **same** type.

The challenge is therefore to find the right categorization of syntactic constituents: the crucial property that defines all preceding constituents as a class as opposed to those that regularly follow.

The first step in this endeavour is to notice that some of the correlations already involve the same constituent classes. Thus, 'Noun and Relative Clause' and 'Noun and Genitive' both involve nouns: the two patterns are covered by the generalization that nouns and their co-constituents in the noun phrase are ordered alike. Similarly, 'Verb and Manner Adverb' and 'Verb and Object' can be subsumed under the generalization that verbs are consistently ordered relative to their co-constituents in the verb phrase. But this still leaves the question of why nouns and verbs should pattern alike; why adpositions should pattern as nouns and verbs; and why question particles should pattern like nouns, verbs and adpositions. Thus, word class labels will not do: they do not spell out the similarities among all the constituents that tend to be ordered the same way across languages.

Of the various proposals in the literature that address the question in (11) and offer answers along the lines of (12), we will single out three. Each envisages a different way in which the constituents whose linear order tends to be correlated across languages are reducible to the same type. Here are the three proposals in a nutshell:

(13) (a) HEADS AND DEPENDENTS
In any one language, all **head** constituents tend to be ordered the same way relative to their **dependents**.

(b) BRANCHING AND NON-BRANCHING CONSTITUENTS
In any one language, all **branching constituents** tend to be ordered the same way relative to their **non-branching** co-constituents.

(c) MOTHER-NODE-CONSTRUCTING AND NON-MOTHER-NODE-CONSTRUCTING CONSTITUENTS
In any one language, all **mother-node-constructing constituents** tend to be ordered the same way relative to their **non-mother-node-constructing co-constituents**.

The next three sections will take up these proposals in turn. In assessing them, we will keep in mind one of the basic metascientific requirements that holds for generalizations: empirical truth. What this means is that an adequate theory must make predictions that are borne out by facts. In our case, the right account must predict cross-linguistic consistency of ordering where such consistency exists; and it must not predict cross-linguistic consistency where there is none.

2.2 HEADS AND DEPENDENTS

Constituents cannot be ordered unless they have been selected to be present in a structure. Thus, a promising place to look for commonnesses among categories that are uniformly ordered in languages is their role in selection. Given that selectors are logically prior to selectees in the selection process, one might hypothesize (1):

(1) In all languages, all selectors tend to precede their selectees.

This guess is supported by the order patterns in OV languages such as Japanese. If we assume that objects are selectors of their verbs and relative clauses are selectors of their noun heads, Japanese bears out (1): it places selectors before selectees. But VO languages such as Easter Island pose a problem: they show the opposite orders, with selectee before selector.

While Easter Island and other VO languages indicate that selectors do not always precede selectees, they do not invalidate the general idea that the ordering of constituents may be based on the division between selectors and selectees. An alternative to (1) is to allow languages to choose between two principles: ordering all selectors before their selectees or ordering all selectees before their selectors.

(2) In any one language, all selectors tend to be uniformly ordered relative to their selectees.

The statement in (2) allows both for languages such as Japanese, where all selectors precede their selectees, as well as for languages such as Easter Island, where all selectees precede their selectors. Given that (2) is stated as a tendency, it also allows for languages such as English, where most – but not all – selectees precede their selectors.

This idea underlies an influential theory of word order: the Principle of Natural Serialization proposed by Theo Vennemann in the early 1970s (see Bartsch and Vennemann 1972: 131–9; Vennemann 1973: 40–7). Here is the statement of the principle (Vennemann 1973: 41; braces flank semantic constituents, square brackets flank syntactic constituents):

(3) THE NATURAL SERIALIZATION PRINCIPLE
(T)he operator-operand relationship tends to be expressed by unidirectional serialization: {Operator {Operand}} tends to be serialized either as [Operator [Operand]] throughout, or as [[Operand]Operator] throughout.

In later work, Vennemann used the term Head for Operand and Specifier for Operator, where Specifier corresponds to the more widely used term Dependent. Thus, we will follow Dryer (1992) by referring to Vennemann's hypothesis as the Head-Dependent theory. Here are some of Vennemann's Heads and Dependents:

(4) HEAD: DEPENDENT:
    Verb   Object
    Verb   Adpositional Phrase
    Verb   Manner Adverb
    Noun   Relative Clause
    Noun   Genitive
    Noun   Adjective

How does Vennemann's generalization stand up in the light of cross-linguistic data? Some of the evidence is certainly consistent with it. Let us take a second look at the list of correlation pairs given in (9) of Section 2.1. The Natural Serialization Principle correctly predicts the uniform ordering of the first five pairs of constituents in Easter Island and Japanese: as seen in Section 2.1, in Easter Island, adpositional object and manner adverb follow the verb, and genitive and relative clause follow the noun, whereas Japanese shows the opposite order for these pairs. The constituent pairs of (9) in Section 1 whose ordering is correctly predicted by Vennemann are shown in bold in (5).

(5) **Verb and Object**
Verb and Adpositional Phrase
Verb and Manner Adverb
Noun and Relative Clause
Noun and Genitive
Adposition and Noun Phrase
Question Particle and Sentence

However, there are two problems with the principle: in some cases, it fails to unambiguously predict cross-linguistic consistency of ordering where such exists and in other cases, it predicts cross-linguistic constituency where it does not exist.

To illustrate the first problem, consider the remaining two pairs of constituents in (5): adposition and noun phrase, and question particle and sentence. In order for the Natural Serialization Principle to correctly predict the cross-linguistically consistent orderings of these pairs, adpositions would have to be viewed as heads vis-à-vis noun phrases and question particles would have to be heads of sentences.

But is this classification independently motivated? Heads can normally stand by themselves with the dependents optional; for example, nouns can stand without relative clauses and many verbs can stand without direct objects. But adpositions generally cannot stand by themselves, nor can question particles. Thus, unless an appropriately broad definition of head and dependent is designed and independently motivated, the principle does not predict the cross-linguistically attested orders of adpositions and question particles.

The second problem with the Natural Serialization Principle is that there are pairs of constituents that meet the definition of Operator and Operand but they do not show the consistency of ordering that the principle predicts. Foremost among these is nouns and adjectives. Just like relative clauses, adjectives, too, delimit the referent of the noun and are therefore dependents of it; yet, relative clause–noun order does correlate with O-V order but adjective–noun order does not. Note, for example, that in English, a VO language, the Natural Serialization Principle would have adjectives follow nouns but the actual order is the opposite. Dryer's extensive cross-linguistic study of adjective-noun order shows that the order of adjectives and nouns does not correlate with the ordering of other constituents (Dryer 1992: 95–6).

In sum, whereas the Natural Serialization Principle makes some correct predictions, it does not predict all cross-linguistically consistent patterns and it makes at least one prediction that is not borne out by evidence.

We will now turn to an alternative approach.

2.3 BRANCHING AND NON-BRANCHING CONSTITUENTS

We have just seen that relative clauses follow nouns in VO languages and precede them in OV languages but that adjectives do not conform to the same pattern even though both relative clauses and adjectives select the noun as head and modify it. This clearly shows that whether a constituent is a selector or a selectee cannot be the only factor accounting for all cross-linguistically consistent order patterns. If it were, adjectives and relative clauses would have to be uniformly ordered relative to the nouns they modify.

So what might be the difference between adjectives and relative clauses that would account for their differential linear behaviour? An answer was suggested by Matthew Dryer (1992): adjectives have a simple syntactic structure in that they are generally single words, whereas relative clauses are complex – they consist of more than one word.

Dryer has proposed that structural simplicity versus complexity is the crucial order-significant property of syntactic constituents. For Vennemann, what defines the classes of uniformly ordered constituents is whether they are Heads or Dependents; for Dryer, the relevant classes are Non-Branching and Branching Categories. Here is his principle (paraphrased from Dryer 1992: 109):

(1) THE BRANCHING DIRECTION HYPOTHESIS
    Given a pair of elements X and Y, where X is non-branching and Y
    is branching, the XY order will show up significantly more often
    than the YX order in VO languages. For OV languages, the
    opposite holds: the YX order will show up significantly more often
    than the XY order.

Let us consider how this principle fares in the light of cross-linguistic evidence. Here is, again, the list of correlation patterns considered above:

(2) Verb and Object
    Verb and Adpositional Phrase
    Verb and Manner Adverb
    Noun and Relative Clause
    Noun and Genitive
    Adposition and Noun Phrase
    Question Particle and Sentence

Note first that the last two correlation patterns on the list, which were problematic for Vennemann, are now accounted for. As we saw above, in Vennemann's theory, the Head-Dependent dichotomy did not seem to apply to adpositions and their noun phrases, nor to question particles and their sentences. However, they do share the characteristic that Dryer suggests is crucial for their ordering: adpositions and question particles are single words as opposed to their respective multi-word co-constituents – noun phrases and sentences. To this extent, the Branching Direction Hypothesis scores better than Natural Serialization: it correctly predicts the cross-linguistically consistent ordering of these two pairs of constituents.

Dryer's theory not only makes correct predictions where Vennemann's seems to make none, but it also avoids making predictions for consistent ordering where it does not occur. As discussed in Section 2.2, Natural Serialization predicts that adjectives and nouns, forming a Dependent-Head pair, should be ordered as object–verb pairs are; but this prediction is false. As already noted above, the Branching Direction Hypothesis avoids this problem because, by Dryer's definition of branching, in most languages, neither adjectives nor nouns branch and thus the order within this pair of constituents is not expected to fall in line with Verb–Object order. Thus, Branching Direction correctly predicts the lack of consistent ordering for this pair of constituents.

But Dryer's hypothesis is not without problems, either. Let us consider the other five correlation pairs in the list. The common characteristic of verb and noun that Vennemann saw was that they were Heads, as opposed to objects, adpositional phrases, manner adverbs, relative clauses and genitives, which were Dependents. For Dryer, the similarity between verbs and nouns is that they are single words, as opposed to objects, adpositional phrases, manner adverbs, relative clauses and genitives, which branch.

But do these constituents really branch? Relative clauses clearly do: they generally consist of more than one word. Objects, adpositional phrases and genitives are generally phrasal and thus multi-word as well. Thus, the Branching Direction Hypothesis correctly predicts the cross-linguistically uniform ordering of verb and object, verb and adpositional phrase, noun and relative clause, and noun and genitive. However, there is a problem with manner adverbs: they are commonly only single words just as verbs are and thus an ordering rule that makes reference to branching versus non-branching constituents cannot differentiate between the two. Yet, manner adverb order follows the pattern of branching constituents. In this case, the Branching Direction Hypothesis fails to predict cross-linguistic constituency where it does exist – a weakness of the same kind as that of the Natural Serialization Principle with respect to adpositions and question particles.

Here is a comparison of the predictions of the two theories. + stands for correct prediction, − stands for false prediction, 0 stands for no prediction even though the constituents in question do show cross-linguistically consistent ordering. NS stands for the Natural Serialization Principle; BD stands for the Branching Direction Principle.

	NS	BD
Noun and Relative Clause	+	+
Noun and Genitive	+	+
Verb and Object	+	+
Verb and Adpositional Phrase	+	+
Verb and Manner Adverb	+	0
Adposition and Noun Phrase	0	+
Question Particle and Sentence	0	+
Adjective and Noun	−	+

Let us now turn to a third theory of constituent order.

2.4 MOTHER-NODE-CONSTRUCTING AND NON-MOTHER-NODE-CONSTRUCTING CONSTITUENTS

Consider the following sentences in English (Hawkins 1994: 65, 70–1):

(1) (a) *Jill **wrote down** the address.*
     (b) *Jill **wrote** the address **down**.*
     (c) *Jill **wrote** the address of the student **down**.*
     (d) *Jill **wrote** the address that her sister had forgotten **down**.*

In (1a), verb and particle are adjacent; in the other three sentences, they are separated by increasingly larger numbers of words. As the distance between the verb and the particle increases, the sentences become more and more awkward.

While common sense tells us that the more distant the parts of a discontinuous construction, the more difficult their interpretation should be, John Hawkins provides a precise explanation for this fact. He analyses sentences from the point of view of the hearer and suggests that the hearer's interest is to be able to see the entire blueprint of the sentence that is coming to him as early as possible. In other words, the hearer wants to be presented with the highest-level constituents of the sentence before getting the details. In the case of the sentences in (1), what this means is that the hearer wants to be given indication right away that

- the sentence consists of a noun phrase and a verb phrase; and then, that
- the verb phrase consists of a verb, a particle and a noun phrase.

In all four sentences, the verb immediately follows the subject noun phrase and thus the highest-level constituents of the sentence – subject noun phrase and verb phrase – are available to the hearer within the space of the first two words that he hears. But the sentences differ in how immediately informative they are regarding the composition of the verb phrase. The sentence in (1a) is optimal in this respect: each of the first three words – *wrote down the* – reveals one of the three immediate constituents of the verb phrase: verb, particle and noun phrase. This is shown in (2a), with the double lines marking the 'recognition domain' – that is, the space within which the three VP constituents are identified.

(2)

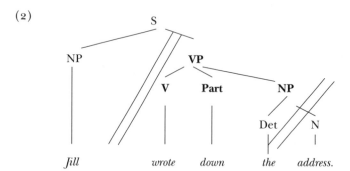

The other three sentences – (1b), (1c) and (1d) – are less forthcoming about the overall blueprint of the verb phrase. In (1b), two of the verb phrase constituents – the verb and the noun phrase – are immediately given: the hearer gets *wrote* first, which is the head verb itself, and then the article *the*, which is an unambiguous identifier – a 'mother-constructing category' – of a noun phrase. But the hearer needs to 'wait out' the word *address* before he learns that there is also a third verb phrase constituent: the particle *down*. In sentences (1c) and (1d) the delay is even longer: there are several words coming the hearer's way before he is able to complete the blueprint of the verb phrase by getting the particle. The diagram in (3) illustrates this for sentence (1d).

(3)

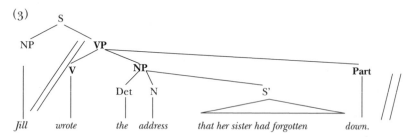

Hawkins proposes a general principle according to which the sooner the immediate constituents of a construction are revealed to the hearer, the easier – and thus the more frequent – the construction. He further suggests that this principle accounts for the varying frequencies of alternative constituent orders not only within a language, as we saw above, but also across languages. Here is the principle (paraphrased from Hawkins 1994: 236):

(4)   THE PRINCIPLE OF EARLY IMMEDIATE CONSTITUENTS
        Constituents are ordered in sentences so as to minimize the
        number of words that it takes, when proceeding from left to right,

to determine the identity of the immediate constituents of a sentence.

Let us see how this principle accounts for the cross-linguistically uniform order of some of the correlation pairs listed in (9) of Section 2.1. Consider the order of verb–object and adposition–noun phrase. In each pair, either constituent may precede the other across languages. The resulting four logical possibilities are given in (5) (see Hawkins 1994: 96, 255–9). The mother-constructing categories – that is, those constituents that are diagnostic of the mother node that they belong to – are in bold. The verb is one of these since a verb unambiguously signals the presence of a verb phrase; the adposition is another since it predicts the presence of an adpositional phrase; but the noun phrase is not since it may or may not be a daughter of an adpositional phrase.

(5) (a) **[Verb [Preposition** NounPhrase]]
  e.g.   *walk*   *in*   *the woods*

  (b) [[NounPhrase **Postposition] Verb**]
  e.g.   *two hours*   *ago*   *called*

  (c) [[**Preposition** NounPhrase] **Verb**]
  e.g.   *in*   *the woods*   *walk*

  (d) [**Verb**   [NounPhrase **Postposition**]]
  e.g.   *called*   *two hours*   *ago*

According to Hawkins' theory, the hearer wants to know as soon as possible that the verb phrase consists of a verb and an adpositional phrase. How forthcoming are these four linearization patterns regarding the internal structure of the verb phrase? The patterns in (5a) and (5b) are optimal. In (5a), in the space of the first two words *walk in*, the hearer gets the entire picture. From *walk*, he identifies one of the immediate constituents of the verb phrase – the verb – and from the preposition *in*, which follows immediately, he constructs the prepositional phrase. Similarly in (5b), he gets the adposition and the verb in immediate sequence.

By contrast, in (5c) and (5d), the two mother-constructing constituents are not adjacent: the intervening words keep the hearer in suspense. In (5c), after the hearer is given the preposition, he has to wait out the noun phrase before he is given the verb. There is a similar waiting involved in (5d).

Given the usefulness of (5a) and (5b) for the hearer and the drawbacks of (5c) and (5d), the following clusters of orders can be predicted to be prevalent:

(6) (5a): Verb & Adpositional Phrase and
     Adposition & Noun Phrase

(5b): Adpositional Phrase & Verb and
      Noun Phrase & Adposition

At the same time the following clusters should be rare:

(7) (5c): Adpositional Phrase & Verb and
        Adposition & Noun Phrase

     (5d): Verb & Adpositional Phrase and
         Noun Phrase & Adposition

In other words, the theory predicts that VO languages should have prepositions rather than postpositions, and that OV languages should have postpositions rather than prepositions. Hawkins' theory thus accounts for two of the pairs of constituents that tend to be uniformly ordered across languages, mentioned in Section 2.1 and repeated below:

(8) Verb and Object
    Verb and Adpositional Phrase
    Verb and Manner Adverb
    Noun and Relative Clause
    Noun and Genitive
    Adposition and Noun Phrase
    Question Particle and Sentence

Hawkins (1994) proposes that several other correlations are also predicted by the theory.

2.5 SUMMARY

We have surveyed three proposals chosen from the literature regarding general principles that constrain constituent order across languages. As stated in Section 2.1, proposals had to address the following conflict:

(1) Why should constituents of **different** types show the **same** ordering across languages?

The challenge for the desired solution was clear: to show that constituents that show the same ordering across languages, diverse as they might appear, are in some sense of the same type. Different things acting the same way is a conflict; same things acting the same way is not.

The three approaches propose three alternative common denominators that cut across syntactic categories to delimit the required order classes. In defining the crucial order-significant properties, all three proposals make crucial use of constituent structure. The Head-Dependent hypothesis highlights the dependency relationship between parts. The other two theories make crucial reference to the relationship between wholes and parts:

Branching Direction sorts constituents depending on whether they have parts or not; and the principle of Early Immediate Constituent Construction classifies them depending on whether a part can or cannot predict its whole.

3 Alternative analyses of relative clause acquisition in second languages

3.1 THE PROBLEM

As noted in Section 1, the central question about learning a language (or about learning anything else, for that matter) is the gap between model and production. Given the model the learner is exposed to, we would expect his output to consist of all and only what the model contains – that is, of error-free replicas of what is heard and nothing else; and we would expect that error-free production happens instantaneously.

However, in actual fact, things are different. The learner does not reproduce all utterances that he has heard; he does not only produce what he has heard but comes up with new utterances of his own as well; and in trying to reproduce model utterances and in creating new ones, he makes mistakes. Furthermore, the learner's production changes over time, gradually approximating the model. The questions that arise are summarized in (1).

(1) (a) Why is the learner's production not the exact replica of the model? In particular,
    (i) why does he say less than what he is exposed to?
    (ii) why does he say more than what he is exposed to?
    (iii) why does he make errors?
  (b) Why does the learner's production change over time?

In what follows, we will not attempt to answer all four of these questions. Our discussion will be limited to (aiii) and (b): why do learners make errors and why are certain aspects of the target language learnt before others. Here are our questions:

(2) (a) THE ORDER IN WHICH SKILLS ARE ACQUIRED
    Which components of the target language will be acquired before other components, and why?
  (b) THE NATURE OF ERRORS
    As the learner tries to cope with yet-unacquired components of the target language, what kinds of errors does he make, and why?

Let us now see some answers to these questions as they emerge from the analysis of second language learners' data.

Learning a new skill involves a change in the mental set of the learner and thus it is generally a difficult and stressful process. It is therefore reasonable to expect the learner to try, unconsciously or consciously, to make the task easier for himself. He will want to minimize the distance between what he already knows and what is to be learnt and in tackling the new, he will 'cut corners'. This attempt to make the learning task easier is likely to determine the sequence in which the learner acquires components of the new skill and the errors that he makes along the way.

But what counts as 'easy' as opposed to 'difficult'? There are two plausible sources of ease. On the one hand, a task is easy if it is like something that is already familiar. We will refer to a skill already known as a **primary skill** and the one to be acquired as the **target skill**. On the other hand, something may be easy if it is simple in an absolute sense, even if it is not familiar.

Here are illustrations of the two concepts outside language. The first source of ease mentioned above is familiarity. Suppose the target skill is not completely new in all its detail: the person already has a skill under his belt that is of a similar kind so that existing knowledge and new knowledge differ only in part. This is so if you learn how to drive a truck after you have learnt how to drive a car; or if you learn how to play ping-pong if you already know how to handle a tennis racket; or if you play the piano and then you begin to play the organ. In such instances, the common features between the old and new task are acquired first, such as the very act of hitting a ball with a racket in both tennis and ping-pong. But a tennis-player's early attempts at hitting the ping-pong ball will show a 'tennis accent': his shots are likely to be too long. Similarly, the hand action needed for playing the organ is likely to be acquired by the pianist before the use of the pedals; and, when first playing an organ, the performance is likely to be plagued by a 'piano accent'.

This '**familiar (be)for(e) unfamiliar**' principle – that is, that familiar aspects of the target skill are learnt before the unfamiliar ones and that the errors made in the new task come from familiar patterns used for the un-familiar ones – is manifested in the language of second-language learners as well. Take pronunciation. An adult second-language learner will have less trouble pronouncing the sounds that are the same in his first language and in the target language. Furthermore, in attempting to pronounce the new sounds of the target language, he is likely to substitute native pronunciation resulting in a 'foreign accent'. For example, German learners of English will have little problem with English /p/ or /t/; but when it comes to pro-nouncing /θ/ and /ð/, as in *thick* or *then*, the familiar German /s/ and /z/ are often used instead.

In the cases just cited, familiarity comes from the primary skill. But some-thing may be familiar also from the target skill if the learner has already acquired aspects of the target. For example, suppose a person is learning how to drive and in the process he is faced with the task of handling the car on an ice-covered road. He has already learnt that, under ordinary road con-ditions, he is to slam on the brakes when he wants to stop; thus, when the car begins to skid on the ice, he applies part of what he already knows about driving to the new situation and hits the brakes. In doing so, he transfers a newly acquired skill that is appropriate under one set of conditions to a situation where it is not appropriate. We will call this kind of error **internal transfer** (because both the model and the erroneous production belong to the target competence), as opposed to transfer from the primary competence to the target, which we will dub **external transfer**. Both kinds of transfer involve applying an aspect of a familiar skill to a domain where it is not appropriate: relying on something familiar under the mistaken assumption that the unfamiliar is like what is already familiar.

A second way, noted above, in which the learner can make the learning task easier for himself is simplification – that is, by cutting down on the components of a structure. The principle involved may be dubbed '**simple (be)for(e) complex**' – that is, that, on the one hand, simple tasks are acquired before complex ones and, on the other hand, the errors in the new task stem from simple patterns substituted for complex ones. This principle is at work in human memory when we retain only the first couple of digits of a phone number and make mistakes on the rest, or when we remember the first name of a person but not the last name. Psychological experiments have shown that in serial recall, the beginnings of sequences are the easiest to remember.

In sum: the order in which new skills are acquired and the errors made in a target area can be reasonably expected to result from the learner's attempt to make his task easier. Ease may come either from familiarity or from simplicity. Familiarity may be derived from the primary area of competence, in which case it is an instance of external transfer; or from an already familiar part of the target skill, in which case it is a case of internal transfer.

In what follows, we will consider the role that external transfer, internal transfer and simplification might play in the second-language acquisition of relative clauses. We will explore how these tendencies help provide answers for the two questions raised in (2): why some aspects of the second language are acquired before others and why the learner makes errors. The next three sections will take up these factors in turn.

3.2 EXTERNAL TRANSFER

Our initial data come from 12 native speakers of Persian learning Swedish as reported by Kenneth Hyltenstam (Hyltenstam 1984). The target structures were Swedish relative clauses; their production was elicited in a picture-describing task. The constructions were of the sort exemplified in (1) (data from Veronica Lundbäck):

(1) (a) SUBJECT RELATIVIZATION
mannen som kom från Iran
the:man that came from Iran
'the man that came from Iran'

(b) DIRECT OBJECT RELATIVIZATION
mannen som jag slog
the:man that I hit
'the man that I hit'

(c) INDIRECT OBJECT RELATIVIZATION
mannen som jag gav mjölk (till)
the:man that I gave milk (to)
'the man that I gave milk to'

Compare these with the corresponding relative clauses in the native language of the subjects: Persian (data from Shigekazu Hasegawa; see also Tarallo and Myhill 1983: 74; Comrie 1989: 147–8).

(2) (a) SUBJECT RELATIVIZATION
mardi ke az Irân âmad
man that from Iran came:S3
'the man that came from Iran'

(b) DIRECT OBJECT RELATIVIZATION
*mardi ke man (**u-ra**) zadam*
man that I (**him-OBJ**) hit:S1
'the man that I hit'

(c) INDIRECT OBJECT RELATIVIZATION
*mardi ke man shir-râ **be u** dadâm*
man that I milk-OBJ **to him** gave:S1
'the man that I gave milk to'

What are the differences between the relative clause structures of the two languages? One difference is the order of constituents: Persian has SOV and Swedish has SVO. We will disregard the question of how the new order of the major sentence constituents is acquired and will focus on the other difference. This other difference is that in Persian, relative clauses where the direct object is relativized may optionally include a pronoun referring back to the head (called a 'resumptive pronoun'); and if the indirect object is relativized, the resumptive pronoun referring back to the head is obligatory. We will use the term 'relativized constituent' for the noun phrase in the relative clause that is co-referential with the head noun phrase. For example, in *the apple which is in the basket*, the relativized constituent is the subject of the relative clause *apple*, represented as *which*; and in *the apple which Jill ate*, the relativized constituent is the object of the relative clause (referred to by *which*).

Given this difference between the relative clause structures of the native language and the target language, the speaker of Persian needs to learn two things about Swedish relative clauses. One is that subject relatives (as in (1a)) are like those in Persian in that they do not use resumptive pronouns. The other is that direct-object and indirect-object relatives (as in (1b) and (1c)) are unlike those in Persian in that Persian allows for or requires resumptive pronouns in the two constructions while Swedish forbids them. How is this information acquired by Persians?

Hyltenstam (1984) found that, while producing subject relatives in Swedish, Persian speakers never used resumptive pronouns, in direct- and indirect-object relatives most of them did. In (3) are illustrated their productions with hypothetical examples (the erroneous resumptive pronouns are highlighted; the examples are constructed on the assumption that Swedish word order was used correctly by the subjects).

(3) (a) SUBJECT RELATIVIZATION
          mannen som kom från Iran
          the:man that came from Iran
          'the man that came from Iran'

     (b) DIRECT OBJECT RELATIVIZATION
          mannen som jag slog **honom*
          the:man that I   hit **him**
          'the man that I hit'

     (c) INDIRECT OBJECT RELATIVIZATION
          mannen som jag gav mjölk till **honom*
          the:man that I   gave milk to **him**
          'the man that I gave milk to'

How can these errors be accounted for? That the Persian speakers correctly opted out of using resumptive pronouns in subject relatives may be for two reasons: either they have already learnt that Swedish does not use them in such constructions, or they simply transferred the absence of resumptive pronouns from their native Persian. It is also possible that both of these factors played a role.

But the erroneous use of resumptive pronouns in direct- and indirect-object relatives is open to only one of these explanations: it must be the result of transfer from Persian – an instance of what we called external transfer above.

That external transfer is indeed the operant factor is suggested by two additional facts. First, as noted above, the resumptive pronoun in direct-object relatives is optional in Persian while in indirect-object relatives, it is obligatory. This frequency difference between the occurrence of the two kinds of pronouns in Persian relative clauses is directly mirrored by the frequency with which the Persian speakers used the pronouns in Swedish. Of Hyltenstam's 12 Persian speakers, seven used resumptive pronouns in all or most of their Swedish direct-object-relative clauses; the other five learners used pronouns in only one case or not at all. In indirect-object relative clauses, however, as many as 10 of the 12 subjects used resumptive pronouns in all their productions; only two used them in one instance or in none. Thus, it is not just that the occurrence of resumptive pronouns in the Swedish spoken by Persians corresponds to the occurrence of resumptive pronouns in the native language but the frequency of their occurrence is also comparable.

The other fact that supports external transfer as the factor in the Persians' use of resumptive pronouns in Swedish comes from speakers of three other native languages also involved in Hyltenstam's study: Greek, Spanish and Finnish. Greek and Spanish, like Persian, have resumptive pronouns in some object-relative clauses and some speakers, just like the Persians, did produce resumptive pronouns in their Swedish sentences. Finnish, however, differs from Persian, Greek and Spanish in that, like Swedish, it does not allow resumptive pronouns in direct-object and indirect-object relatives. Correspondingly, the Finnish speakers did not produce any such pronouns in either type of Swedish relative clause. The erroneous use of resumptive pronouns by learners whose native languages had them and the correct non-use of resumptive pronouns by learners whose native language did not have them strongly suggests that the erroneous use of resumptive pronouns was indeed the result of external transfer.

In sum: the Hyltenstam data cited so far support the conclusion that the occurrence and extent of the erroneous use of resumptive pronouns by learners of Swedish in the study is the result of external transfer.

However, additional data from other studies indicate that external transfer is not always the reason for the mistaken use of resumptive pronouns by language learners. Below, three kinds of facts will be adduced showing that resumptive pronouns can be erroneously used by learners even when the primary language is not likely to, or cannot possibly, be the source.

First, consider evidence presented by Stephen Matthews and Virginia Yip (2003) about their two Cantonese-speaking children acquiring English. They found that both children (between the ages of two and five) used resumptive pronouns in their English relative clauses. Here are some examples.

(4) (a) **I got that red flower dress that Jan gave **it** to me.*
    (b) **This is the homework that I do **it**.*

Could the use of these pronouns be the result of external transfer? Although Cantonese does allow resumptive pronouns in non-subject relatives, Matthews and Yip argue that the use of such pronouns in the English sentences cannot possibly be the result of external transfer (pp. 59–60). For one thing, while Cantonese does allow resumptive pronouns, the children did not use them in their Cantonese sentences. It would be strange if the use of resumptive pronouns in their English came from the Cantonese model but the pronouns did not show up in the children's Cantonese.

Also, the children generally did not use resumptive pronouns in English when, because of transfer from Cantonese, they erroneously preposed relative clauses to their heads. (For example, for 'Daddy, which tape is the one that you recorded?', one of the children said *Daddy, which that you record tape?* and not *Daddy, which that you record **it** tape?* (p. 58)). The pronouns occurred only when the children attempted the unfamiliar English order of relative clause following the head. If the use of resumptive pronouns came from Cantonese, we would not expect them to be used in those English relative constructions that were otherwise unlike the Cantonese constructions. Thus, in this case, even though the primary language does have the structures that could have served as the model for the errors, it is unlikely that the primary language did in fact serve as a model.

The second, more startling piece of evidence to show that erroneous resumptive pronouns in learners' languages cannot always be attributed to transfer from the primary language is that learners sometimes insert resumptive pronouns in a target language even if their primary language does not have them at all. As noted above, Hyltenstam's Finnish speakers did not produce resumptive pronouns in their Swedish and this makes sense since Finnish does not have them. But Fernando Tarallo and John Myhill's study (1983: especially 63–4, 70–2) yielded different results.

Tarallo and Myhill elicited grammaticality judgements from 99 university students whose native language was English and who were studying different foreign languages, including German, Portuguese, Mandarin Chinese and Japanese. None of these languages allow resumptive pronouns in direct-object and indirect-object relative clauses. Nonetheless, Tarallo and Myhill found that, when learners were given relative clauses in their respective target languages with resumptive pronouns inserted, some of the learners did deem the constructions grammatical. This could not possibly have been due to transfer from the primary language since English of course does not allow resumptive pronouns (nor could it have been because of the target languages of course since those languages did not use resumptive pronouns, either).

The third and most striking piece of evidence to show that the erroneous use of resumptive pronouns is not always the result of external transfer is that it also occurs in the speech of children acquiring their first language. Ana Teresa Pérez-Leroux (1995) summarizes evidence about resumptive pronouns in the speech of children acquiring French and English as their first language – languages that do not have resumptive pronouns. Examples are in (5) (Pérez-Leroux 1995: 121).

(5) (a) *I hurt my finger that Thomas stepped on **it**.*
(b) *Smoky is an engine that **he** pulls a train.*

Clearly, external transfer is not even an option to explain the errors since there is no primary language present at all.

In sum: while the erroneous use of resumptive pronouns by Hyltenstam's Persian speakers in Swedish may be explained by external transfer, these errors must have different sources in other cases. The erroneous use of resumptive pronouns in English by the Cantonese-dominant children in the study by Matthews and Yip, the erroneous grammaticality judgements of resumptive pronouns in German, Portuguese, Mandarin and Japanese by native English learners as reported by Tarallo and Myhill – and, of course, the occurrence of these pronouns in the first language of children – cannot be attributed to external transfer.

What explains, then, the occurrence of resumptive pronouns in these cases? As noted in Section 3.1, there are alternative explanatory avenues to explore. We identified three ways in which learners may try to render the target easier and thus may lapse into errors. External transfer (relying on skills from the primary domain) is only one of them; the others are internal transfer (applying patterns already known in the target domain) and simplification. The question is: could the use of the resumptive pronouns by the two Cantonese-dominant children and the erroneous sanctioning of these pronouns by the Tarallo and Myhill subjects be a result of either of these two factors: internal transfer or simplification?

Internal transfer would be a possible explanation if it could be shown that relative clauses that contained resumptive pronouns were like some target-language structures that were already familiar to learners. Simplification would be a possibility if relative clauses with resumptive pronouns could be shown to be simpler than relative clauses without such pronouns. We will explore each option in turn.

3.3 INTERNAL TRANSFER

Let us first consider internal transfer. Relative clauses with erroneously used resumptive pronouns may echo a construction in a target language that learners are likely to be familiar with: main clauses. Compare relative clauses with and without resumptive pronouns in English – the target language in the Matthews and Yip study – with the corresponding main clauses with and without pronouns:

(1) (a) *the books that [I read **them**]$_S$
      (b) [I read **them**.]$_S$
      (c) the books that [I read]$_S$
      (d) *[I read.]$_S$

It is clear that the ungrammatical presence of the resumptive pronoun in (1a) makes the relative clause look like the corresponding main clause in (1b), whereas the grammatical absence of the resumptive pronoun in the relative clause in (1c) calls for a new type of clause that is unlike main clauses (see (1d)). The same would hold for German, one of the target languages involved in the Tarallo and Myhill study, although not necessarily for the other languages – Portuguese, Mandarin and Japanese – since these languages are 'pro-drop': they do not require explicit noun phrase arguments in main clauses.

Thus, internal transfer is a possible explanation for the results in the Matthews and Yip study and for the students in the Tarallo and Myhill studies who evaluated German sentences: in these cases, learners may have generalized the presumably familiar structure of main clauses in the target language to relative clauses.

Regarding the Cantonese children: internal transfer explains not only why the children used resumptive pronouns in their English relative clauses but also why they used them only in those English relative clauses that followed the head. Since this is the correct order in English, they may have been more influenced by target-internal data than when, following the Cantonese order, they placed their English relative clauses before the head.

Let us take stock. We have encountered three sets of facts about the erroneous use of resumptive pronouns in a second-language learner's language:
- Hyltenstam's Persian speakers learning Swedish
- Matthews' and Yip's Cantonese-dominant children learning English
- Tarallo's and Myhill's English speakers learning German, Portuguese, Mandarin and Japanese.

External transfer can account for the Persians' pronouns in direct- and indirect-object relatives. Internal transfer can be the source of the pronouns in the Matthews and Yip study and of the German data in the Tarallo and Myhill study. But neither external nor internal transfer can account for the resumptive pronouns judged grammatical in Portuguese, Mandarin and Japanese in the Tarallo and Myhill study. This is because in these cases, neither did the native language, English, have resumptive pronouns in relative clauses nor did main clauses in the target language offer a strict model for the explicit representation of all noun phrase arguments.

In search of an explanation of these facts, let us turn to the last of the three explanatory avenues that we envisaged in Section 3.1: simplification. Could it be that relative clauses with resumptive pronouns have a simpler structure than relative clauses without them and this is why learners prefer them even if neither the primary language nor the target language models their use?

3.4 SIMPLIFICATION

At first, the idea that relative clauses with resumptive pronouns are simpler than those without them does not hold much promise. Compare (1a), a sentence from Matthews' and Yip's Cantonese children (repeated from Section 3.2 (4a)) and (1b):

(1) (a) *I got that red flower dress that Jan gave **it** to me.*
    (b) *I got that red flower dress that Jan gave to me.*

The relative clause in (1a) seems more complex than the one in (1b) since it includes an extra word: the pronoun *it*. But there is nonetheless a sense in which (1a) is simpler than (1b): the semantic argument structure of the verb *give*, which selects both a subject and an object, is made explicit in (1a) while the object of *give* is lacking in (1b). In other words, the relative clause in (1a) is compositional while the relative clause in (1b) is not. Thus, even though (1a) has a more complex syntactic form than (1b), from the point of view of meaning–form correspondence, it is simpler. Resumptive pronouns turn elliptical clauses into compositional ones.

If relative clauses with resumptive pronouns are indeed simpler than relative clauses without them, a prediction would follow: we would expect resumptive pronouns to be more abundant in some kinds of relative clauses than in other kinds. In particular, we would expect them to be preferentially used in relative clause constructions that are otherwise difficult so that the pronouns can compensate for the difficulty.

That resumptive pronouns are indeed used in more difficult relative clauses is suggested by the distribution of resumptive pronouns over various types of relative clauses in primary languages. In a cross-linguistic study of relative clauses, Edward Keenan and Bernard Comrie found the following (1977: 92–3):

(2) (a) If in a language, resumptive pronouns are used in **direct-object** relative clauses, they are also used in **indirect-object** relative clauses.

(b) If in a language, resumptive pronouns are used in **subject** relative clauses, they are also used in **direct-object** relative clauses.

John A. Hawkins has subsequently tested this claim for a sample of 24 languages (1999: 259). He found that 17 languages allowed for or required resumptive pronouns in indirect-object relatives and, of those, only nine allowed or required them in direct-object relatives. For example, Persian and Arabic have resumptive pronouns in both indirect-object and direct-object relatives and Greek and Hausa have them in indirect-object relatives but not in direct-object relatives. No language was found with resumptive pronouns in direct-object relatives but not in indirect-object relatives.

This so far just shows that in primary languages, resumptive pronouns preferentially occur in indirect-object relatives over direct-object relatives, and in direct-object relatives over subject relatives. But there is also indication that this has to do with their varying degrees of difficulty: indirect-object relatives are more difficult than direct-object relatives and the latter more difficult than subject relatives. Keenan and Comrie found the following implicational regularities concerning their occurrence in languages (1977: 68–73):

(3) (a) All languages have **subject** relative clauses.
(b) If a language has **indirect-object** relative clauses, it also has **direct-object** relative clauses.

For example, Malagasy has only subject relatives; Welsh has subject and direct-object relatives; and Basque has subject, direct-object and indirect-object relatives. No language has only direct-object relatives, or only indirect-object relatives, or only subject and indirect-object relatives.

Now, it is reasonable to. assume that the cross-linguistic frequency of a construction correlates with relative ease: the easier the construction, the more widespread it is across languages. If this is so, direct-object relatives are easier than indirect-object relatives and subject relatives are the easiest of the three.

This difference in degree of difficulty among types of relative clauses has also been borne out by various experiments. In one of them, English speakers were asked to repeat relative-clause constructions of various kinds. The accuracy rate of their repetitions was found to mirror the scale: subject relatives were more accurately repeated than direct-object relatives and the repetitions of the latter had fewer errors that the repetitions of indirect-object relatives (Keenan and S. Hawkins 1987).

Why should subject, direct-object and indirect-object relative clauses differ in difficulty in just the way their cross-linguistic distribution and experimental data suggest? As pointed out by Tarallo and Myhill (1983: 71) and argued most extensively by Hawkins (1999: 257–61), it is by no means an accident. The hearer's task is to identify the referent of the co-referential noun phrase in the relative clause. The difficulty of this task increases with the distance between the head and the slot where the co-referential noun phrase would stand if it were a main clause. In languages where the order of major constituents is Subject & Direct Object & Indirect Object and the relative clause follows the head, this distance turns out to be small for subject relatives, larger for direct-object relatives and still larger in indirect-object relativization. This is shown in (4).

(4)   NP-HEAD   Subject   Direct Object   Indirect Object

The scale in (4) can be used to predict both the occurrence of the three relative clause types in primary languages as stated in (3), and the distribution of resumptive pronouns over these clause types as stated in (2). The cross-linguistic availability of relative clause types increases from right to left corresponding to the decreasing difficulty of these constructions in that direction on the scale. The cross-linguistic availability of resumptive pronouns in turn increases from left to right in proportion to the increasing difficulty of relative clause constructions in that direction. Thus, in primary languages, resumptive pronouns appear to step in to aid comprehension where relative clause structure gets more difficult to process.

But if resumptive pronouns have this function in primary languages, they are likely to play the same role in learners' languages. This assumption sheds light on some of the observations made above.

First, it renders the results in the Tarallo and Myhill study less mysterious – namely, that learners accepted resumptive pronouns in the relative clauses of languages that did not use them and where even main clauses did not always spell out all noun phrase arguments. They did so because the construction with the relative pronoun seemed simpler to them.

Second, the hypothesis that resumptive pronouns are employed by the speaker as a crutch in more difficult constructions also provides an alternative explanation for why the resumptive pronouns in the English constructions of the Cantonese-dominant children occurred only when the relative clause followed the head. Earlier, we suggested that this was so because the head & relative clause order was the correct English order and thus they may have been influenced by the structure of English main clauses. But here is an alternative explanation. Recall that the children had to learn two facts about English relative clauses: that they followed the head noun rather than, as in Cantonese, preceded it, and that they did not include resumptive pronouns. The fact that the children used resumptive pronouns in their English relatives, which, because of their linear position, were less like the Cantonese ones and thus presumably difficult for them, suggests that the children used the pronouns as an aid to help them produce relative clauses in the unfamiliar position.

And third, if resumptive pronouns make relative clause structures easier, this also explains why they turn up in children's first-language data.

The fact that resumptive pronouns are elements of choice in complex relative clauses can be captured by saying that resumptive pronouns are the unmarked option in marked relative clauses. That this seems to hold both for primary languages and for learners' languages suggests that these two forms of language obey, at least to an extent, the same universal principles. In other words, rather than being arbitrary assemblages of deviant structures, learners' languages can be viewed as members of the family of human languages, at least somewhat on a par with primary languages.

3.5 LANGUAGE ACQUISITION AND HISTORICAL CHANGE

Change in language takes place on two levels. On the micro-level, it happens in the life of a single individual, as in learning first or second languages. In addition, language also changes on a larger scale: in the life of entire speech communities in the course of centuries and millennia. The two kinds of change are different in many ways but the three tendencies that we have seen operative in shaping second-language acquisition are also at work in historical change.

One of the tendencies that we identified above is external transfer: the second-language learner applies knowledge appropriate for his native language to the target language. What corresponds to this in historical change is borrowing: a language changes by taking over a pattern from another. This is most obvious in vocabulary: languages borrow words, as English has taken *government* from French, *algebra* from Arabic, *pizza* from Italian and *burrito* from Spanish. In addition to loanwords, the borrowing of syntactic patterns is also well documented. For example, Amharic, a language of

Ethiopia, differs from other Semitic languages in that it has SOV order and the genitive precedes the noun, while Semitic is generally verb-initial with the genitive following the noun. The reason is the influence on Amharic of neighbouring Cushitic languages that are SOV and GN.

The historical parallel to the second tendency that we have seen in second-language acquisition – internal transfer – is analogy: exceptional forms are made to conform to the more widespread general mould. Just as a learner of English may apply the regular plural marking to an irregular word – *foots* rather than *feet*, *sheeps* rather than *sheep* – native speakers, too, do the same when they use *antennas* instead of the earlier *antennae*, or *vertebras* instead of *vertebrae*. In the case of the learner of English, these analogical extensions are errors and he/she will have to learn to use the correct forms. In the case of native speakers, provided the regularized forms are used widely enough, it is the language that 'yields': the regularized forms become acceptable.

The third factor that we have seen involved in second-language learning – simplification – looms very large in historical change. Its role is paramount in one of the most pervasive types of historical change: grammaticalization. As briefly discussed in Section 3.3 of Chapter 2, this process consists of a lexical item – a noun, a verb, a demonstrative or a numeral – being reduced in the course of time to a grammatical marker: a negative marker, an auxiliary verb, or a definite or indefinite article. Here are some examples of grammaticalization:

- the lexical verb *have* in English and its equivalents in Germanic and Romance languages have turned into auxiliaries;
- the lexical verb *will*, originally meaning 'want', has turned into a future marker in English;
- the lexical verb *go* has taken on the function of future marking in English (e.g. in *I am going to read*) as did its equivalent in French;
- some occurrences of distal demonstratives meaning 'that' have evolved into definite articles in Romance, Germanic and other languages (e.g. English *the* has evolved from *that*);
- the numeral meaning 'one' has given rise to indefinite articles in Romance and Germanic languages, as well as in Hungarian, Turkish, Hebrew and many other languages (e.g. English *a(n)* has evolved from *one*).

That grammaticalization is an instance of simplification is clearly shown by what happens to the meaning of the grammaticalized words and what happens to their phonological form: meaning becomes thinner and form becomes smaller. Take the verb *will*. From the original meaning, which indicated intended future action, what is left is simply reference to the future: the component of intention has been lost. And in its contracted form as in *I'll*, the form is also simplified. Similarly, when the Latin demonstrative *ille, illa, illud* (masculine, feminine and neutral 'that') has given rise to the Romance definite articles, such as *le* and *la* in French, the original meaning – reference to a specific item located at a distance from the speaker – became simplified with the deictic (pointing) component fading out. As with the case of *will*, the original form was shortened as well.

All in all, the speaker's tendency to make language easier by generalizing known patterns (whether by importing them from another language or taking them from the language itself) and by simplifying expressions is a significant force driving both micro- and macro-change in language.

3.6 SUMMARY

As stated in Section 3.1, a basic issue in second-language learning (and, mutatis mutandis, in the learning of any skill) is the gap between model and production: second-language learners do not produce all and only what is in the ambient language, they make errors, and their output improves over time. We have focused on two of the issues: the sequence in which the target skills are acquired and the nature of errors made in the process.

(1)   (a)   THE ORDER IN WHICH SKILLS ARE ACQUIRED
              Which components of the target language are acquired
              before other components, and why?
      (b)   THE NATURE OF ERRORS
              As the learner tries to cope with yet-unacquired
              components of the target language, what kinds of errors
              does he make, and why?

In the course of our analysis of acquisitional data, we identified three factors that may play a role in determining both the sequence of acquisition and the nature of the errors made along the way and thus help explain the gap between model and production. These factors are external transfer, internal transfer and simplification.

The answers emerging to the two questions are these. First, regarding acquisitional sequence (1a): learners acquire sooner those aspects of the target language that are familiar to them (whether from the native language or from already acquired parts of the target language) and/or that are simple. Second, regarding errors (1b): learners will make errors by replacing unfamiliar patterns with familiar ones and/or complex patterns with simple ones.

Here is a summary to show which of the three factors – external transfer, internal transfer and simplification – are most likely to account for the data considered from relative clause acquisition above, whether singly or jointly.

(a)   FACT: Hyltenstam's Persian speakers erroneously used resumptive
        pronouns in their Swedish direct-object and indirect-object
        relative clauses.
        OPERANT FACTOR: **external transfer**.

(b) FACT: Matthews' and Yip's Cantonese-dominant children erroneously used resumptive pronouns in their postposed English relative clauses.
OPERANT FACTOR:
- either **internal transfer** (from English main clauses)
- or **simplification** (indicated by the fact that resumptive pronouns were used only in relative clauses in the presumably more difficult, target-like Head & RelCl order)
- or **both**.

(c) FACT: Tarallo's and Myhill's English subjects erroneously judged resumptive pronouns in German, Portuguese, Mandarin and Japanese relative clauses as grammatical.
OPERANT FACTOR:
- either **external transfer** (from English main clauses)
- or
  - for German:
    internal transfer (from German main clauses)
  - for Portuguese, Mandarin, and Japanese:
    simplification
- or a combination of the above.

Our discussion of second-language acquisition has been far from comprehensive. The three factors considered help explain why learners fall short of replicating all and only what they hear: why they acquire some aspects of the target language before acquiring others aspects of it and what kinds of errors they make.

However, these factors do not address other aspects of the problem of second-language acquisition mentioned in (1) in Section 3.1. In particular, they do not even begin to explain why learners go beyond the data they are exposed to by constructing completely novel utterances; nor why learner's output changes in time gradually approximating the model. Some of the factors that may play a role are the learner's need to communicate, the frequency of his exposure to particular constructions, what is taught to him, his emotional approach to the learning task and his individual learning style.

4 Conclusions

In this chapter, we considered alternative analyses of cross-linguistic variation and change. The conflicts that we encountered all revolved around the taxonomic concepts of 'same' and 'different'. Why do different pairs of constituents show the same ordering across languages? How are aspects of the second language that are learnt first differ from other aspects that are learnt later and what is the source of errors that differentiate the learner's production from the model? Most if not all of these questions boil down to asking how different things can nonetheless be the same, and how things that are the same can also be different.

Notes

2   Alternative analyses of word order variation across languages

- Examples from Easter Island are from Chapin 1978 and Du Feu 1996. In some cases, the original data are given here in simplified form.
- Japanese case-markers are transcribed here as postpositions rather than suffixes – a controversial issue.
- On whether adpositions and question particles are operands or operators, see Dryer 1992: 100, 102–3.
- On the ordering of manner adverbs, see Dryer 1992: 122–4.

3   Alternative analyses of relative clause acquisition in second languages

- For relevant discussions, I am grateful to Min Sook Kim.
- For a discussion of Keenan and Comrie's Accessibility Hierarchy and some of its exceptions, see Newmeyer 1998: 316–20.
- Results similar to those by Tarallo and Myhill (1983) were arrived at by Georgette Ioup and Anna Kruse (1977): in their study, some native speakers of Japanese – a language that does not use resumptive pronouns in relative clauses – did consider English relative clauses with resumptive pronouns grammatical.
- For drawing the distinction between external and internal transfer, see Gass 1979.
- For a highly influential theory about how markedness governs both primary-language and learners' language structures, see Fred Eckman's Markedness Differential Hypothesis (Eckman 1977). For summary discussions on the relationship between typological implications for primary languages and acquisitional sequences in second-language learning, including discussions of relative clause structures, see Braidi 1999: 79–98; and Song 2001: 326–33.
- From the large literature on grammaticalization, see for example the highly interesting books by Heine and Kuteva (2002) and Traugott and Heine (1991).

Exercises

1. Consider the following order patterns of English:
   - Article & Noun (e.g. *the horse*)
   - Numeral & Noun (e.g. *two horses*)
   - Auxiliary & Verb (e.g. *must go*)
   - *want* & complement clause (e.g. *Mary wants to move to Florida*)
   - Comparative Adjective & Standard (e.g. *later than usual*)
   - Subject & Verb (e.g. *Jill left.*)

Which – if any – of the three proposals discussed in Section 2 predicts the co-occurrence of these orders in English?

2. Dryer (1992) reports on an additional pair of constituents whose ordering correlates with the ordering of verb and object across languages: Complementizer and Sentence. Here is an example from English and one from Japanese, with the complementizer in bold (see Hawkins 1994: 66–7).

(a) ENGLISH
*Mary said [**that** John got married yesterday]$_S$.*
(b) JAPANESE
[Mary ga John ga kekkonsita **to**$]_S$ *itta.*
Mary SBJ John SBJ got:married that said
'Mary said that John got married yesterday.'

Is the correlation between verb and object order and the order of these two constituents explained by any of the three theories of word order discussed?

3. Using Hawkins' theory, how do you account for the marginality of sentence (d)?

(a) *I gave Mary the book.*
(b) *I gave the book to Mary.*
(c) *I gave Mary the book that everybody has been talking about in town.*
(d) *?I gave the book that everybody has been talking about in town and that I know will be a great hit in New York City to Mary.*

4. Consider the order of verb and object, and of noun head and relative clause in the six languages of the Appendix. (The relevant sentences are 4, 5, 6, 9, 10 and 11). Are these orders predicted by the head-dependent hypothesis, or by the branching-non-branching hypothesis, or by both?

5. It was mentioned in Section 3.3 that some languages – e.g. Mandarin and Portuguese – were 'pro-drop' languages.

(a) Looking at the data in the Appendix, find two other languages that are 'pro-drop'.
(b) When the subject pronoun is not present in the sentences of these languages, how does the addressee know who is meant to be the subject?
(c) Although subject pronouns are not in parentheses in the Japanese sentences of the Appendix, Japanese, too, is a 'pro-drop' language. When the subject pronoun is not present, how do you think the addressee can nonetheless tell who the subject is?

6. Look up the grammar of a creole language, e.g. Tok Pisin (Papua New Guinea) or Jamaican Creole. Identify the source languages and consider the role that simplification may have played in deriving the creole grammar from that of the source language.

7. Collect phonological, morphological and syntactic errors from the English of foreign-language speakers. How can they be explained? Consider external transfer, internal transfer, simplification and perhaps other factors.

8. Think of examples of 'cultural accents'. Can a person's 'odd behaviour' in an unfamiliar culture be explained by transferring cultural habits from his primary culture or from other areas of the target culture, or by simplification?

Chapter Six

Four Contemporary Approaches to Syntax

A theory which involves a contradiction is therefore entirely useless **as a theory**.

(Popper 1962: 319, emphasis original)

1 Preliminaries

In the preceding chapters, we considered alternative analyses of selected syntactic patterns derived from various frameworks. In this chapter, we will take up a sample of the contemporary approaches to syntactic description, some of them already mentioned before, and attempt to provide overall characterizations for each in terms of their basic assumptions.

Four families of syntactic frameworks will be discussed: transformational grammars, dependency grammars, construction grammars and optimality theory. The most fundamental difference among them is how they view the differences and similarities among syntactic structures. Here are the four distinctive hypotheses:

(1) TRANSFORMATIONAL GRAMMARS
Structures that are **different** in surface structure may be **the same** in underlying structure.

(2) DEPENDENCY GRAMMARS
Structures that are **different** in terms of word categories may be **the same** in that they include a head and its dependants.

(3) CONSTRUCTION GRAMMARS
Different structures have **different** meanings.

(4) OPTIMALITY THEORY
Structures may **differ** in and across languages because of the **different** rankings of the **same** rules.

The next four sections will take up the four frameworks in turn.

2 Transformational grammars

2.1 BASIC ASSUMPTIONS

As already seen in our earlier discussions (Chapter 1, Section 3.3 and 3.4; Chapter 2, Section 2; Chapter 4, Section 3.3), the central proposal of transformational grammars is that sentences must be assigned multi-level syntactic representations. The analyst should not take sentences 'at face value' and represent the words only as they appear selected and ordered in the pronounced form of the sentence. Instead, they should assume a second structural representation as well that is less like the pronounced form. This is because sentences that seem idiosyncratic in 'surface' structure can be shown to manifest more general patterns on an 'underlying' level. The mission of the underlying representation is thus to construct a common denominator for certain sets of superficially different sentences.

For an example, take the sentences in (1).

(1) (a) *There arrived two girls.*
    (b) *Two girls arrived.*

In addition to the difference in the order of words, the two sentences also differ in word selection: the first includes the word *there* but the second does not. Thus, if we only consider their surface structures – the words as selected and ordered for purposes of pronunciation – the two sentences would have to be described as different even though they are similar in that they both include the verb *arrived* and the subject *two girls*. Since surface structure obscures this similarity, transformational grammars posit a single underlying structure that is the same for both. The shared underlying structure for the two sentences is identical to the surface structure of (1b). Rules inserting *there* and changing the order of words optionally convert this underlying structure to the surface structure of *There arrived two girls*.

Accordingly, the syntactic accounts in transformational grammar utilize two kinds of rules. First, there are rules that form underlying structures. In most versions of this approach, these rules – called phrase structure rules – specify part–whole relations and linear order among syntactic categories. For example, a rule might stipulate that a sentence must consist of a noun phrase and a verb phrase in this order. Second, there are the rules that transform these underlying structures into surface structures, generally in more than one step.

The example given above illustrates the force of the assumption of underlying structures. An underlying structure manages to subsume different sentences under the same general pattern by 'splitting' the structural account of sentences into two distinct representations. It reveals one-ness where there is superficial 'many-ness'.

But how can a single sentence – such as (1b) *There arrived two girls* – be claimed to have two structures whose properties are contradictory – such as one showing an element absent (*there* in the example above) and the other showing it present? How can we get away with claiming that a word is both there and is not there, or that the phrase *two girls* both precedes and follows *arrived*, without getting embroiled in a fatal contradiction, which, as Popper remarks in the motto of this chapter, is the bane of scientific theories? There has been a two-pronged attack on this problem.

First, there has been a persistent attempt to **constrain the differences** that are allowed to hold between underlying and surface representations and thus limit the inconsistency between the two. For example, some transformational frameworks insist on what is called monotonous derivations: they allow only the adding of constituents in the process of converting underlying representation into surface structure but not their deletion and substitution. In other words, no derivational 'backtracking', or the cancelling of earlier steps, is allowed. There is 'adding bricks' but no 'removing bricks' or 'replacing bricks'; there is construction but no demolition. For example, under the assumption of monotony, the derivational addition of the word *there* is permitted, as in the example discussed above; but the derivational re-ordering of *two girls* and *arrived* is not. Similarly, neither the deletion of the 'you'-subjects of imperative sentences nor the movement of wh-words to the front of the sentence (see Chapter 1 (Sections 3.3 and 3.4)) is allowed in monotonic grammars.

Second, transformational syntacticians have been striving to find **multiple motivation** for both surface and underlying structures. The idea is that if we can find lots of evidence to show that underlying structure and surface structure are different, their very existence is justified and contradictions between the two are to be expected rather than to be condemned. The argument is similar to one used in psychotherapy. To claim that a person is both gentle and violent is a contradiction; but to claim that the person has two personalities one gentle and one violent and that the distinctness of the two personalities is borne out in several different ways mitigates the contradiction. As we saw in Chapter 1 (Section 3.2), facing an object that has contradictory properties poses a conflict; splitting that contradictory object into parts each internally consistent resolves the conflict.

There is an obvious solution to the question of how to establish the fundamentally different nature of surface and underlying structures. Sentences, by their very nature of being symbolic objects, have two conceptually necessary representations: phonetic structure that shows pronunciation and meaning structure that shows how the sentence is understood. But if so, why not just equate 'underlying structure' with meaning and 'surface structure' with sound form? Under such a view, contradictions between the surface and underlying levels are fully justified because meanings and sounds are obviously different kinds of things and thus they can be expected to have contradictory properties.

For example, in the sentence *There arrived two girls*, the contradiction between the word *there* being present in pronunciation but not present in meaning does not pose a contradiction. It is not present in semantic structure because it does not mean anything and it is present in surface structure because it is pronounced. This reasoning does not explain why a meaningless word such as *there* is present in pronunciation but it resolves what would otherwise appear to be a contradiction. Instead of saying that a single constituent – the word *there* – is both syntactically present and syntactically absent, we are splitting *there* into two distinct entities – its meaning and its pronunciation – and we are saying that the word is present as a bit of form but not as a bit of meaning.

While the idea of equating underlying representation with semantic representation was proposed as early as the 1970s by practitioners of a trend called generative semantics, most of transformational syntax has until recently assumed that underlying structure (also called deep structure, or D-structure) is distinct from semantic representation. However, as we will see shortly, the most recent version of transformational grammar – the Minimalist Program – rejects the existence of any level of representation other than phonetic and semantic. The highly motivated, economical nature of syntax as envisaged by the Minimalist Program forms a rigorous filter that notions such as syntactic underlying and surface structures cannot pass: these levels of representation fall by the wayside.

For documenting the workings of transformational grammars in more detail, we will return to the topic of passive constructions discussed in Chapter 4 (especially Sections 2.1 and 5.2) and take a look at various analyses of the English passive in the course of the evolution of this framework. One of the prominent trends in the history of transformational grammar has been towards formulating increasingly more and more general statements encompassing more and more sentence types of a single language and, in many cases, of different languages. We will highlight four major steps in the evolution of the transformational account of passives that differ from each other by increasing generality.

2.2 THE PASSIVE CONSTRUCTION IN ENGLISH

2.2.1 The Passive Transformation

Consider the active–passive pairs in (1) and (2).

(1) (a) *The cat caught the squirrel.*
     (b) *The squirrel was caught by the cat.*

(2) (a) *Her course grade disappointed Mary.*
     (b) *Mary was disappointed by her course grade.*

The basic insight of early transformationalists was that active and corresponding passive sentences, while different in some ways, show certain characteristics in common. The differences lie in the form of the verb and the form of its complement. The verb is a single word in the active sentence while it consists of an auxiliary and a verb form in passives. The complement is an obligatory direct object in the active sentence but it is an optional prepositional phrase in the passive sentence.

   The similarities are both semantic and syntactic. For one thing, corresponding active and passive sentences are roughly equivalent in meaning: they are synonymous at least truth-conditionally. In addition, they both include a verb with a subject and a complement. The selectional constraints on the choice of the active subject and the passive *by*-phrase are the same, as are the selectional constraints on the active object and the passive subject. This is shown by the parallelism in decreasing levels of grammaticality of the following active–passive pair (Radford 1997a: 342):

(3) (a) *They arrested the students/?the camels/?!the flowers/!the ideas.*
     (b) *The students/?The camels/?!The flowers/!The ideas were arrested.*

The passive verb *be arrested* requires a human subject just as the active verb *arrest* requires a human object.

   The first transformational accounts sought to capture the resemblances between active and passive sentences by positing the surface structure of active sentences as the underlying structure for both actives and passives. Passives were then derived from actives by a transformational rule that moved the active object to the front, moved the active subject to the back, inserted *by* in front of the latter, and changed the form of the verb. If we disregard several details including the change in the verb form, the rule is as follows:

(4) THE PASSIVE TRANSFORMATION
$$NP_1 - V - NP_2 \Rightarrow NP_2 - V - by\ NP_1$$

> In prose: given a noun phrase followed by a verb and another noun phrase, put this second noun phrase to the beginning of the sentence and place the first noun phrase at the end of the sentence inserting *by* in front of it.

For example, given the underlying structure *Bill ate the cherries*, where *Bill* is NP1 and *the cherries* is NP2, the rule yields the passive surface structure *The cherries were eaten by Bill.*

2.2.2 *NP-Movement*

How general is the Passive Transformation? Since it is stated on categories rather than individual lexical items, it has a degree of generality: it derives all passive sentences in English regardless of the specific words they contain. However, it is strictly construction-specific: it does not encompass constructions other than the passive. It thus depicts the passive as unique among sentence patterns.

A subsequent insight addressed this point: it was the recognition of similarities between the passive construction and so-called 'raising' sentences, as (1b) and (2b). (See Chapter 2, Section 3.3.)

(1) (a) *It seems that the weather is improving.*
    (b) *The weather seems to be improving.*

(2) (a) *It is likely that Fred will accept the offer.*
    (b) *Fred is likely to accept the offer.*

In (1b), *the weather* is the subject of *seems*; but semantically, it is an argument of *is improving*. Given that there is also (1a) – a sentence where *the weather* actually appears as the subject of the verb that it is a semantic argument of – one can posit the same underlying structure for both sentences and then derive (1b) by a movement rule that displaces *the weather* from its semantically appropriate argument position into the position of the subject of *seems*. The embedded subject is thus raised to become the subject of the higher clause. The same holds for *the offer* in (2b).

But if so, a partial similarity between the raising rule and the passive rule emerges: both involve the movement of a noun phrase from a lower position in constituent structure into a higher position to the left – into the position of the subject of the (main) verb. Thus, the process of NP-Movement, as it came to be known, can be seen as a common denominator to passivization and raising.

(3) THE NP-MOVEMENT TRANSFORMATION
Move a lower noun phrase into the subject position of the (main) verb.

Furthermore, as was discussed in Chapter 4 (Section 3.3.2), the movement of the Dative Recipient in Patient–Recipient sentences such as *The butler brought tea to Aunt Lilly* to object position, to yield a double-object construction *The butler brought Aunt Lilly tea*, which was originally conceived as a construction-specific rule, can also be taken care of by a generalized form of NP-Movement.

The message of this account, which posits the single rule of NP-Movement in the derivation of passives, raising structures and double-object sentences, is that the passive is not a unique structure: it bears a partial resemblance to these other constructions. The train of thought that leads to advancing from a unique passive rule to a more general NP-Movement rule is based on a simple recognition widespread in all sciences as well as in everyday thought: an object may be unique in its entirety but it may be non-unique in its components.

Further research led to even broader generalizations pointing the way to a third major development in the transformational account of passives.

2.2.3 *Move Alpha*

There are also other constructions in English whose transformational analysis involves movement. An example is Wh-Movement. It applies to wh-questions such as *Who(m) did you talk to?*, where – as discussed in Chapter 1, Section 3.4 – *who(m)* is moved from its underlying post-verbal position to the beginning of the sentence. Wh-Movement also applies in relative clause constructions such as *the seeds which the sparrows are eating*, where *which* – the object of *are eating* – is analysed as having undergone the same leftward movement.

Common to all movement rules is the fact that they specify two things: the target constituent of the rule – the one that moves – and the landing site – the position into which the target constituent moves. If there were general constraints on targets and landing sites, NP-Movement and Wh-Movement might become predictable instances of a general rule schema for movement and thus the passive, along with raising sentences and double-object constructions, would be shown to be related to wh-questions and relative clauses.

Several general principles have been proposed regarding constraints on targets and landing sites. The principle that is most relevant here is called the Case Filter in the Government and Binding version of transformational syntax.

The Case Filter is a constraint on syntactic surface structures. It is an 'exit requirement' for noun phrases which says that before they can 'graduate from syntax', all noun phrases must be assigned case. The notion of case referred to here is not necessarily overt morphological marking: it is simply a possibly null marker indicating that the noun phrase occupies a legitimate position in a sentence; in particular, that it occurs adjacent to a constituent that is designated as a case-assigner. Case assigners are prepositions, active verbs and an abstract verbal constituent called Infl(ection), which in English directly precedes the main verb. Since passive verbs are assumed not to be case-assigners, noun phrases that directly follow a passive verb are prompted by the Case Filter to move into a position where they can acquire case, such as directly preceding Infl.

For an illustration, here is the underlying structure of the agent-less passive sentence *The book was borrowed by Mary* (see Culicover 1997: 93).

(1)

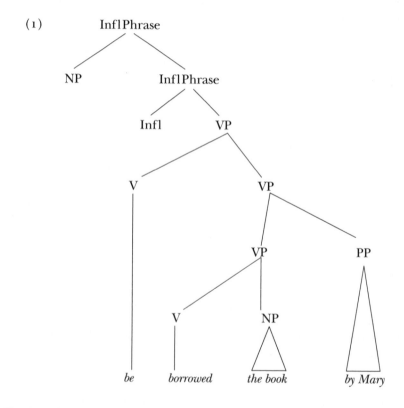

The Case Filter, stating the necessity of case marking for all noun phrases, and the stipulation regarding what constituents can and cannot assign case jointly determine the target of the movement: it should be *the book*, which is a case-less complement of the non-case-assigning verb *be borrowed*. The two principles also zero in on the landing site: it must be the only empty NP position where *the book* could be assigned case: the position in front of Infl. And, because of the relentless nature of the Case Filter, the obligatoriness of the movement does not need to be stipulated, either.

Given several additional constraints that have been proposed on targets, landing sites and the modality of movement (obligatory or optional), nothing about the terms and the modality of any specific movement needs to be spelled out anymore. The result is a single, maximally general movement rule given in (2), where 'Alpha' is a variable for the target of the rule: the constituent that is to move.

(2) THE GENERAL MOVEMENT TRANSFORMATION
    Move Alpha.

The rule in (2) simply says: perform a movement within the limits defined by general constraints regarding the target, the landing site and the modality of movement rules. The rule only serves as a trigger for movement to take place: what would move, where and whether obligatorily or optionally are derivable from general principles.

But, one might ask, what is the motivation for the linchpin of this account: the Case Filter? Why should all noun phrases be assigned case? The answer within the Government and Binding framework was given simply by appeal to syntactic surface structure: compliance with the Case Filter was declared to be a constraint on syntactic well-formedness. But this is where the explanation had to stop: in a syntactic framework that represents syntax divorced from the entirety of grammar, syntactic surface structure itself has few if any independent justifications.

The Minimalist Program, however – the most recent version of transformational grammar – provides a more satisfying answer to the need for proper case assignment. It forms the fourth major step in the development of the account of passives in transformational grammar.

2.2.4 Why move?

Evolving since the 1990s, Minimalist Syntax has represented a fresh start within the transformationalist tradition. Norbert Hornstein, one of its prominent practitioners and theorists, characterized one of his own studies within the minimalist framework as 'grammatical downsizing' (1999: 69). After decades of painstaking research on particular aspects of syntax, Noam Chomsky – who originated the transformational approach back in the 1950s – took a fresh look at the concept of syntax. He started out with an assumption about the overall purpose of grammar. He said the call of grammars was to provide for three and only three kinds of well-formedness: the well-formedness of semantic structure, the well-formedness of phonetic structure and the well-formedness of the pairings between the two. In other words, a sentence is grammatical if it has a legitimate meaning and a legitimate sound form, and if it properly associates meaning with form.

Given this view, what is syntax? It is a means to mediate between the conflicting requirements of two entities of vastly different properties – meaning and sound form – by providing a viable compromise between the two. All the conceptual devices assumed in syntactic analysis must then be evaluated from the point of view of how well they serve this purpose; everything extraneous to this goal must be thrown overboard.

According to the Minimalist Program, the derivation of a sentence starts out with the random selection of words from the lexicon. An operation called MERGE puts the words together into larger units in accordance with the selectional constraints specified for the words in the lexicon. For example, a lexical item such as *resemble* must be merged with a noun phrase that forms its object, whereas a verb such as *hover* must not be merged with an object. MERGE includes the assignment of case as well.

According to general rules of phrase-building (to be discussed in Section 3.4), words are subsumed under phrases. At that point – called SPELL-OUT – the derivation of the sentence splits into two branches. On the one hand, the phonetic specification of the individual lexical items is subjected to rules that eventually yield terminal phonetic representations, that is, complete sound strings. The meanings and syntactic features of lexical items, on the other hand, are subject to rules of movement that convert these structures into terminal semantic representations, that is, well-formed meanings.

A fundamental requirement of terminal semantic and phonetic representations is that they must contain only elements that are 'fully interpretable' in the respective domains – that is, that are necessary for yielding the meaning and the sound form of the sentence. Thus, semantic structures cannot include phonetic elements, phonetic structures cannot include semantic elements, and neither can include syntactic terms and relations that do not directly translate into either sound or meaning.

This means that syntactic features that have no semantic content must be eliminated in order for terminal semantic structures to be well-formed. Such syntactic features are grammatical gender of the kind that exist in Spanish, French, German and many other Indo-European languages, and features of case morphology, such as those on English pronouns (*he* versus *him* and so on). These features are necessary for syntactic and morphological purposes but they are semantically irrelevant.

The mechanism that is responsible for eliminating such semantically uninterpretable features is called CHECKING: heads of phrases check the features of their specifiers (e.g. subjects of verb phrases) and complements (e.g. objects of verbs) for compatibility. If the features are found to be compatible, they are eliminated, thereby preparing the structure for semantic interpretation.

For example, the sentence *She saw him* would pass Case Checking: both the form *she* and the form *him* have the proper case forms that the verb *saw* requires of its subject and object. As the result of the successful 'examination', the case features are erased since they have no further relevance. However, the sentence *She saw he* would not pass the Case Checking test since the nominative form is not the right one for the object of *saw*. As a result, its case feature cannot be eliminated and the offending syntactic feature prevents full semantic interpretation. The sentence is thus judged ill-formed by the grammar: the derivation is said to 'crash'.

Case Checking corresponds in its function to the Case Filter in the earlier versions of transformational grammar. The Case Filter sent case-less noun phrases into positions where they would be assigned case. Case Checking similarly motivates NP-Movement for noun phrases but in a more principled way. It assumes a principle called GREED, which says that constituents take care to ensure their own well-formedness. This principle motivates noun phrases to move into positions where the case features specified in their lexical entries can be checked and eliminated for purposes of full semantic and phonetic interpretation.

One can immediately see the implications of this grammatical framework for the account of passive sentences – our main focus in this section. As noted above, the Minimalist Program assumes that nouns come from the lexicon with their cases specified; thus, the goal to receive case is not a motivation for the underlying object to move, as it is in Government and Binding discussed in Section 2.2.3. There is, however, as we have just seen, a more basic motivation for the same movement supplied by the requirement of Full Interpretation.

For an example, let's take the passive sentence *He was punished by someone*. In the underlying structure, *he* is represented as following the passive verb: *was punished he*. This is because *he* is a Patient argument of the verb and the position of Patient is assumed to be the one immediately following the verb, as in the corresponding active sentence *Somebody punished him*. Moved by GREED, the pronoun *he* strives to shed its semantically irrelevant nominative case feature in order to ready itself for semantic interpretation. Since the elimination of syntactic features is possible only if they are first checked for legitimacy and passed, *he* has to be able to prove to the case-checker that its nominative form is legit. However, its underlying position does not allow it to do so because there is a conflict between its nominative case and its position following the verb. Therefore it moves into a position where nominative pronouns are supposed to occur: the subject position of the sentence.

Thus, the rule Move Alpha now has a very concrete motivation as it applies in the derivation of passive sentences. It is an instrument of enabling the sentence to pass the checkpoint at the syntax-semantic border and thus to receive a semantic reading. Semantic interpretation is clearly a conceptually necessary requirement in a framework that defines itself as responsible for showing how meanings and sound forms of sentences are related.

The analysis of passive sentences documents the progressive search for more and more general rules across the sentences within a language. Furthermore, the conceptual devices proposed in transformational grammar for generalizing over sentences of a single language have also been proposed to be instrumental in generalizing across languages. The component of transformational grammar that is responsible for accounting for cross-linguistic similarities and differences is called Principles and Parameters. Principles are universals of language; parameters are dimensions along which languages differ.

The basic idea of Principles and Parameters is typology. If we compare members of any class of objects – whether tables, dogs, societies or religions – we will find some universally occurring characteristics and other features that vary. The latter will naturally fall into classes; for tables, these classes are shape, size, colour and so on. The Principles and Parameters framework is an explicit articulation of this general logic of typology as applied to languages. The empirical force of the framework lies in the specific choice of patterns that are claimed to be principles – that is, universals – and in the specific choice of parameters.

Universal principles are assumed to include rules such Move Alpha and the various associated constraints on movement discussed above. Examples of parameters have to do with selection, linear order and meaning–form relations, such as whether pronoun subjects are obligatory, as in English, or optional, as in Spanish and other 'pro-drop languages', and whether the wh-word in questions must be sentence-initial, as in English, or not, as in Turkish.

2.3 SUMMARY

The principal tools proposed in Transformational Grammar for generalizing about sentences are underlying and surface structures, and rules that mediate between the two. Its historical evolution shows the increasing generality of the principles that are invoked for deriving sentences and it culminates in the assumption that the structures that the rules mediate between are meaning and phonetic form.

Alec Marantz' discussion of the Minimalist Program concludes with a section entitled *The End of Syntax* (1995: 380–1). What Marantz means is that the Minimalist Program announces the end of syntax as 'the end of a sub-field of linguistics' because it views these rules as mere instruments in mediating between meanings and sound forms. Syntax is construed as the set of rules that ensure full phonetic and semantic interpretability of sentences as well as the proper matching of semantic and phonetic structures.

3 Dependency grammars

3.1 BASIC ASSUMPTIONS

The central claims that define the family of dependency-based grammars have to do with similarities and differences among parts and wholes. Consider the following:

(1) noun and prepositional phrase
     (a) *Jean from France*
     (b) *apples from Washington*

(2) verb and object
    (a)   *visit France*
    (b)   *pick apples*

The diagrams in (3) and (4) present two alternative analyses of such phrases.

(3) Analysis 1:
    (a) N and PP: (b) V and NP:

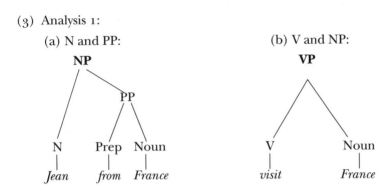

(4) Analysis 2:
    (a) N and PP: (b) V and NP:

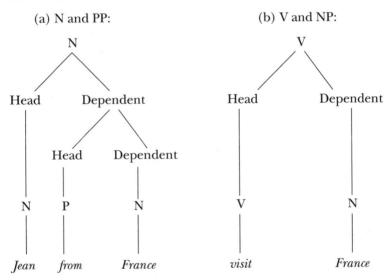

The two analyses have two things in common. First, the bottom lines of the diagrams are the same: they both classify the word-level parts of the phrases by using the same word-level category labels: noun, verb, preposition. Second, both analyses assume a single root node: they both represent the respective word sequences as forming phrases.

But there are also two differences between the two tree diagrams, highlighted in bold in (3). First, while the different word-category labels acknowledge the differences between noun, verb and preposition in analysis 1, analysis 2 interposes a level of analysis where there are samenesses across word categories: both noun and verb are **Heads** and both the preposition–noun sequence and the post-verbal noun are **Dependents**. The two terms 'Head' and 'Dependent' thus claim cross-categorial identities across distinct word categories.

Second, the root nodes are different in the two analyses: in 1, the root nodes – NP and VP – are distinct from any of the word-level categories included in the phrase but in 2, the root nodes N and V are identical to one of the word categories in the phrase. Structures of type 1 are known as **constituency structures**; structures of type 2 are known as **dependency structures**.

Here is an extralinguistic analogy to show how the two differ. In (5a) the relationship between a physician and his assistant is represented; in (5b) the relationship between a teacher and a teacher's aid.

(5) (a)   (b)

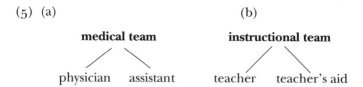

Contrast this with (6) displaying a somewhat different analysis of the same relations:

(6) (a)   (b)

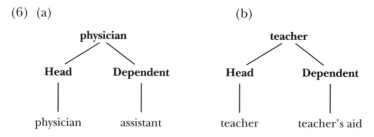

The diagram in (5) is like the constituency structure of (3); (6) is like the dependency structure of (4). In contrast to (5), (6) employs the categories Head and Dependent to subsume otherwise distinct kinds of individuals – a physician and a teacher – under the label Head and a medical assistant and a teacher's aid under the label Dependent. Also, in (6), each team is labelled the same as its head: when you say 'The doctor has seen me', the term 'the doctor' may include reference to his assistant as well.

Let us now review the distinctive empirical claims made by dependency structures in more detail. Looking at things from a general partonomic (whole–part) perspective, dependency structure is a more constrained subtype of partonomy: it makes two claims about sameness that constituent structure does not.

One of the categorial identities claimed by dependency structure holds **within any one phrase**: between the whole and one of its parts.

In principle, there are three possible relations between whole and parts:

(7) (a) the whole is the same as each of its parts
    (b) the whole is different from each of its parts
    (c) the whole is the same as some but not all of its parts

There are examples for each possibility outside language. The relation in (7a) is exemplified by the chemical structure of, say, water: no matter how many H_2O molecules you put together, the chemical composition of the resulting mass is still H_2O. The taste of bread illustrates (7b): bread does not taste like any one of its ingredients. Chocolate frosting, however, is somewhat like (7c): if you mix melted chocolate with butter to add creaminess, the taste of chocolate will override that of the butter.

Syntactic constituent structure is of type (7b): the phrasal category VP is labelled as different from all of its parts – verb and noun. Syntactic dependency structure adopts option (7c): the nature of the Head part and the nature of the entire phrase is claimed to be the same.

The other categorial identity claimed by dependency structure holds **across phrases**: it is suggested that certain parts of different phrases are of the same ilk: they are Heads or they are Dependents no matter what their specific word category.

How can the claims of dependency structure be tested? As in all instances of categorial claims, there is a single criterion of evaluation: the validity of a category stands or falls with its utility in stating generalizations. Thus, dependency structure is valid if (8) and (9) are true:

(8) THE CATEGORIAL IDENTITY OF HEAD AND PHRASE
    Grammatical rules that apply to the Head also apply to the entire phrase, and vice versa.

For example, patterns that hold true for nouns should also hold true for noun phrases; and vice versa.

(9) THE CATEGORIAL IDENTITY OF HEADS ACROSS PHRASES
    AND DEPENDENTS ACROSS PHRASES

    (a) Grammatical rules that apply to the Head of one phrase type also apply to the Heads of all other phrase types.
    (b) Grammatical rules that apply to the Dependent(s) of one phrase type also apply to the Dependent(s) of all other phrase types.

For example, patterns that are true for nouns should also be true for verbs since they are both heads; and what is true for adjectives should also be true for adverbs since they are both dependents.

Let us now see to what extent these claims hold true.

3.2 Categorial identity across phrases

We will begin with the cross-phrasal claim given in (9) above. Is it true that Heads of different phrases are subject to the same grammatical generalizations and that Dependents of different phrases similarly obey the same constraints? There is indeed multiple evidence to support this claim.

Let us first consider a single phrase type, such as a noun phrase consisting of a noun and an adjective in English. There are certain ways in which the two categories differ. First, note that in most instances, the adjective is dispensable but the noun is not. It would be logically possible that neither of the two should be dispensable or that either should be; but, in actuality, the dispensability pattern is skewed, as shown in (1).

(1) (a) *Yellow pansies cover the hillside.*
     (b) *Pansies cover the hillside.*
     (c) **Yellow cover the hillside.*

In addition to omissibility, there are also other grammatical characteristics whose distribution within the noun phrase is similarly skewed. Take plural marking. For indicating plurality, there are several logical possibilities: the noun could bear the plural marker with the adjective remaining unmarked; the adjective could be marked for plurality with the noun unmarked; or both noun and adjective could be plural-marked. These options are shown in (2); English opts for (a).

(2) (a) *yellow pansies*
     (b) **yellows pansy*
     (c) **yellows pansies*

Notice that the two properties – obligatory occurrence and plural marking – which both single out one of the two constituents of the noun phrase, single out the same constituent: the noun is the element that is required to be present and the one that carries plural marking in English. Of course, one might expect the two characteristics to converge on the noun: if the dispensable constituent – the adjective – carried the plural marking, there would be no plural marking when the adjective is not present. Nonetheless, there is no necessary connection between the two characteristics since there is no reason why a noun phrase should be marked for plurality by any of its parts. In many languages – such as Chinese or Japanese – nothing in the noun phrase is required to carry plural marking.

So far we have seen that two characteristics – obligatory presence and number marking – both single out the same constituent of the noun phrase: the noun. But this simply corroborates a categorial distinction between nouns and adjectives: the fact that they are different in these two respects may be accounted for by the two belonging to different categories.

However, notice what happens in verb phrases. The properties of obligatory occurrence and morphological marking are asymmetrically distributed in the verb phrase as well. In verb phrases, too, obligatory occurrence and morphological marking converge on the same constituent: the verb. The examples in (3) show that the verb, rather than the object, is obligatory. The examples in (4) show that the verb, rather than the object, is affixed – this time, for tense.

(3) (a) *Bill was reading the New York Times.*
    (b) *Bill was reading.*
    (c) **Bill the New York Times.*

(4) (a) *Jill plant-ed spinach.*
    (b) **Jill plant spinach-ed.*
    (c) **Jill plant-ed spinach-ed.*

Taking verb phrases by themselves, this difference between verbs and their objects could again be chalked up to their categorial difference. But since the convergence of the same two characteristics on one constituent holds for both the noun phrase and the verb phrase, a cross-phrasal generalization emerges. In spite of their distinct categories, nouns and verbs are alike in that they are the obligatory members of their phrases and in that they carry the morphological marking appropriate for the whole phrase. To resolve the paradox of different categories acting alike, we need a single super-category to subsume both. This is where the concept Head proves its usefulness. We can then make use of the category Head to formulate a general statement according to which it is Heads that are both obligatorily present and carry morphological marking for the entire phrase.

The justification of the notion Head would be greatly boosted if there were additional ways in which they were alike across phrases. One such additional characteristic that shows a degree of uniformity across phrases is constituent order. As seen in Section 2.2 of Chapter 5, there is a tendency for Heads and Dependents to show the same linear precedence relations across phrases. This holds for languages such as Turkish or Japanese, where Heads uniformly follow Dependents, and for Easter Island and Irish, where Heads uniformly precede. It also holds to a limited extent in English in that verbs precede their objects and nouns precede their relative clauses; although the adjective-before-noun order and the fact that possessive constructions can go either way (*John's cousin* and *a cousin of John's*) break the uniformity.

Here is, then, the summary of the evidence for the claim that there are two cross-phrasal super-categories: Head and Dependent, that include constituents of different grammatical types. The first two points have to do with the asymmetric relation among constituents of a single phrase.

(a) There is **more than one grammatical characteristic** – such as obligatory occurrence, morphological marking – that show a skewed, asymmetric distribution between constituents of a given phrase.

(b) These characteristics converge on the **same constituent** of the phrase: the same constituent that is obligatory is the one that is marked.

The remaining two points have to do with the same asymmetry among constituents of a phrase holding across phrase types.

(c) There is **more than one phrase type** for which the pattern described above is true.

(d) The ordering of the distinguished constituent and its co-constituent tends to be the **same** across phrase types.

However, there is evidence that, in spite of their similarities, Heads of different phrases do not have exactly the same characteristics: they are similar in some ways but different in other ways. Categorial differences lurking behind the general labels Head and Dependent are still significant. For example, as seen in Chapter 3, nouns and verbs cannot be co-conjuncts even though they are both heads. Similarly, adjectives and adverbs are different in their morphological composition as well as in their linear constraints even though they are both Dependents. Examples to show this are (5) and (6).

(5) (a) *Jill ate and left.*
    (b) *Jill ate cookies and ice cream.*
    (c) **Jill ate and cookies.*

(6) (a) *slow runner*
    (b) *run slowly*

Thus, Heads of different phrases do not behave the same way: they are only similar. Dependents, too, are alike in some ways across phrases in some ways but different in other ways. The cross-phrasal identity claim about Heads and about Dependents stated in (9) of Section 3.1 thus needs to be relaxed so as to claim only partial identity.

We now turn to the testing of the other claim made by dependency grammars: that the category of the Head is also the category of the entire phrase.

3.3 CATEGORIAL IDENTITY WITHIN PHRASES

In constituent structures, there is room for any arbitrary category label for the phrase. In dependency representations, however, there is no choice regarding the category of the phrase: as stated in (9) of Section 3.1, it must be the same as that of the Head. Thus, in dependency representations, the label of the whole phrase is redundant and thus may be omitted: it is predictable from the label of the Head. (For a dependency diagram where the phrase labels are omitted, see the representation of *Susan expected him to succeed* cited in Chapter 1, Section 1, (10).)

Note that the claim about the categorial identity of the Heads and the phrase is independent of the claim about a cross-phrasally congruent Head-Dependent relation that we considered in the preceding section: one could be true without the other. It could be that Heads and Dependents have shared characteristics across phrases while at the same time the category of the Head and the category of the whole phrase are not the same. The opposite scenario is also conceivable.

What empirical evidence would justify or defeat the 'Head category equals phrase category' claim? One piece of evidence discussed above is crucial here. Among the characteristics that distinguish Heads and Dependents is obligatory occurrence. This means that the Head can stand for the entire phrase all by itself while its Dependents cannot. But if so, it follows that the Head's category is the same as that of the entire phrase; if the two were different, the Head could not form the same kind of phrase all by itself.

But is it really true that the part of the phrase that, by other criteria, is characterized as the Head of the phrase, can always stand by itself in the same position? As we saw above, this is sometimes true: some nouns and verbs may function as full phrases. However, this is not always so. For example, while some transitive verbs can stand by themselves, others cannot:

(1) (a) *Jill ate a pumpkin.*
    (b) *Jill ate.*

(2) (a) *Jill accused Fred.*
    (b) **Jill accused.*

Note also the evidence coming from conjoining. As discussed in Section 3.2.1 of Chapter 3, it is generally true that constituents that are of the same kind can be conjoined. However, Heads and their phrases are not always conjoinable. In (3a) they are but in (3b) they are not.

(3) (a) *The brown chairs and table have just arrived.*
    (b) **Table and the brown chairs have just arrived.*

Thus, the claim about Heads and phrases belonging to the very same class does not always hold.

The conclusion that we have arrived at regarding the relationship between Head and phrase is like the one we arrived at in connection with the relationship between Heads and Dependents of different phrases stated at the end of the preceding section. The grammatical properties of Heads and phrases are only partially alike, just as the grammatical properties of Heads of different phrases and Dependents of different phrases are also the same only in part. How could this partial but not full identity be represented?

The problem exists as long as we adopt a particular conceptualization of classes, which we will call 'slotting'. 'Slotting' means classifying things in such a way that once an object is assigned to a category, it cannot be assigned to any another category on the same level of the taxonomic system.

For example, if we classify living beings in terms of life form as animals and plants, dogs and fish are in the animal slot and turnips and water lilies in the plant slot. But this rigid classificatory system misses out on the similarities that hold between some animals and some plants. Thus, both dogs and turnips are land-based while both fish and water lilies are water-based. In order to do justice to similarities among living things from the point of view of both life form and habitat, we need to classify them by 'tagging' rather than slotting. The difference is that while any one object can only be placed in a single slot, it may have more than one tag attached to it.

The difference between the two concepts of classification is shown in (4) and (5).

(4) CLASSIFICATION BY SLOTTING

    (a) Classification of living beings by life form:

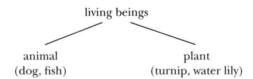

living beings

animal   plant
(dog, fish)   (turnip, water lily)

    (b) Classification of living beings by habitat:

living beings

land-based   aquatic
(dog, turnip)   (fish, water lily)

(5) CLASSIFICATION BY TAGGING

Classification of living beings by both life form and habitat:
dog [animal], [land-based]
fish [animal], [aquatic]
turnip [plant], [land-based]
water lily [plant], [aquatic]

In linguistics, tags of this kind – properties of constituents used for classifying them – are called **features**.

Let us now return to the question raised above. We saw that Heads and their phrases are partially but not fully alike; and that Heads across phrases were also both similar and different as were Dependents across phrases. The question was how could partial identity be represented. Thinking of classification in terms of features rather than rigid categories – tags rather than slots – offers a solution.

3.4 X-BAR THEORY

A proposal along these lines, implicit already in traditional dependency grammar, has been made in generative transformational grammar under the label 'X-bar theory'. The diagram in (1) contrasts traditional dependency structure with X-bar theory's view regarding adjective–noun and verb–object constructions:

(1) (a) TRADITIONAL DEPENDENCY STRUCTURE

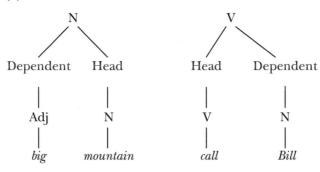

(b) X-BAR THEORY

In X-bar theory, syntactic categories are represented as pairs of features of two kinds: categorial features and rank features. The Head and the phrase share their categorial feature – such as N or V – but are distinguished by their rank feature (called 'bar level' in the literature) indicated by different numbers of strokes. In the above examples, the phrase is a one-bar constituent while the Head is zero-bar.

X-bar notation makes available the following classes:

(2)   (a)   Within a single phrase:
 – joint reference to head and phrase is possible by reference to their shared categorial feature (e.g. N′ and N share the categorial feature N)
 – distinct reference to Head and phrase is possible by reference to their different bar levels (e.g. N is zero-bar and N′ is one-bar).

(b)   Across phrases:
 – joint reference to Heads is possible by reference to their shared bar level (e.g. both N′ and V′ are one-bar)
 – distinct reference to Heads is possible by reference to their different categorial features (N′ is an N and V′ is a V).

The availability of these classes makes the following predictions regarding similarities and differences among constituents within and across phrases:

(3)   Constituents of the **same category within phrases** (e.g. N and N′)
(a)   are alike in some ways because of their shared categorial feature (e.g. N); and
(b)   are different in other ways because of their different bar levels (e.g. zero-bar and one-bar).
Constituents of the **same bar level across phrases** (e.g. N′ and V′)
(c)   are alike in some ways because of their shared bar level (e.g. one-bar); and
(d)   are different in other ways because of their different categorial features (e.g. N and V).

At the same time, X-bar theory predicts that certain constituents should have no uniquely shared properties. These are constituents that are neither of the same category nor of the same bar level; for example, a verb and a noun phrase.

There is evidence to support each of the four claims in (3). Let us start with (3a). That phrases and their Heads are in some ways alike is shown by the similar occurrence privileges of adjectival phrases and single adjectives in (4):

(4) (a) *The coffee is **very hot**.*
     (b) *The coffee is **hot**.*

They may also be conjoinable: *Jill likes coffee fresh and very hot.* Such facts support (3a).

However, (3b) is also true: phrases and their Heads also differ in some ways. The examples in (1) and (2) in Section 3.3 showed that some Heads cannot take the same position as the entire phrase (e.g. in *Jill accused Fred,* the Head of the verb phrase is the verb but it cannot form the verb phrase all by itself: *Jill accused*). And (3) in Section 3.3 showed that Heads may not be conjoinable with their phrases (**table and the brown chairs*).

Additional evidence for the distinctness of Heads and their phrases comes from pro-forms. Noun phrases and their Heads call for different pro-forms in English. As (5) shows, the pro-forms for full noun phrases are *he, she, it* etc. while the pro-forms for noun heads are *one* or *ones*.

(5) (a) *Peter bought a new car. **It** is in the garage.*
     (b) *Peter bought a new car but Paul bought a used **one**.*
     (c) **Peter bought a new car_1. **One_1** is in the garage.*
     (d) **Peter bought a new car but Paul bought a used **it**.*

Turning to the comparison of constituents of the same bar level in categorially different phrases, we again find evidence bearing out both similarities (3c) and differences (3d).

Similarities are shown by cleft constructions and questions. Both noun phrases and prepositional phrases can be the first constituents in so-called cleft sentences:

(6) (a) *It is **the dog** that needs to be fed.*
     (b) *It is **in the fridge** that you can find the dog food.*

And noun phrases, adjectival phrases, adverbial phrases, prepositional phrases and quantifier phrases can all function as question phrases (Radford 1981: 108):

(7) (a) ***What book** did you read?*
     (b) ***How long** is it?*
     (c) ***How quickly** did you read it?*
     (d) ***In what way** do you think the author is wrong?*
     (e) ***How much** did it cost?*

However, shared bar level allows for differences as well (3d). For example, as discussed in Chapter 3 and illustrated in (8), verb phrases and noun phrases cannot be conjoined.

(8) (a) *The cats drank the milk and lay down to sleep.*
     (b) **The cats drank the milk and the laying down to sleep.*

Thus, all four generalizations facilitated by X-bar notation (given in (3)) have empirical support: categorial identity and shared bar level predict some similarities among constituents and both leave room for differences as well.

In sum: X-bar theory provides a convenient feature notation for formulating generalizations over constituents that are different by category but the same in bar level, as well as generalizations about constituents that are different by bar level but the same by category.

3.5 SUMMARY

Dependency grammars propose that there is a cross-categorially uniform asymmetric relationship between parts of phrases. Two claims are made: that one of the constituents of the phrase – called the Head – is identical or at least similar to the whole phrase; and that the Head and its Dependents in one phrase bear some similarities to their counterparts in other phrases. Both claims have empirical support.

4 Construction grammars

4.1 BASIC ASSUMPTIONS

In ordinary linguistic usage, a construction is simply a unit of structure: a verb phrase is a construction (e.g. *water the plants*) and so is a question (e.g. *Why don't you water the plants?*). In this sense, every syntactic framework assumes constructions. Construction grammars are special, however, because of the specific properties they attribute to constructions. In what follows, we will consider two constructionist claims.

The first claim is partonomic, having to do with how meaning is construed by form.

(1) ALL CONSTRUCTIONS HAVE MEANINGS
    Part of the meaning of every construction is contributed by its structural frame.

The other claim is taxonomic, having to do with relations among constructions.

(2) ALL CONSTRUCTIONS HAVE UNIQUE MEANINGS
    Constructions that differ in structure also differ in meaning.

Let us take a closer look at each proposal.

4.2 ALL CONSTRUCTIONS HAVE MEANINGS

This claim relates to the fundamental issue of compositionality: how do the parts relate to the whole? Every syntactic approach acknowledges that the choice of the parts contributes to the meaning of the whole. Thus, the two sentences *Eve **baked** a cherry pie* and *Eve **ate** a cherry pie* mean different things and the difference arises from the different verbs. Furthermore, no syntactic approach will deny that in addition to semantic differences resulting from the selection of words, **some** structural differences are also meaning-bearing. For example, the difference between the readings of *Jill ran up a large hill* and *Jill ran up a large bill* is attributable to a structural difference: *up* in the first sentence is part of the prepositional phrase *up a large hill* while it is part of the complex verb *ran up* in the second sentence.

However, many syntacticians would consider other structural differences as immaterial to the meaning of the entire construction. As was discussed in Section 2.1 and in more detail in Chapter 4 (Section 3.3), transformational grammar represents some constructions that are distinct in surface structure as the same on the level of underlying structure. An example is the Patient–Recipient sentences in (1) and (2).

(1) Object-dative construction
    (a) *Bill gave some money to the Heart Association.*
    (b) *The teacher told a story to the children.*

(2) Double-object construction
    (a) *Bill gave the Heart Association some money.*
    (b) *The teacher told the children a story.*

In transformational grammar, the structural difference of corresponding sentences – (1a) and (2a), (1b) and (2b) – is considered non-meaning-bearing and the two sentences are represented as being the same on an underlying level. Thus, as discussed in Chapter 4, V NP NP is derived from V NP *to* NP by a rule called Dative Movement (later subsumed in part under NP-Movement, subsequently part of Move Alpha), which takes *to the children* in (1b) and inverts it with *a story* while deleting the preposition *to*, yielding (2b).

In contrast with such accounts, construction grammar claims that not just some but **every** structural difference is meaning-bearing. Examples of this approach are Adele Goldberg's and Ronald Langacker's analyses of Patient–Recipient sentences, presented in Chapter 4 (Sections 4.3 and 4.4). Both Goldberg and Langacker propose that object-dative and double-object sentences differ in meaning in that they represent alternate construals of the same event – that is, different perspectives.

Similarly, a careful analysis of the members of the following sentence pairs shows that while they may be roughly synonymous, there are subtle differences in emphasis and implication so that in some instances even truth-conditional equivalence is doubtful.

(3) (a) *He loaded hay onto the wagon.*
    (b) *He loaded the wagon with hay.*

(4) (a) *He stacked boxes onto the shelves.*
     (b) *He stacked the shelves with boxes.*

The (b)-sentences imply that the entire space – the whole wagon and all the shelves – were filled while the (a)-sentences lack this interpretation (Goldberg 1995: 107, 175–9).

A similar slight semantic difference can be detected in the following pair of sentences:

(5) (a) *That Don will leave is likely.*
     (b) *Don is likely to leave.*

Langacker remarks that in the second sentence, where *Don* is the subject of *is likely*, 'Don's volition is critical', while the first sentence 'is more neutral in this regard' (1995a: 23–4). More will be said about these sentences below.

As a further example of subtle semantic differences arising from structural frame, consider the following sentences:

(6) (a) *I find that this chair is uncomfortable.*
     (b) *I find this chair to be uncomfortable.*
     (c) *I find this chair uncomfortable.*

As Langacker points out, the judgement in (6a) may be based on indirect evidence while (6b) suggests more direct evidence and (6c) 'implies that the speaker has actually sat in the chair.' (1995a: 5).

Another argument for the semantic significance of structural frames is offered by exceptional but nonetheless clearly interpretable uses of verbs, as in (7) (Goldberg 1995: 70):

(7) (a) *Pat sneezed the foam off the cappuccino.*
     (b) *My father frowned away the compliment.*

The verbs *sneeze* and *frown* are not normally transitive; yet a transitive sentence frame enables them to function as such. This suggests that the lexical meaning of a verb does not fully determine the syntactic contexts where it can be used: structural frame can override lexical specification and impose a lexically anomalous but nevertheless well-formed interpretation.

Attributing semantic significance to constructions relates to the question of whether constructions are compositional or not. Some construction grammar frameworks assume compositionality of constructions (see Goldberg 1995: 13–16). Their point is that, as in the case of the *sneeze* and *frown* examples, the parts taken by themselves may not account for the meaning but if structural meaning is added, the whole is still compositional. But other versions of constructional grammar maintain that constructions are not fully compositional. Langacker points out that there is no fully compositional analysis possible for the word *pencil sharpener*.

This latter view of the relationship between wholes and parts in constructions shows an interesting parallel with current ideas in other scientific fields. Physicist Fritjof Capra describes a new way of thinking about partonomic relations called 'systems thinking', which has become prominent in physics, biology and psychology. The physical theory of quantum mechanics, the biological analysis of animal and plant communities, and Gestalt psychology have all grappled with non-compositionality in their respective domains and they all settled on non-compositionality being the rule rather than the exception. Capra writes:

> According to the systems view, the essential properties of an organism, or living system, are properties of the whole, which none of the parts have. They arise from the interactions and relationships among the parts. These properties are destroyed when the system is dissected, either physically or theoretically, into isolated elements. Although we can discern individual parts in any system, these parts are not isolated, and the nature of the whole is always different from the mere sum of its parts.
>
> In this view, the properties of the parts are not intrinsic properties but can be understood only within the context of the larger whole. Thus the relationship between the parts and the whole has been reversed. In the systems approach, the properties of the parts can be understood only from the organization of the whole. Accordingly, systems thinking concentrates not on basic building blocks, but on basic principles of organization. Systems thinking is 'contextual', which is the opposite of analytical thinking. Analysis means taking something apart in order to understand it; systems thinking means putting it into the context of a larger whole. . . .
>
> Whereas in classical mechanics the properties and behavior of the parts determine those of the whole, the situation is reversed in quantum mechanics: it is the whole that determines the behavior of the parts.
>
> (1996: 29–31)

A concrete illustration of non-compositionality in the physical world is given in the following passage:

> At each level of complexity, the observed phenomena exhibit properties that do not exist at the lower level. For example, the concept of temperature, which is central to thermodynamics, is meaningless at the level of individual atoms, where the laws of quantum theory operate. Similarly, the taste of sugar is not present in the carbon, hydrogen, and oxygen atoms that constitute its components. In the early 1920s, the philosopher C.D. Broad coined the term 'emergent properties' for those properties that emerge at a certain level of complexity but do not exist at lower levels.
>
> (ibid.: 28–9)

The fact that construction grammars pay full tribute to semantic differences among constructions has an interesting consequence: some syntactic patterns that are problems in other frameworks because they pose analytic conflicts are problem-free in construction grammar. Here are two examples.

First, consider the sentences in (8). They both include a noun phrase modified by a relative clause but they differ in whether the relative clause is adjacent to the noun phrase it modifies or whether it is separated from it.

(8) (a) ***The letter that you were waiting for*** *came.*
    (b) ***The letter*** *came* ***that you were waiting for.***
        (Langacker 1997: 24–7)

If we assume that semantic coherence between constituents must be paralleled by adjacency (see Chapter 2, Section 2), then (8a) is not a problem since it conforms to this expectation: the Head and the modifying clause form a conceptual unit and, correspondingly, they are adjacent. Sentence (b), however, is in violation: it is an instance of discontinuous ordering because the relative clause does not stand next to the Head.

The type of tree structure where selectional and linear relations are inseparable cannot show the relative clause as both adjacent to the Head – as suggested by selection – and as non-adjacent to it (as shown by pronunciation) because A and B cannot be both adjacent and non-adjacent at the same time. As we saw in Chapter 2, to solve the problem of (8b), frameworks that allow for multiple levels of syntactic representation associate this sentence with two distinct structures. Its surface structure represents the order of Head and relative clause as pronounced but its underlying structure has the relative clause next to the Head – that is, the underlying structure of (8b) would be identical to the surface structure of (8a). The surface structure is then derived from the underlying structure by a movement rule that extraposes the relative clause to the end of the sentence (see Radford 1988: 448–56).

In this manner, the conflict between meaning and form is resolved by identifying two distinct facets of the sentence – underlying structure and surface structure – with each showing only one of the two facets that would be in conflict if both were present in the same structure. The selectional coherence between Head and relative clause is shown on the underlying level and the formal coherence of the two is shown on the surface level.

In Ronald Langacker's Cognitive Grammar – a framework that belongs to the broad class of construction grammars – 'the problem in effect never arises in the first place' (Langacker 1997: 24). The reason is that in this approach, sentence diagrams are, by definition, bipolar (Langacker 1991: 287). This means that all representations of syntactic units – whether lexical items or syntactic constructions – have both a semantic and a phonological side. Thus, they can conveniently accommodate both meaning and form at the same time, including whatever mismatches they may exhibit. The diagram of (8b): *The letter that you were waiting for came* below makes this clear (taken from Langacker 1997: 25):

(9)

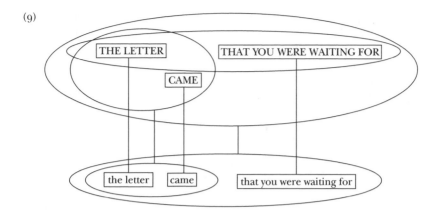

The bottom part of the figure, in lower-case letters, shows the pronuncia-tion of the sentence. The top part, in capital letters, is the semantic, or con-ceptual, side which is free of linear relations. Symbolic correspondence relations among the elements are shown by vertical ties. The crucial dif-ference between phonological and conceptual representations lies in the relations that *the letter* bears to the other parts of the sentence. In the phonological representation, *the letter* forms a constituent with only one word: *came*. Thus, in this representation, noun phrase head and relative clause do not form a unit. In conceptual structure, THE LETTER and CAME form a constituent just as in phonological structure; but in addi-tion, THE LETTER also forms a unit with THAT YOU WERE WAITING FOR. This is shown by two ovals intersecting in the constituent THE LETTER: one encompassing THE LETTER and CAME and the other, THE LETTER and THAT YOU WERE WAITING FOR. In other words, the relative clause and its Head are separated in pronunciation but unified in conceptual structure.

Thus, bipolar representations proposed in cognitive grammar re-conceptualize the apparent conflict in form – that the relative clause is selec-tionally related to the head but is not adjacent to it – as one holding between form and meaning. While form is 'one thing' and thus it must not be self-contradictory, meaning and form are two different things and thus there is no expectation that they should show congruent structures. The basic idea is akin to that of Sadock's Autolexical Grammar discussed in Section 2.3 of Chapter 2.

A second example to illustrate how the existence of analytic problems is the result of the assumptions that the analyst makes and how construction grammars avoid certain problems by adopting alternative assumptions is 'subject-to-subject raising' sentences (discussed in Chapter 2, Section 3.3). Let us return to the examples in (5) repeated here as (10).

(10) (a) *That Don will leave is likely.*
     (b) *Don is likely to leave.*

Once again, one of the two sentences shows a discrepancy between form and meaning, here having to do with the arguments of the predicate *is likely*. In sentence (10a), the subject of the predicate is the clause *that Don will leave* and within this clause, the subject is *Don*. This is shown, among others, by the fact that the clause is in pre-verbal position and that it answers a subject-question *What is likely?* In sentence (10b), however, the constituent that precedes the predicate *is likely* and that answers a subject-question is *Don*; the predicate *will leave* appears as an infinitive at the end of the sentence. The conflict is that, while *Don* is semantically and selectionally the subject of *will leave*, in terms of form, it is the subject of *is likely*.

Langacker succinctly summarizes the solution proposed in multi-level frameworks (Langacker 1995a: 22). Here is the argument adapted to our examples:

1. In (10a), the subject of *is likely* is an embedded clause: *that Don will leave*.
2. Thus, it is assumed that in all other uses of *is likely* as well (such as in (10b)), its subject must be clausal.
3. However, in (10b), the subject of *is likely* is not the embedded clause *Don will leave* but only part of that clause: the noun phrase *Don*.
4. In order to resolve this conflict, an abstract structure needs to be posited for (10b) where *Don will leave* **is** shown to be the subject of *is likely*.
5. Since that structure does not reflect the pronunciation of the sentence, a rule is needed to subsequently raise *Don* to be the subject of *likely* since this is how it is pronounced.

The crucial point where Cognitive Grammar departs from the train of thought above is 2. As already noted in connection with (5) above, Langacker points out that (10a) and (10b) are not completely synonymous: (10b) – *Don is likely to leave* – encourages the interpretation that Don will leave intentionally while (10a) is non-committal in this regard. Thus, he posits two distinct lexical entries for *be likely*, one taking clausal subjects as in (10a), and the other taking nominal subjects as in (10b).

While the multi-level analysis assumes that all occurrences of *be likely* are occurrences of the same lexical item, Langacker's account denies this. The example shows that verbs can have slightly different meanings depending on the choice of their focal constituents – such as the choice of the subject (called 'trajector' in Cognitive Grammar). If a nominal constituent – *Don* – is made into the subject of *be likely*, as in (10b), rather than just being part of the clause that is the subject of *be likely*, the referent of that nominal is understood as having a more direct participation in the state described by *be likely*. Instead of one of the two constructions – (10a) and (10b) – being derived from the other and thus being a deformed version of the other, in Cognitive Grammar the two constructions are alternatives on a par. The two lexical items for *be likely* both select the clause as their conceptual subject but differ in whether the formal subject is the clause itself or the clause's conceptual subject.

In both examples just discussed – alternative orders of noun phrase head and relative clause, and alternative subjects of *be likely* – the basic argument is the same. In the first example, there is a mismatch between selectional and linear relations; in the second example, there is a mismatch between selectional relations and grammatical functions. In both cases, multi-level syntactic analyses posit an abstract level of syntactic form which 'sets things right' by replacing surface mismatch with alignment. In contrast, construction grammars acknowledge and highlight the mismatches and show that they hold not within form but between form and meaning.

There are also other expectations that are relaxed in Langacker's Cognitive Grammar. Part–whole relations – constituent structure – are not held to the requirement that the parts should not overlap. Thus 'subject-to-object raising sentences', such as *I expect Bill to return soon*, where the main clause and the subordinate clause overlap in *Bill* in that this noun is the object of the main verb and the subject of the subordinate verb at the same time, are not problematic. In fact, overlap of constructions is claimed to be more the rule than the exception: subject–verb agreement, for example, is also analysed as a case of overlap between the subject and the verb. In general, composite constructions are seen as a collage and not as a mosaic picture (Langacker 1997: 11).

Let us now turn to the second claim of construction grammars.

4.3 ALL CONSTRUCTIONS HAVE UNIQUE MEANINGS

Claiming that constructional frames carry meaning does not necessarily imply that two different constructions could not contribute the same meaning. But, as noted in our discussion of the Constructional Grammar account of Patient–Recipient sentences (Section 4.3 of Chapter 4), Construction Grammar does make this additional claim: not only do constructions have meaning but their meanings are unique. In other words, no two constructions are synonymous.

The way to account for similarities among constructions is perhaps the key difference between constructional grammars and transformational grammars. Our discussion of the various descriptions of active and passive constructions in transformational grammars in Section 2 illustrated the continued striving after more general accounts within that framework. In that example, this was achieved by breaking down the basic active and passive constructions into increasingly smaller and more general components in an attempt to relate them to an increasingly broader range of grammatical constructions.

Chomsky characterizes this endeavour in the following way (Chomsky 1995: 175). In early generative grammar, he says, rules were 'construction-particular and language-particular'. In the more recent versions, '(t)he notion of grammatical construction is eliminated, and with it, construction-particular rules. Constructions such as verb phrase, relative clause, and passive remain only as taxonomic artifacts, collections of phenomena explained through the interaction of the principles of (universal grammar)'.

This view differs from that of construction grammars, where constructions are units that are not indivisible but nonetheless basic in some sense of the word. While transformational grammars strive for generalizations even at the price of disregarding some differences, constructional grammars take differences very seriously and insist on representing them as such.

If constructions are different both within and across languages, the question is how the similarities between constructions can nonetheless be accounted for. That constructions are not wholly distinct from each other is acknowledged by construction grammars: constructions are arranged in a taxonomy to point up their similarities (Goldberg 1995: 67–100; Croft 2001: 25–6). Thus, unlike in transformation grammars, differences among constructions are not reduced to full identity but only to partial sameness, or similarity. For example, both the construction 'Subject *kick* Object' and the construction 'Subject *kiss* Object' are seen as subtypes of the type 'Subject, Transitive Verb, Object' (Croft 2001: 26).

Since it is also claimed that constructions are different across languages, the question is what, if anything, can be said to be the same across languages. Radical Construction Grammar (ibid.) focuses on syntactic variation both within and across languages. As discussed earlier, variation is itself a paradoxical notion: two things are seen both as the same and yet different. The way the paradox of variation is addressed in Radical Construction Grammar is the same as the way the paradox of non-compositionality is solved.

As noted above, non-compositionality is a problem only as long as compositionality is expected; once the underlying assumption that the desired norm is compositionality is eliminated, the problem of non-compositionality melts away. Similarly, variation is a problem only as long as the different tokens are classified as tokens of the same thing; once their categorial sameness is given up, there is no conflict. And this is exactly what Radical Construction Grammar proposes.

Although Croft does not explicitly deny the validity of the category 'human language', he sees the similarities among languages as much less extensive than other language typologists do. His claim is that there are two areas of universals. One pertains to one of the cardinal poles of symbolic correspondence: conceptual structure – that is, the thoughts that people communicate by language. The other has to do with how ideas are expressed in syntactic form. In this latter domain, Croft proposes no unrestricted universals – that is, features that are present in all languages. Instead, he proposes that there are implicational relationships among syntactic patterns such that the occurrence of one pattern entails the occurrence of another pattern in the same language. Furthermore, he suggests that these implications make sense in that they all conform to 'markedness hierarchies'.

4.4 Summary

The overall message of construction grammars is that conflicts do not need to be resolved; instead, they can be removed by changing the assumptions that cause them.

5 Optimality Theory

5.1 Basic assumptions

Optimality Theory addresses the problem of conflicts in grammatical analysis head-on. As discussed earlier (Chapter 1, Section 3), conflicts can be dealt with in several different ways, one of which is ranking: the temporary suspension of one of the conflicting principles. This is the approach to conflict resolution that Optimality Theory takes.

Five hypotheses are central to this approach.

(1) GRAMMARS CONSIST OF CONSTRAINTS RATHER THAN RULES
Grammatical statements are constraints. Unlike rules, which are positively stated, constraints are negative statements barring certain structures while allowing others.

(2) CONSTRAINTS ARE UNIVERSAL ACROSS LANGUAGES
Any constraint that the grammar of one language includes is part of the grammars of all human languages. Thus languages do not differ in the constraints that their grammars contain.

(3) CONSTRAINTS MAY BE IN CONFLICT
Constraints are not necessarily consistent with each other: one may contradict the other.

(4) CONFLICTS AMONG CONSTRAINTS ARE RESOLVED BY RANKING
Conflicts among constraints are resolved by ranking one constraint over the other.

(5) THE RANKING OF CONSTRAINTS IS VARIABLE
Constraints may be ranked differently for purposes of different constructions of a language and in different languages. This is where differences among languages come from.

The application of these assumptions will be shown next in a specific example. The data and argumentation are taken from Judith Aissen's study (2003).

5.2 THE CASE MARKING OF DIRECT OBJECTS

Languages differ in how they case-mark direct objects. Hungarian is a language that case-marks all direct objects, shown in the example in (1).

>   (1)   *A   kutya megharapja az   **ember-t.***
>   the dog   bites   the **man-ACC**
>   'Dogs bite men.'

However, Lisu marks no direct objects. Since subjects are not case-marked either nor are they differentiated from direct objects in other ways, this may result in subject–object ambiguity as in (2) (Li and Thompson 1976: 472; TM = topic marker; DECL = declarative marker; transcription simplified).

>   (2)   *Làthyu nya **ánà** khù-a.*
>   people TM **dog** bite-DECL
>   'People, dogs bite them.' OR
>   'People, they bite dogs.'

The picture becomes more complex if we look at languages like Hebrew. Hebrew falls between Hungarian and Lisu in that it marks some direct objects but not others. In particular, definite direct objects must be case-marked by the prepositional clitic *et* but most indefinite ones may not (Aissen 2003: 453).

>   (3)   (a)   *Ha-sere   her'a   '**et-ha-milxama**.*
>   the-movie showed **ACC-the-war**
>   'The movie showed the war.'
>
>   (b)   *Ha-sere   her'a   **milxama**.*
>   the-movie showed **war**
>   'The movie showed a war.'

There is additional variation among languages. Some – for example, Catalan and Pitjantjatjara – are more restrictive than Hebrew: they obligatorily case-mark only certain definite direct objects – (strong) personal pronouns (Catalan) and personal pronouns and proper names (Pitjantjatjara). The rule in Turkish, on the other hand, is more relaxed than the one in Hebrew: Turkish case-marks not only all definite direct objects but also indefinite objects provided they refer to a specific individual.

How can we make sense of these cross-linguistic differences regarding the case marking of direct objects? Working within the framework of Optimality Theory, Aissen provides the following account.

First, in line with the basic assumption that grammatical rules are constraints (see (1) in Section 5.1), Aissen proposes that there are two constraints at work here: Iconicity and Economy. In accordance with a second assumption of Optimality Theory (see (2) in Section 5.1), both are universal.

(4) (a) THE ICONICITY CONSTRAINT
For all languages: given a markedness opposition of two noun phrases, the marked member should be case-marked.

(b) THE ECONOMY CONSTRAINT
For all languages: no noun phrase should be case-marked.

The two constraints are in conflict (see (3) in Section 5.1). They are at cross-purposes because Iconicity allows case marking under certain conditions while Economy bans case marking under all conditions.

According to Optimality Theory, conflicts between constraints should be resolved by ranking (see (4) in Section 5.1). Now, were conflicting constraints ranked the same way in all languages, some constraints would never come into play: they would always be suppressed by those ranked higher. For example, if Iconicity were universally ranked over Economy, the latter would be universally suppressed and would never have a say on the matter of direct-object case marking. If so, all languages would case-code all marked objects. If in turn Economy were universally ranked over Iconicity, no object would ever be case-marked in any language.

As we saw above, neither of the two scenarios holds: some languages do case-mark some kinds of objects and others do not. This is where the fifth claim of Optimality Theory ((5) in Section 5.1)) comes in: constraints are universal but their ranking may vary across languages. Given that the constraints themselves are universal, the burden of the variability of syntactic structures across languages is placed entirely on the shoulders of the variable ranking of the invariable constraints.

How exactly do the two constraints – Iconicity and Economy – account for the cross-linguistic variability of direct object case marking?

The facts that need to be correctly predicted by the account can be stated in terms of a chain of implications:

(5) Personal Proper Definite Indefinite Indefinite
    pronoun name common specific   non-specific
               noun   noun   noun

If in a language, direct objects of a certain kind are case-marked, so are all other kinds to the left on the scale.

How can we relate this observation to the Iconicity Constraint? This constraint says: case-mark objects that are marked. If the hierarchy in (5) is to be predicted by the Iconicity Constraint, object types to the left of the scale would have to be more marked than object types to the right.

There is indeed independent evidence for this. The evidence comes from the cross-linguistic distribution of the various kinds of nominals that can function as direct objects. The maximally restricted distribution of pronominal direct objects is shown by the fact that in some languages – for example, Chamorro – pronouns cannot be direct objects (unless the subject, too, is a pronoun). The relatively restricted distribution of definite objects – both pronouns and nouns – is shown by Tagalog, where definite noun phrases cannot be direct objects (Aissen 2003: 445–6). At the other end, indefinite non-specific noun phrases are universally allowed to be direct objects. There are no languages that allow only pronominal objects or only definite ones but none lower on the scale.

Since greater cross-linguistic distribution is one of the symptoms of the unmarked member of an opposition, the distributional facts just cited show that the hierarchy in (5) is indeed one of markedness: the object types to the left are more marked than those to the right.

Given this recognition, a set of specific constraints may be derived from the Iconicity Constraint regarding case marking. In (6), these are given in the order of more binding to less binding.

(6) • Avoid the lack of case marking on personal-pronoun direct objects.
   • Avoid the lack of case marking on proper-name direct objects.
   • Avoid the lack of case marking on definite common noun direct objects.
   • Avoid the lack of case marking on indefinite specific direct objects.
   • Avoid the lack of case marking on indefinite non-specific direct objects.

Since constraints are assumed to be universal, (6) would still predict that all languages should case-code all objects – a prediction that is incorrect. The differences among languages come from alternative rankings of the Economy Constraint relative to the five constraints in (6). Some languages will assign greater priority to compliance with the markedness constraints derived from the Iconicity Constraint, which encourage case marking, than to compliance with the Economy Constraint, which bans them. Other languages will in turn bow to the force of the Economy Constraint over some or all of the iconicity requirements.

The alternative rankings are shown in (7). The languages are listed on top (CAT stands for Catalan, PITJ for Pitjantjatara, TUR for Turkish, HUNG for Hungarian). The placement of ECON in the chart shows the point in the hierarchy of constraints where the Economy Principle steps in for that language.

(7)

	LISU	CAT	PITJ	HEBR	TURK	HUNG
	ECON					
Avoid lack of case on pronoun objects		ECON				
Avoid lack of case on proper-name objects			ECON			
Avoid lack of case on definite objects				ECON		
Avoid lack of case on specific indefinites					ECON	
Avoid lack of case on non-specific indefinites						ECON

For Lisu, the Economy Constraint reigns supreme: the language complies with it on all levels of markedness in that it does not case-mark even the most marked types of direct objects and thus it violates all the requirements of Iconicity. Catalan, which case-marks pronominal direct objects only, is less parsimonious: it ranks the Economy Constraint lower than the top requirement of markedness that calls for case marking on the most marked direct objects: personal pronouns. Pitjantjatjara, Hebrew and Turkish accord less and less role to Economy in favour of Iconicity. Finally, Hungarian discards Economy altogether and case-marks all objects since they are the marked member of the opposition Subject–Object.

5.3 SUMMARY

The issue of conflicting demands on language structure is at the very core of Optimality Theory. It proposes that conflicts among constraints can be resolved by ranking – that is, by the suppression of one of the two conflicting principles in favour of the other. The constraints posited are claimed to be universal but violable in that a constraint may be ranked lower than another and thus be prevented from surfacing in a language.

6 Conclusions

The first three approaches surveyed above – transformational grammars, dependency grammars and construction grammars – centre on partonomic issues: given a set of co-occurring words, are they 'one' or are they 'many'; and if they make a single whole, what exactly is the relationship between the whole and the parts? All three approaches are compatible with the fourth approach discussed – Optimality Theory – which claims that grammatical principles are universal and differences among the constructions of a single language and of different languages result from the differential ranking of conflicting principles.

Notes

1 Preliminaries
For comprehensive multi-theory surveys, see Moravcsik and Wirth 1980; Sells 1985; Horrocks 1987; Mahmoudian 1993; Edmondson and Burquest 1992; Droste and Joseph 1991; Van Valin 2001: 172–226; Borsley 1999; Brown and Miller 1996; Newmeyer 1986, 1998; Sag *et al.* 2003: 525–42; and the publishing house Routledge's Linguistic Theory Guides series edited by Dick Hudson.

2 Transformational grammars
- The half-a-century-long history of Transformational Grammar began in the 1950s when, expanding on the ideas of his teacher Zellig Harris, Noam Chomsky first proposed multi-level syntactic representations and transformations to connect the levels. The proposal's first published version was *Syntactic Structures* (Chomsky 1957). Subsequent major milestones in the development of the idea are marked by additional books by Chomsky: the Extended Standard Theory proposed in his *Aspects of the Theory of Syntax* (Chomsky 1965), followed by *Lectures in Government and Binding* (Chomsky 1984) followed by *The Minimalist Program* (Chomsky 1995). The principal changes had to do with the role of meaning in grammar, the homogeneous versus modular view of syntax, the role of the lexicon in syntax, and the form and function of transformational rules. Parallel to these developments, a framework called Principles and Parameters emerged to encounter cross-linguistic syntactic variation head-on (see Culicover 1997). Chomsky's proposals were elaborated, applied and modified by many other linguists, resulting in a huge body of literature.
- For detailed histories of Transformational Grammar, see Newmeyer 1986; two of Andrew Radford's excellent textbooks (Radford 1981, 1988); and the relevant articles in Brown and Miller 1996. For a very brief but very clear statement, see Roberts 2000. On Government and Binding theory, see also Haegeman 1994; on the Minimalist Program, see also Webelhuth 1995; and, once again, Andrew Radford's more recent texts (Radford 1997a, 1997b). A concise overview of the various versions of Transformational Generative Grammar is given in Jackendoff 2002: 107–11.
- This discussion about transformational analyses of the passive relies on Culicover 1997: 89–101; Radford 1981: 420–47, 1988: 180–206 and 1997a: 341–9.

2.2.2   NP-Movement

(7) is an imprecise statement of the rule as a result of the necessarily skeletal nature of the present discussion of passives in transformational theory. For more detail, see Radford 1981: 180–206, 1988: 420–65.

2.2.4   Why move?

A much earlier, comprehensive theory of grammar that proposes that full interpretation drives grammatical derivations of sentences and thus the application of all syntactic, lexical and phonological rules is Gerald Sanders' *Equational Grammar* (Sanders 1972).

3.1   Basic assumptions

- The modern-day roots of the general framework of dependency grammars go back to Lucien Tesnière (Tesnière 1959). A contemporary version of dependency grammar is provided by Richard Hudson; for book-length accounts, see Hudson 1984, 1990; a concise version is given in Hudson 1996. Other contemporary dependency-based grammars are Igor Mel'čuk 1988 and Head-Driven Phrase Structure Grammar (see, for example, Sag *et al.* 2003). For a brief overview of X-bar theory, see Cann 1996.
- On just what grammatical characteristics are properties of Heads, see the papers in Corbett *et al.* 1993.

4.1   Basic assumptions

For a survey of the various frameworks that adopt constructionist principles, see Goldberg 1995: 219–24 and Croft 2001: 14–29.

4.2   All constructions have meanings

- An early suggestion for the bipolarity of both lexical items and syntactic constructions was made in Sanders' *Equational Grammar* (Sanders 1972).
- Figure (9) is reproduced by permission from Mouton de Gruyter and Ronald W. Langacker.

5   Optimality Theory

For a comprehensive account of Optimality Theory, see Kager 1999.

Exercises

1. Consider the phrases Article + N and Demonstrative + Noun. Do they form Head–Dependent constructions? If so, by what criteria?

2. In Transformational Grammar, the following sentences are considered synonymous and thus assigned the same underlying structure. In

Construction Grammar, they are not viewed as synonymous and are not brought to a single common semantic denominator. Analyse their meanings and decide whether they are indeed fully synonymous. (Examples from Langacker 1995a.)

(a) *They wanted to adopt a child.*
      They wanted a child to adopt.
(b) *It is easy to talk to him.*
      He is easy to talk to.

3. How does English case marking fit in with the Markedness Principle and the Iconicity Principle? Consider both nominal direct objects and pronominal ones (such as *me, you, him, her, it, us, you, them, whom*).

4. Identify the direct-object markers in the Latin, Hungarian and Japanese data in the Appendix.

5. Classify the courses offered by your department in terms of topic, level, number of credits etc., first by using the 'slotting' method and then 'tagging' (see the discussion in Section 3.3). Evaluate the two methods from the point of view of their usefulness in making generalizations about the courses.

Chapter Seven

Where do Conflicts Come From?

> It is wrong to think that the task of physics is to find out how nature **is**. Physics concerns only what we can **say** about nature.
>
> (Niels Bohr, as quoted in Gregory 1988: 95, emphasis original)

1 Two sources of conflict

Conflicts in syntax and syntactic theory have been the focus of discussion in this book. Why do they arise? What are their root causes?

A syntactic description is the product of two factors. On the one hand, it reflects the knowledge that, in some form or another, speakers of languages have about sentence structure. On the other hand, it must conform to the requirements regarding what scientific descriptions should be like. Thus, syntactic descriptions reflect the mind of the speaker of the language and at the same time they hold up a mirror to the mind of the linguist: the mental apparatus the linguist brings to analysing the data.

Conflicts arise on both levels: in ordinary linguistic expression and in linguistic analysis. We will consider the roots of the two types of conflict in turn.

2 Conflicts in language

2.1 MEANING AND FORM

There are two principal sources of conflict in linguistic expression: conflict between meaning and form, and conflict between the needs of the speaker and those of the hearer.

First, consider meaning and form. They are two distinct entities; yet they are being brought together by the relation of symbolic correspondence. For meaning to be outwardly accessible, it must be carried by form.

The problem of how to make form convey meaning looms large in all kinds of communication whether linguistic or artistic. Thoughts are devoid of any publicly perceptible material existence and when they are to be cast in some kind of material form – whether clay or marble or paint or gesture or musical sound or speech – there is a clash.

The principal source of the mismatch between thought and linguistic form has to do with temporal organization. Linguistic form is linear but the structure of thoughts is not. There is some temporal sequencing in our thought processes: you may think of one thing first and then of something else. But individual propositions are not linearly structured: predicates and their arguments do not follow a temporal sequence as they do when they are put into words.

This mismatch between the linear nature of linguistic form and the non-linear nature of thoughts is witnessed by the many differences in how languages order words. To be sure, word order is not completely unrelated to semantic relations. First, the adjacency of words, phrases or clauses tends to convey semantic coherence; for example, adjectives and the nouns they modify are generally adjacent. Second, linear precedence, too, can be iconic. In a sentence such as *The kitten climbed into the basket and went to sleep*, the order in which the two acts took place is reflected by the order in which the two acts are mentioned.

Even apart from such cases of iconic adjacency and precedence, word order patterns across languages are not completely random. As we saw in Chapter 5 (Section 2), it is possible to identify large superclasses of syntactic constituents – such as heads and dependents, or branching and non-branching constituents, or mother-node-constructing and non-mother-node-constructing constituents – that show a somewhat consistent ordering within a language. However, the fact still remains that some languages will order these supercategories one way – say, Heads before Dependents – while others do it the other way – Dependents before Heads. This shows that meaning does not call for a single temporal sequencing of constituents.

In sum, meaning and linguistic form are different kinds of entities and thus, when form is pressed into the service of conveying thoughts, the conflict between temporally unsequenced thought and temporally sequenced form needs to be resolved.

2.2 SPEAKER AND ADDRESSEE

What determines the exact meaning that the speaker is to convey? On the one hand, his utterance is expected to be truthful: the meaning has to match the facts. But, on the other hand, there is also the speaker's own perspective: the angle from which he views the experience he is describing.

These two determinants of meaning became evident as we considered the alternative alignments of semantic participant roles and grammatical functions in active and passive sentences and object–dative and double-object sentences. Active and passive sentences both describe the same state of affairs but they convey different perspectives. The statement *Bill was given the job* shows the speaker's interest in what happened to Bill, whereas *The job was given to Bill* is about what happened to the job. The same has been shown for object–dative and double-object constructions, as well as for the two orders in verb–particle constructions, for 'raised' and 'unraised' constructions and for others.

In addition to the actual facts to be described and the speaker's take on them, there is a third factor that affects the **meaning** to be conveyed by the speaker: the addressee's perspective. The content of the message must be shaped so as to match the hearer's assumptions. For example, in referring to a person, the speaker generally cannot start his message by using a pronoun, such as *he*, or using a definite noun phrase such as *the man*. The identity of the referent may be clear to the speaker; but the question is will the referent be clear to the addressee? A certain amount of empathy on the part of the speaker is needed. He/she must be able to put himself in the shoes of the addressee and shape the content of the message so that there is a tight fit between what he/she wants to say and what can be assumed to be already known by the hearer.

The tension between the speaker's and the hearer's needs is even more clearly apparent in the choice of **form**. What does the speaker want the form of a sentence to be like and what does the addressee want in this regard? Depending on the choice of interlocutors and speech situation, the needs of speakers and of hearers may vary. Loquacious speakers may want to use elaborate form and hearers may impatiently wish to put a dam on what seems like excess verbiage. Yet, normally, the speaker wants to use as little form as possible to express what he wants to say. He is after economy. The hearer in turn values redundancy: he wants to get as many clues as possible so that he can decipher the intended meaning. The conflict is between the requirement of least effort in saying things and the requirement of least effort in deciphering the message.

The conflict may be settled in favour of one or the other interlocutor. Take elliptical and full forms of co-ordinate structures as in (1).

(1) (a) *The computers came from Korea and the printers came from Japan.*
    (b) *The computers came from Korea and the printers, from Japan.*

From the viewpoint of the hearer, (1a) is a better expression of the intended meaning since it is more complete: it is compositional. But (1b) is easier for the speaker since he gets away with saying less. Here, the speaker seems to have won the tug-of-war.

Speech forms that arise in the course of the historical process of grammaticalization (discussed in Chapter 2, Section 3.3 and Chapter 5, Section 3.5) also appear to favour the speaker. Contracted forms such as *can't* as opposed to *cannot* are easier to pronounce but may be less easily comprehended.

More often than not, however, the hearer's needs are favoured over the speakers (Gundel *et al.* 1988). This was shown in the course of our discussion in Chapter 5 (Section 3) of the distribution of resumptive pronouns in relative clauses. Compare the two sentences in (2).

(2)   (a)   *The letter that I mailed yesterday was lost.*
      (b)   ** The letter that I mailed **it** yesterday was lost.*

The sentence in (2b) is ungrammatical in English but common in some languages as well as in the speech of language learners. As we have seen, resumptive pronouns are preferentially used in relative clauses that are more difficult to comprehend. Thus, even though their production is an extra task for the speaker, their use is an aid for the hearer.

Another instance of syntax leaning towards the needs of the hearer is John Hawkins' analysis of word order patterns. As discussed in Chapter 5 (Section 2.4), Hawkins proposes that the prime principle that determines constituent order is to allow the hearer to receive the basic layout of the sentence as early as possible.

In yet another construction type, neither party is a clear winner. Take wh-questions in English. Why are question pronouns sentence-initial? On the one hand, their emphatic, sentence-initial position may have the beneficial function of alerting the hearer to the fact that the sentence is a question rather than a statement and of highlighting the particular bit of information that is being asked about. But at the same time, the displaced ordering of the question pronouns may make the addressee's job more difficult to figure out the semantic relationship between the verb and the question word.

The choice between favouring the addressee and favouring himself is in some cases a free choice of the speaker: a given language may provide means to shape the form of a construction in alternative ways. In other cases, the speaker is not free to make this choice: the language has made the choice for them by allowing only one of the alternative expressions. For example, resumptive pronouns in relative clauses serving the needs of the hearer are ungrammatical in most varieties of English but optional or even obligatory in many other languages. Also, question pronouns are sentence-initial in English but they appear in their verb complement positions in other languages such as Turkish or Chantyal. Cross-linguistically available options are often turned into necessities within a given language.

The opposing forces related to the needs of the encoder (the speaker) and the decoder (the hearer) are at work in any kind of communication, linguistic or artistic. The conflict does not pitch one person against the other in language since all users of language are both speakers and hearers: when we speak we monitor what we say.

In sum: speakers of a language must cope with two kinds of mismatch: that between meaning and form, and that between the speaker's needs and those of the addressee.

3 Conflicts in metalanguage

As we saw in Chapter 1 (Section 2.1.1), syntactic descriptions – as all scientific accounts – must meet four requirements: empirical adequacy, generality, simplicity and consistency.

Some of these criteria correspond to the requirements that speakers of ordinary languages have to meet. What corresponds to the criterion of empirical adequacy in ordinary language use is the expectation that the speaker will speak the truth: that he does not lie. Scientific descriptions must provide a truthful image of some segment of reality: a close fit with the facts, just as speakers in ordinary language are supposed to tell us about true facts. Simplicity and consistency have to do with making the descriptions palatable for the addressee. The hearer should not be confronted by a complex-to-decipher form that burdens his mind, and he should not be given conflicting information that twists the mind. Thus, as in ordinary language, both the needs of the encoder and those of the decoder play a role in shaping scientific communication as well.

But there is also a criterion that applies to scientific descriptions but not to ordinary discourse: generality. Scientific accounts seek explanations and thus they must place the observed phenomena within a network of facts so that they shed their uniqueness and become derivable from comprehensive principles. In ordinary discourse, generality is rarely if ever called for: people prefer to talk about individual events and objects that are rooted in human contexts and that paint pictures for the mental eye. I am more likely to provide a specific, picturesque description to a friend, such as *Hear this, last night I knocked the lovely crystal vase that Aunt Betty gave me off the shelf and it shattered to pieces*, than to offer a generalization, *Glass breaks when it falls to the ground*.

It is the requirement of generality when taken together with the other three criteria that gives rise to conflicts in linguistic accounts. The most prominent conflict is between generality and empirical adequacy. It is difficult to fit facts into generalizations and often when we do so, the account violates empirical adequacy and if the conflict is not resolved, the description falls short of simplicity and consistency.

Generalizing about a set of things involves categorizing them: viewing them as tokens of a single type. As Cecil Brown put it, categorization involves 'the treatment of two or more distinguishable entities as if they were the same' (1990: 17). But facts are often recalcitrant: they resist the likeness forced upon them when they are lumped into a single class. We may wish to consider them *as if* they were the same; but they are not in fact the same.

How conflicts arise when disparate things are conceptualized as one thing and how they can melt away was evident in our discussions of certain sentence pairs, such as those in (1)–(3).

(1) Object–dative and double-object sentences
    (a) *Bill gave fish to the penguins.*
    (b) *Bill gave the penguins fish.*

(2) Active and passive sentences
    (a) *The penguins ate the fish.*
    (b) *The fish were eaten by the penguins.*

(3) 'Unraised' and 'raised' sentences
    (a) *I believe that my puppy is hungry.*
    (b) *I believe my puppy to be hungry.*

The conflict here is between two forms having the same meaning. The solutions proposed in the literature make it clear that what is 'one thing' and what are 'two things' are negotiable claims. As we saw in Chapter 4, one set of approaches takes issue with the contention that the forms of the members of each pair of sentences are two different forms. They argue that, on some level of syntactic analysis, they are the same form. The other line of argument acknowledges that there are two forms involved but reviews the claim that members of each pair have the same meaning. Instead, it is proposed that the meanings are different: rather than one meaning being involved, there are two meanings. Either way, the mismatch between two forms conveying one meaning is resolved, either into one (underlying) form conveying one meaning, or into two forms conveying two meanings.

What this shows is that conflicts are not inherent in reality: they arise and disappear depending on the assumptions and expectations with which the scientist approaches reality. What Niels Bohr said about physics in the epigraph to this chapter holds more generally: scientific accounts do not offer a true image of reality but present only what we can say about it.

4 Conclusion

This book has been about human thought and its expression on two levels. On the one hand, it has been about how people use language to convey their thoughts about the world. On the other hand, it has been about how linguists design metalanguages to formulate their analyses of language.

Both endeavours are fraught with conflicts. Every human language is a record of how speakers manage to accommodate mismatches between meaning and form and conflicts between the speaker's needs and those of the hearer. Every description of a language is in turn a record of how the linguist has been able to accommodate the often conflicting demands of empirical truth, generality, simplicity and consistency. Finding productive solutions for conflicts may be the central task in linguistic theory, as it may be in life in general, surpassed only by the even greater challenge of learning to simply embrace conflicts and live with them productively.

Appendix: Parallel Data from Six Languages

This appendix contains data from the following languages:

1. English
2. Latin
3. Russian
4. Hungarian
5. Japanese
6. Chantyal

1 English

1. *The boy is running.*
2. *I am running.*
3. *You$_S$ are running.*
4. *The young boy is eating bread.*
5. *I am eating old bread.*
6. *You$_S$ are eating fresh bread.*
7. *The bread is being eaten by the boy.*
8. *The fresh bread is being eaten by you$_S$.*
9. *The tall boy who baked the bread is running.*
10. *The boy is eating old bread that you$_S$ baked.*
11. *The bread which the boy baked is fresh.*
12. *I know that the boy is young.*
13. *You$_S$ know that the boy baked the bread.*
14. *Is the boy running?*
15. *Are you$_S$ eating bread?*
16. *Who is running?*
17. *Who baked the bread?*
18. *What did the boy bake?*

2 Latin (Indo-European, Italic; extinct)

Note: Alternative word order variants are possible.

1. 'The boy is running.'
   Puer   curri-t.
   boy.MSC.SG.NOM run-PRS.S3

2. 'I am running.'
   (Ego)   curr-o.
   I.NOM run-PRS.S1

3. 'You_S are running.'
   (Tu)   curri-s.
   you_S.NOM run-PRS.S2

4. 'The young boy is eating bread.'
   Puer   iuven-is   pan-em
   boy.MSC.SG.NOM young-MSC.SG.NOM bread-MSC.SG.ACC
        ed-it.
        eat-PRS.S3

5. 'I am eating old bread.'
   (Ego)   pan-em   senect-em   ed-o.
   I.NOM bread-MSC.SG.ACC old-MSC.SG.ACC eat-PRS.S1

6. 'You_S are eating fresh bread.'
   (Tu)   pan-em   nov-um   ed-is.
   you_S.NOM bread-MSC.SG.ACC new-MSC.SG.ACC eat-PRS.S2

7. 'The bread is being eaten by the boy.'
   Panis   a puer-o   ed-itur.
   bread.MSC.SG.NOM by boy-MSC.SG.ABL eat-PASS.PRS.S3

8. 'The fresh bread is being eaten by you.'
   Panis   nov-us   a te
   bread.MSC.SG.NOM new-MSC.SG.NOM by you_S.ABL
        ed-itur.
        eat-PASS.PRS.S3

9. 'The tall boy who baked the bread is running.'
   Puer   alt-us,   qui
   boy.MSC.SG.NOM tall-MSC.SG.NOM who.SG.NOM
        pan-em   coxi-t,   curr-it.
        bread-MSC.SG.ACC cook.PST-S3 run-PRS.S3

10. 'The boy is eating old bread that you$_S$ baked.'
    Puer   *pan-em*   *senect-em*
    boy.MzSC.SG.NOM bread-MSC.SG.ACC old-MSC.SG.ACC
        ed-it,   *quem*   *tu*   *coxi-s.*
        eat-PRS.S3 which.SG.ACC you$_S$.NOM cook.PST-S2

11. 'The bread which the boy baked is fresh.'
    Panis   *quem*   *puer coxi-t,*
    bread.MSC.SG.NOM which.MSC.SG.ACC boy bake.PST-S3
        nov-us   *est.*
        fresh-MSC.SG.NOM be.PRS.S3

12. 'I know that the boy is young.'
    (Ego)   *puer-um*   *iuven-em*   *esse*
    I.NOM boy-MSC.SG.ACC young-MSC.SG.ACC be.INF
        sci-o.
        know-PRS.S1

13. 'You$_S$ know that the boy baked the bread.'
    (Tu) puer-um   *pan-em*   *cox-isse*
    you$_S$ boy-MSC.SG.ACC bread-MSC.SG.ACC cook.PST-INF.PST
        sci-s.
        know-PRES.S2

14. 'Is the boy running?'
    Curr-it   *puer?*
    run-PRS.S3 boy.MSC.SG.NOM

15. 'Are you$_S$ eating bread?'
    (Tu) ed-is   *pan-em?*
    you$_S$ eat-PRS.S2 bread-MSC.SG.ACC

16. 'Who is running?'
    Quis   *curr-it?*
    who.SG.NOM run-PRS.S3

17. 'Who baked the bread?'
    Quis   *pan-em*   *coxi-t?*
    who.SG.NOM bread-MSC.SG.ACC cook.PST-S3

18. What did the boy bake?
    Quid   *puer*   *coxi-t?*
    what.SG.ACC boy.MSC.SG.NOM cook.PST-SG3

3 Russian (Indo-European, Slavic; Russia)

Contributed by Olesya Ostapenko.
Note: Alternative word order variants are possible.

1. 'The boy is running.'
   mal'čik   *bež-it*
   boy.MSC.SG.NOM run-PRS.S3

2. 'I am running.'
   ja   *beg-u*
   I.NOM run-PRS.S1

3. 'You$_S$ are running.'
   ty   *bež-iš*
   you$_S$.NOM run-PRS.S2

4. 'The little boy is eating bread.'
   mal'en'k-ij   *mal'čik*   *es-t*
   little-MSC.SG.NOM boy.MSC.SG.NOM eat-PRS.S3
       xl'eb
       bread.MSC.SG.ACC

5. 'I am eating old bread.'
   ja   *e-m*   *ne-sv'ež-ij*   *xl'eb*
   I.NOM eat-PRS.S1 not-fresh-MSC.SG.ACC bread.MSC.SG.ACC

6. 'You$_S$ are eating fresh bread.'
   ty   *e-š*   *sv'ež-ij*   *xl'eb*
   you$_S$.NOM eat-PRS.S2 fresh-MSC.SG.ACC bread.MSC.SG.ACC

7. 'The bread is being eaten by the boy.'
   /awkward/
   x'leb   *est-sja*   *mal'čik-om*
   bread.MSC.SG.NOM eat-REFL.PRS.S3 boy-MSC.SG.INS

8. 'The fresh bread is being eaten by you$_S$.'
   s'ež-ij   *xl'eb*   *est-sja*
   fresh-MSC.SG.NOM bread.MSC.SG.NOM eat-REFL.PRS.S3
       toboj
       you$_S$.INS

9. 'The tall boy who baked the bread is running.'
   vysok-ij   *mal'čik*   *kotor-yj*
   tall-MSC.SG.NOM boy.MSC.SG.NOM who-MSC.SG.NOM
       isp'ok   *xl'eb*   *bež-it*
       baked.PST.S3 bread.MSC.SG.ACC run-PRS.S3

10. 'The boy is eating the old bread that you_s baked.'
    mal'čik   *es-t*   *ne-sv'ež-ij*
    boy.MSC.SG.NOM eat-PRS.S3 not-fresh-MSC.SG.ACC
       xl'eb   *kotor-yj*
       bread.MSC.SG.ACC which-MSC.SG.ACC
       ty   *isp'ok*
       you_s.NOM baked.PST.MSC

11. 'The bread which the boy baked is fresh.'
    x'leb   *kotor-yj*   *mal'čik*
    bread.MSC.SG.NOM which-MSC.SG.ACC boy.MSC.SG.NOM
       isp'ok   *sv'ež-ij*
       baked.PST.MSC.SG. fresh-MSC.SG.NOM

12. 'I know that the boy is young.'
    ja   *zna-ju*   *što mal'čik*   *mal'en'k'-ij*
    I.NOM know-PRS.S1 that boy.MSC.SG.NOM little-MSC.SG.NOM

13. 'You_s know that the boy baked the bread'
    ty   *zna-eš*   *što mal'čik*   *isp'ok*
    you_s.NOM know-S2 that boy.MSC.SG.NOM baked.PST.MSC
       xl'eb
       bread.MSC.SG.ACC

14. 'Is the boy running?'
    (a) *mal'čik*   *bež-it*
         boy.MSC.SG.NOM run-PRS.S3

    (b) *bež-it*   *li mal'čik*
         run-PRS.S3 Q boy.MSC.SG.NOM

15. 'Are you_s eating bread?'
    (a) *ty*   *eš*   *xl'eb?*
         you_s.NOM eat.PRS.S2 bread.MSC.SG.ACC

    (b) *eš*   *li ty*   *xl'eb?*
         eat-PRS.S2 Q you_s.NOM bread.MSC.SG.ACC

16. 'Who is running?'
    kto bež-it?
    who run-PRS.S3

17. 'Who baked the bread?'
    kto isp^jok   *xl'eb?*
    who baked.PST.MSC.SG bread.MSC.SG.ACC

18. 'What did the boy bake?'
    što   *isp'ok*   *mal'čik?*
    what.ACC baked.PST.MSC.SG boy.MSC.SG.NOM

4 Hungarian (Uralic, Finno-Ugric; Hungary)

Note: Alternative word order variants are possible; the versions given are those least dependent on context.

1. 'The boy is running.'
   A fiú   szalad.
   the boy.SG.NOM run.PRS.S3

2. 'I am running.'
   (Én)   szalad-ok.
   (I.NOM) run-PRS.S1

3. 'You₅ are running.'
   (Te)   szalad-sz.
   (you₅.NOM) run-PRS.S2

4. 'The young boy is eating bread.'
   A fiú   kenyer-et   esz-ik.
   the boy.SG.NOM bread.SG-ACC eat-PRS.S3.INDEFOBJ

5. 'I am eating old bread.'
   (Én)   régi kenyer-et   esz-em.
   (I.NOM) old bread.SG-ACC eat-PRS.S1.INDEFOBJ

6. 'You₅ are eating fresh bread.'
   (Te)   friss kenyer-et   esz-el.
   (you₅.NOM) fresh bread.SG-ACC eat-S2.PRS.INDEFOBJ

7. 'The bread is being eaten by the boy.'
   /no equivalent/

8. 'The fresh bread is being eaten by you.'
   /no equivalent/

9. 'The tall boy who baked the bread is running.'
   A magas fiú,   aki   a   kenyer-et
   the tall   boy.SG.NOM who.SG.NOM the bread.SG-ACC
   süt-ött-e,   szalad.
   bake-PST-S3.DEFOBJ run.S3.PRS

10. 'The boy is eating old bread that you₅ baked.'
    A fiú   esz-i   a   kenyer-et,
    the boy.SG.NOM eat-PRS.S3.DEFOBJ the bread-ACC
    amely-et   (te)   süt-tt-él.
    which-SG-ACC (you₅.NOM) bake-PST-SG2.INDEFOBJ

1 1. 'The bread which the boy baked is fresh.'
   A   kenyér,   amely-et   a   fiú
   the bread.SG.NOM which.SG ACC the boy.SG.NOM
       süt-ött,   friss.
       bake-PST.S3.INDEFOBJ fresh.SG.NOM

1 2. 'I know that the boy is young.'
   (Én)   tud-om,   hogy a   fiú   fiatal.
   (I.NOM) know-S1.DEFOBJ that the boy.SG.NOM young.SG.NOM

1 3. 'You_S know that the boy baked the bread.'
   (Te)   tud-od,   hogy a   fiú
   (you_S.NOM) know-S2.DEFOBJ that the boy.SG.NOM
       süt-ött-e   a   kenyer-et.
       bake-PST-S3.DEFOBJ the bread.SG-ACC

1 4. 'Is the boy running?'
   Szalad   a   fiú?
   run.PRES.S3 the boy.SG.NOM

1 5. 'Are you_S eating bread?'
   (Te)   kenyer-et   esz-el?
   (you_S.NOM) bread.SG-ACC eat-PRS.S2.INDEFOBJ

1 6. 'Who is running?'
   Ki   szalad?
   who.SG.NOM run.PRS.S3

1 7. 'Who baked the bread?'
   Ki   süt-ött-e   a   kenyer-et?
   who.SG.NOM bake-PST-S3.DEFOBJ the bread.SG-ACC

1 8. 'What did the boy bake?'
   Mi-t   süt-ött   a   fiú?
   what.SG-ACC bake-PST.S3.INDEFOBJ the boy.SG.NOM

5 Japanese (Altaic; Japan)

Translation by Motomi Kajitani.

Notes:

- Some sentences might sound somewhat unnatural for pragmatic reasons.
- The form *-te-i-ru* indicates progressivity when it is attached to a verb depicting an action that can be continued (such as 'eat'); but when it is attached to a verb that depicts an action that cannot be continued (such as 'get to know'), it indicates a state.
- The/sign in 9, 10 and 11 indicates alternative case markings.

1. 'The boy is running.'
   sono otoko-no-ko-wa   *hashit-te-i-ru*
   the man-GEN-child-TOP run-GER-PROG-PRS

2. 'I am running.'
   watashi-wa hashit-te-i-ru
   I-TOP   run-GER-PROG-PRS

3. 'You$_S$ are running.'
   anata-wa hashit-te-i-ru
   you$_S$-TOP run-GER-PROG-PRS

4. 'The young boy is eating bread.'
   (a) /preferred/
       sono waka-i   *otoko-no-ko-wa*   *pan-wo*
       the young-PRS man-GEN-child-TOP bread-ACC
       tabe-te-i-ru
       eat-GER-PROG-PRS

   (b) *pan-wo*   *sono waka-i*   *otoko-no-ko-wa*
       bread-ACC the young-PRS man-GEN-child-TOP
       tabe-te-i-ru
       eat-GER-PROG-PRS

5. 'I am eating old bread.'
   (a) /preferred/
       wahatshi-wa furu-i   *pan-wo*   *tabe-te-i-ru*
       I-TOP   old-PRS bread-ACC eat-GER-PROG-PRS

   (b) *furu-i*   *pan-wo*   *wahatshi-wa tabe-te-i-ru*
       old-PRS bread-ACC I-TOP   eat-GER-PROG-PRS

6. 'You$_S$ are eating fresh bread.'
   (a) /preferred/
       anata-wa yaki-tate-no   *pan-wo*
       you$_S$-TOP bake-freshly.done-GEN bread-ACC
       tabe-te-i-ru
       eat-GER-PROG-PRS

   (b) *yaki-tate-no*   *pan-wo*   *anata-wa*
       bake-freshly.done-GEN bread-ACC you$_S$-TOP
       tabe-te-i-ru
       eat-GER-PROG-PRS

7. 'The bread is being eaten by the boy.'
   (a) *sono pan-wa*   *sono otoko-no-ko-ni*
       the bread-TOP the man-GEN-child-DAT
       tabe-rare-te-i-ru
       eat-PASS-GER-PROG-PRS

(b) *sono otoko-no-ko-ni*   *sono pan-wa*
    the man-GEN-child-DAT the bread-TOP
    tabe-rare-te-i-ru
    eat-PASS-GER-PROG-PRS

8. 'The fresh bread is being eaten by you$_S$.'
   (a) *sono yaki-tate-no*   *pan-wa*   *anata-ni*
     the bake-freshly.done-GEN bread-TOP you$_S$-DAT
     tabe-rare-te-i-ru
     eat-PASS-GER-PROG-PRS

   (b) *anata-ni sono yaki-tate-no*   *pan-wa*
     you$_S$-DAT the bake-freshly.done-GEN bread-TOP
     tabe-rare-te-i-ru
     eat-PASS-GER-PROG-PRS

9. 'The tall boy who baked the bread is running.'
   sono pan-wo   *yai-ta*   *(sono) se-ga/no*   *taka-i*
   the bread-ACC bake-PST (the) height-NOM/GEN tall-PRS
   otoko-no-ko-wa   *hashit-te-i-ru*
   man-GEN-child-TOP run-GER-PROG-PRS

10. 'The boy is eating old bread that you$_S$ baked.'
   (a) *sono otoko-no-ko-wa*   *anata-ga/no*   *yai-ta*
     the man-GEN-child-TOP you$_S$-NOM/GEN bake-PST
     furu-i   *pan-wo*   *tabe-te-i-ru*
     old-PRS bread-ACC eat-GER-PROG-PRS

   (b) *anata-ga/no*   *yai-ta*   *furu- i* *pan-wo*   *sono*
     you$_S$-NOM/GEN bake-PST old-PRS bread-ACC the
     otoko-no-ko-wa   *tabe-te-i-ru*
     man-GEN-child-TOP eat-GER-PROG-PRS

11. 'The bread which the boy baked is fresh.'
   sono otoko-no-ko-ga/no   *yai-ta*   *sono pan-wa*
   the man-GEN-child-NOM/GEN bake-PST the bread-TOP
   yaki-tate-da
   bake-freshly.done-PRS

12. 'I know that the boy is young.'
   (a) /preferred/
     watashi-wa sono otoko-no-ko-wa   *waka-i*   *to*
     I-TOP   the man-GEN-child-TOP young-PRS that
     shit-te-i-ru
     get.to.know-GER-STATE-PRS

(b) *sono otoko-no-ko-wa*   *waka-i*
    the man-GEN-child-TOP young-PRS
       to   *watashi-wa shit-te-i-ru*
       that I-TOP   get.to.know-GER-STATE-PRS

13. 'You_S know that the boy baked the bread.'
    (a) /preferred/
        sono otoko-no-ko-ga   *sono pan-wo*   *yai-ta*   *to*
        the man-GEN-child-NOM the bread-ACC bake-PST that
        anata-wa shit-te-i-ru
        you_S-TOP know-GER-STATE-PRS

    (b) *anata-wa sono otoko-no-ko-ga*   *sono pan-wo*
        you_S-TOP the man-GEN-child-NOM the bread-ACC
        yai-ta to   *shit-te-i-ru*
        bake-PST that know-GER-STATE-PRS

14. 'Is the boy running?'
    sono otoko-no-ko-wa   *hashit-te-iru-ka*
    the man-GEN-child-TOP run-GER-PROG-PRS-Q

15. 'Are you_S eating bread?'
    (a) /preferred/
        anata-wa pan-wo   *tabe-te-i-ru-ka*
        you_S-TOP bread-ACC eat-GER-PROG-PRS-Q

    (b) *pan-wo*   *anata-wa tabe-te-i-ru-ka*
        bread-ACC you_S-TOP eat-GER-PROG-PRS-Q

16. 'Who is running?'
    dare-ga   *hashit-te-i-ru-ka*
    who-NOM run-GER-PROG-PRS-Q

17. 'Who baked the bread?'
    (a) /preferred/
        dare-ga   *sono pan-wo*   *yai-ta-ka*
        who-NOM the bread-ACC bread-PST-Q

    (b) *sono pan-wo*   *dare-ga*   *yai-ta-ka*
        the bread-ACC who-NOM bake-PST-Q

18. 'What did the boy bake?'
    (a) /preferred/
        sono otoko-no-ko-wa   *nani-wo yai-ta-ka*
        that man-GEN-child-TOP what-ACC bake-PST-Q

    (b) *nani-wo*   *sono otoko-no-ko-wa*   *yai-ta-ka*
        what-ACC the man-GEN-child-TOP bake-PST-Q

6 Chantyal (Tibeto-Burman, Himalayan; Nepal)

Contributed by Michael Noonan.

Notes:

- The sentences could be translated in a variety of ways depending on the context; only one version is given below for each.
- The Chantyal do not bake bread; the only bread-like item they make is a sort of pancake that is not baked.
- Regarding sentences 7, 8: Chantyal has no passive.
- Regarding sentence 12: Chantyal has no verb meaning 'know' that takes sentential complements. A factive particle is used in lieu of the verb 'know'.

1. 'The boy is running.'
   kyata dugri-gðy   mu
   boy   run-PROG be.NPST

2. 'I am running.'
   na dugri-gðy   mu
   I   run-PROG be.NPST

3. 'You$_S$ are running.'
   kɦii   dugri-gðy   mu
   you$_S$ run-PROG be.NPST

4. 'The young boy is eating panbread.'
   tðnnðri kyata-sð kɦiyaŋ   ca-m
   young boy-ERG panbread eat-NPST

5. 'I am eating old [i.e., cold] panbread.'
   na-sð basi kɦiyaŋ   ca-m
   I-ERG cold panbread eat-NPST

6. 'You$_S$ are eating fresh panbread.'
   kɦii-sð   char kɦiyaŋ   ca-m
   you$_S$-ERG new panbread eat-NPST

7. 'The panbread is being eaten by the boy.'
   (no equivalent)

8. 'The fresh panbread is being eaten by you$_S$.'
   (no equivalent)

9. 'The tall boy who made the panbread is running.'
   kfiyaŋ   kara-si-wa   ∂lko kyata dugri-g∂y   mu
   panbread put.in-ANT-NOM tall boy   run-PROG be.NPST

10. 'The boy is eating the old panbread that you_s made.'
    Kyata-s∂ kfii-s∂   kara-si-wa   basi kfiyaŋ   ca-m
    boy-ERG you_s-ERG put.in-ANT-NOM cold panbread eat-NPST

11. 'The panbread that the boy made is fresh.'
    kyata-s∂ kara-si-wa   kfiyaŋ   char mu
    boy-ERG put.in-ANT-NOM panbread new be-NPST

12. 'I know that the boy is young.'
    kyata   t∂nn∂ni mu   t∂
    boy-ERG young   be.NPST fact

13. 'You_s know that the boy made the panbread.'
    (literally: 'Did the boy make the panbread? You know this.')
    kyata-s∂ kfiyaŋ   kar-la?   kfii-ra   thaa   mu
    boy-ERG panbread put.in-PERF.Q you_s-DAT knowledge be.NPST

14. 'Is the boy running?'
    kyata dugri-g∂y   mu-ẽ
    boy   run-PROG be.NPST-Q

15. 'Are you_s eating panbread?'
    kfii-s∂   kfiyaŋ   ca-m-ẽ
    you_s-ERG panbread eat-NPST-Q

16. 'Who is running?'
    su   dugri-g∂y   mu-ẽ
    who run-PROG be.NPST-Q

17. 'Who made the panbread?'
    su-s∂   kfiyaŋ   kar-la
    who-ERG panbread put.in-PERF.Q

18. 'What did the boy make?'
    (literally: 'What did the boy put in?')
    kyata-s∂ ta   kar-la
    boy-ERG what put.in-PERF.Q

Glossary

For definitions of additional grammatical terminology, see for example,

- James R. Hurford. 1994. *Grammar. A Student's Guide.* Cambridge: Cambridge University Press
- Robert Lawrence Trask. 1994. *A Dictionary of Grammatical Terms in Linguistics.* 1993. London: Routledge.

ablative
see case

absolutive
see case

accusative
see case

active sentence
a sentence where the more active semantic participant is expressed as the subject and the less active one is expressed as a direct object; such as in *The man fixed the computer.* In passive sentences, the less active participant is the subject, as in *The computer was fixed by the man*

adjacency
the 'next to' relation; for example, *The garage is next to the house*

adjunct
a phrase that is present in a sentence even though it is not obligatorily selected by the verb; for example, *The hen laid two eggs **last night***

adposition
a cover term for prepositions (e.g. English *about*) and postpositions (e.g. English *ago*)

agent
see semantic participant role

agreement

a pattern of word-form selection: one word (the 'target') has an affix or clitic whose feature value co-varies with that of another word in the sentence ('the controller'); for example, the English demonstrative agrees with the noun in number (*this boy, these boys*)

alignment

the correspondence relation between semantic participant roles and grammatical relations; for example, active and passive sentences represent different alignment patterns

anaphoric pronoun

a pronoun that takes its referent from another noun phrase in the sentence or discourse, called the antecedent; for example, in *Jill said **she** was tired*, *she* is an anaphoric pronoun and *Jill* is its antecedent

antecedent

see anaphoric pronoun

argument

a noun phrase whose referent is semantically associated with a predicate; for example, ***The bird** ate **the spider***

bimorphemic

consisting of two morphemes; for example, *happi-ly*

bridge statement

it establishes the link between an explanatory principle and a fact that the principle explains; for example, *The Earth is a planet* is a bridge statement between *All planets move* and *The Earth moves*

case

a formal marker (affix or adposition or a special form of the word stem) that indicates the role of a noun phrase in a sentence.

- Nominative: the case of the subject (e.g. ***He** left*)
- Accusative: the case of the direct object (e.g. *Jill left **him***)
- Genitive: the case of the possessor (e.g. ***John's** brother*)
- Dative: the case of the indirect object (e.g. *John gave a book **to him***)
- Ablative: the case indicating origin (for example, *I took the book **from him***)
- Oblique: any case other than the nominative
- Ergative: the unique case of the active participant in two-argument clauses
- Absolutive: the shared case of the patient of two-argument clauses and of the intransitive subject
- Vocative: the case of the name of a person addressed

category (class, type)
a set of items grouped together because of some shared properties (e.g. birds)

chomeur
used in Relational Grammar to label a term that has been demoted from subject or object, as the *by*-phrase in *The building was destroyed by the wind*

clause-mate
two constituents are clause-mates if they occur in the same clause; in the sentence *Jill told Sue that Tom was promoted, Jill* and *Sue* are clause-mates but *Jill* and *Tom* are not

cleft sentence
an English sentence structure where a focused constituent stands in the front of the sentence preceded by *it is*; for example, *It is spring that I like*

clitic
a stressless word that forms a phonological unit with a stressed word: *He's tall*

complement
non-subject noun phrases that are selected by a verb, adjective or noun; such as *Jill* in *I envy Jill,* or in *I am envious of Jill*

complementizer
a conjunction introducing a subordinate clause, such as *that* in *He said that he was going to be late*

compositional
a whole is compositional if its characteristics are the sum of the characteristics of its parts and of the relations of the parts; for example, the number 15 is compositional relative to its parts 10 and 5 and the additive relation between them

configuration
the hierarchical and linear position of a constituent in a tree structure; such as that English subjects are immediately dominated by a sentence node and precede the verb

conjuncts
terms of a co-ordinate structure; for example, the the phrase *John and Jill* consists of two conjuncts

constituent
part of a whole; for example, constituents of *The sun rose* are the phrases *the sun* and *rose*

constituent structure
see partonomy

controller
see agreement

co-occur
occur together; for example, nouns and articles co-occur

co-reference
two noun phrases having the same referent, such as an anaphoric pronoun
and its antecedent

dative
see case

demonstrative
see determiner

dependency
a syntagmatic relationship between two things where one (the 'Head') can
stand without the other (the 'Dependent'); for example, the verb is a Head
and its adverb is the Dependent

dependent
see dependency

determiner
cover term for article (*the, a(n)*) and demonstrative (*this, that*); *that* is termed
distal demonstrative

discontinuity
a linear pattern where two things that belong together are separated;
for example, a cup on the table and its saucer left in the kitchen

discourse
a set of connected sentences, such as a lecture, a poem or a conversation

distal
see determiner; *that* is a distal determiner

distribution
the description of the various locations where members of a class of objects
can be found; for example, the distribution of lions in Africa

ditransitive
a verb that takes two objects; for example, *give* in *I gave the puppy milk*

ellipis
a construction where a constituent is understood but not expressed; for example, *Joe sat down and ___ fell asleep*

ergative
see case

explanandum
a fact to be explained; for example, that things fall

explanans
a principle that explains a fact; for example, gravity explains that things fall

finite verb
a verb that can be a predicate of a main clause; for example, *He is working*

gender
a grammatical class of nominals – it may or may not be based on sexual gender; for example, Spanish *manzana* 'apple' is feminine gender

genitive
see case

governee
see government

government
a pattern of word-form selection: a word, such as a verb or an adjective (the 'governor'), calls for a particular case of a nominal (the 'governee'); for example, *love* requires the accusative – *love her*

governor
see government

grammatical functions
the morphosyntactic classes of noun phrases in a sentence from the point of view of how they relate to the predicate; for example, subject, direct object, indirect object (also called grammatical relations)

iconic
a form is iconic if it depicts the referent that it stands for – the traffic light for 'walk' showing the image of walking figure is iconic but a plain green light is not

immediate constituent
a highest-level part of a whole, with no intermediate parts between the two; for example, the subject noun phrase is an immediate constituent of the sentence but an article is not

immediate precedence
the relationship of one item coming directly before another; for example, *the* immediately precedes *plum* in *the plum*

implicans
see implication

implication
one item (the 'implicans') predicting the presence of another (the 'implicatum'); for example, rain implies wet ground

implicatum
see implication

interlocutor
participant of a conversation or of an exchange of letters

intransitive
a verb that takes no object; for example, *exist*

lexeme
a meaningful unit of form that is listed in the lexicon because it cannot be further broken down into meaningful parts that would account for the meaning of the whole; it may be a morpheme or a word or an idiomatic expression

lexicon
dictionary

linearization
placing items in order in a one-dimensional arrangement; for example, arranging people in a single line

linear order
see linearization

main clause
a clause that can form a sentence by itself; for example, ***Jill likes the house** that I am going to buy*

metalanguage
the terminology used for talking about language

markedness
the asymmetric relationship between two items forming an opposition, where one member (the 'unmarked') is simpler and more frequent than the other (the 'marked'); for example, of active and passive sentences, the active is unmarked and the passive is marked in English

marker
an affix, clitic or word indicating a grammatical category such as tense or case; for example, *baked*

modality
cover term for 'must', 'may' or 'must/may not'

monomorphemic
consisting of one morpheme; for example, *book*

negative polarity item
words like *anyone* or *anywhere* that can attract the negative element from the verb; for example, *I did not see anyone* and *I saw no one*

nominal
cover term for nouns and pronouns

nominative
see case

nomological explanation
an explanation that predicts something with absolute certainty; for example, gravity predicts the falling of objects

oblique case
see case

ontogenesis
changes within the life of an individual; for example, the development of a child

paradigmatic relation
the relationship among items in an inventory; for example, among the consonants of English

parameter
dimension, or scale of variation; for example, animals differ along the parameter of whether they eat plants or meat

partonomy (same as mereonomy, mereology, meronomy, constituent structure)
whole–part relations; for example, a corporation consists of departments and the departments consist of subsections

passive
see active

passivize
the object of an active sentence is said to be passivized when the sentence is converted into a passive; for example, when the sentence *Joe hired Bill* is made into a passive (*Bill was hired by Joe*), *Bill* has been passivized

patient
see semantic participant role

permissive explanation
an explanation that says something is possible (but not necessary or even probable); for example, meteorological principles of temperate climates allow for rain in September

phylogenesis
evolutionary change; for example, the evolution of apes

phrasal verb
a verb plus particle construction; for example, *call up*

phrase
a set of words that form a grammatical unit; for example, **The blue bird** *is nearby*

polymorphemic
consisting of more than one morpheme; for example, *un-pleasant-ness*

possessor
designates an entity that owns or is otherwise dominant over another; for example, **the book's** *cover*

possessum
designates an entity that is owned or is otherwise dominated by another; for example, *the book's* **cover**

precedence
the relationship of one item coming before another, whether directly or indirectly; for example, *the* precedes both *blue* and *plum* in *the blue plum*

predicate
part of the sentence that describes the action, event or state that the sentence is about; for example, *The plane **arrived late***

primary language
a language native to a substantial speech community (i.e. English, Ojibwe); as opposed to secondary languages such as pathological speech or the interlanguage of second-language learners

probabilistic explanation
an explanation that says something is likely (but not necessary); for example, meteorological principles of temperate climates render snow likely in December

proform
a word that provides brief reference to another constituent in the sentence or discourse; such as anaphoric pronouns

proper inclusion
a set is properly included in another set if the latter includes all the former plus some additional members; for example, the set of mixed gender students properly includes the set of male students

referent
a person or thing that a word or phrase designates; for example, the referents of *Jill* and *herself* are the same in *Jill hurt herself*

reflexivization
the process of using a reflexive pronoun for a full noun phrase to refer to somebody or something; for example, *Sue hurt herself* is an instance of reflexivization

relativize
the noun phrase in a relative clause that is co-referential with the head of the clause is said to be relativized (often replaced by a relative pronoun); for example, in *the house that I want to build*, the object of the relative clause ('house') has been relativized

resumptive pronoun
an anaphoric pronoun used in relative clauses of some languages in reference to the head of the clause; in '*the man that I never want to see **him** again*'

schema
a statement or name formulated in terms of symbols; for example, H_2O for water

selection
a decision regarding what items should be part of a structure; for example, selecting tiles for covering the walls of a bathroom

semantic participant role (also called thematic role)
the role that noun phrase referents play in an action or happening; for example, in *Jonas gave the horse to his cousin,* Jonas is an Agent, the horse is a Patient and his cousin is a Recipient

standard of comparison
the item that something is compared with; for example, *John is taller than **Bill***

subordinate
an item dominated by another, 'superordinate' item; for example, the boss is superordinate to employees, who are subordinates

superordinate
see subordinate

symbolic correspondence
the relationship between the form and meaning of a symbol, such as of a hand gesture or a word

syntagmatic relation
the relationship among co-occurring items; for example, between *s* and *p* in *span*

target
see agreement

taxonomy (classification, categorization, typology)
placing items in groups based on some shared characteristics; for example, the taxonomy of schools includes primary, middle and high schools

temporal relation
the relation between items on the timescale; see precedence and immediate precedence

token
individual members of a class; for example, this computer is a token of the class of computers

topic
a known item of which something is said; for example, *My **brother**, he is in Chicago*

transitive
a verb that takes an object; for example, *resemble*

type
see category

univerbation
two or more words merging into one in historical change; for example, *alright*

utterance
a cover term for a sentence or a sequence of sentences forming a discourse

valence
the number of obligatory arguments a verb or other word takes; for example, *give* has three valences (*Jill gave the bone to her dog*)

well-formedness
the property of being constructed according to the given set of rules; for example, *the world* is well-formed, **world the* is ill-formed

References

Aikhenvald, Alexandra Y., R.M.W. Dixon and Masayuki Onishi (eds). 2001. *Non-canonical Marking of Subjects and Objects*. Amsterdam and Philadelphia: John Benjamins.

Aissen, Judith. 1991. 'Relational Grammar'. In F.G. Droste and J.E. Joseph (eds), 63–102.

Aissen, Judith. 2003. 'Differential object marking: iconicity vs. economy'. *Natural Language and Linguistic Theory* 21: 435–83.

Allan, Keith. 2001. *Natural Language Semantics*. Oxford and Malden, MA: Blackwell.

Anderson, Stephen R. and Sandra Chung. 1977. 'Grammatical relations and clause structure in verb-initial languages'. In P. Cole and J.M. Sadock (eds), 1–25.

Atkinson, Martin. 1996. 'Generative grammar: the Minimalist Program'. In K. Brown and J. Miller (eds), 137–47.

Baltin, Mark. 1987. 'Degree complements'. In G.J. Huck and A. Ojeda (eds), 11–26.

Baltin, Mark and Christ Collins (eds). 2001. *The Handbook of Contemporary Syntactic Theory*. Malden, MA: Blackwell.

Barlow, Michael and Suzanne Kemmer (eds). 2000. *Usage-based Models of Language*. Stanford, CA: CSLI.

Bartsch, Renate and Theo Vennemann. 1972. *Semantic Structures. A Study in the Relation between Semantics and Syntax*. Frankfurt am Main: Athenäum.

Blake, Barry J. 1990. *Relational Grammar*. (Linguistic Theory Guides) London: Routledge.

Borsley, Robert. 1999. *Syntactic Theory. A Unified Approach*. 2nd edn. London and New York: Arnold.

Braidi, Susan M. 1999. *The Acquisition of Second-language Syntax*. London: Arnold.

Bresnan, Joan. 2001. *Lexical-functional Syntax*. Oxford and Malden, MA: Blackwell.

Brown, Cecil H. 1990. 'A survey of category types in natural language'. In S.L. Tsohatzidis (ed.), *Meanings and Prototypes. Studies in Linguistic Categorization*. London and New York: Routledge, 17–47.

Brown, Keith and Jim Miller (eds). 1996. *Concise Encyclopedia of Syntactic Theories*. Oxford and New York: Pergamon.

Bunt, Harry and Arthur van Horck (eds). 1996. *Discontinuous Constituency*. Berlin: Mouton de Gruyter.

Cann, R. 1996. 'X-bar syntax'. In K. Brown and J. Miller, 379–85.

Capra, Fritjof. 1996. *The Web of Life*. New York and London: Doubleday.

Chapin, Paul. 1978. 'Easter Island: a characteristic VSO language'. In W.P. Lehmann (ed.), 139–68.

Chomsky, Noam. 1957. *Syntactic Structures*. The Hague: Mouton.

Chomsky, Noam. 1965. *Aspects of the Theory of Syntax*. Cambridge, MA: The MIT Press.

Chomsky, Noam. 1984. *Lectures in Government and Binding*. Dordrecht: Foris.

Chomsky, Noam. 1995. *The Minimalist Program*. Cambridge, MA and London: The MIT Press.

Christie, Daniel J., Richard V. Wagner and Deborah Du Nann Winter. 2001. *Peace, Conflict, and Violence. Peace Psychology for the 21st Century*. Upper Saddle River, NJ: Prentice Hall.

Cole, Peter and Jerrold M. Sadock (eds). 1977. *Grammatical Relations*. (Syntax and Semantics, Volume 8). New York: Academic Press.

Comrie, Bernard. 1978. 'Ergativity'. In W.P. Lehmann (ed.), 329–94.

Comrie, Bernard. 1982. 'Grammatical relations in Huichol'. In Paul J. Hopper and Sandra A. Thompson (eds). *Studies in Transitivity*. (Syntax and Semantics 15) New York: Academic Press, 95–115.

Comrie, Bernard. 1989. *Language Universals and Linguistic Typology*. 2nd edn. Chicago: The University of Chicago Press.

Coombs, Clude H. and George S. Avrunin. 1988. *The Structure of Conflict*. Hillside, NJ: Erlbaum.

Corbett, Greville G. 1999. 'Introduction'. *Folia Linguistica* (Special issue on agreement) 33, 2: 103–7.

Corbett, Greville G., Norman M. Fraser and Scott McGlashan (eds). 1993. *Heads in Grammatical Theory*. Cambridge: Cambridge University Press.

Croft, William. 2001. *Radical Construction Grammar. Syntactic Theory in Typological Perspective*. Oxford and New York: Oxford University Press.

Culicover, Peter W. 1997. *Principles and Parameters. An Introduction to Syntactic Theory*. Oxford: Oxford University Press.

Dehé, Nicole, Rau Jackendoff, Andrew McIntyre and Silke Urban (eds). 2002. *Verb-Particle Explorations*. Berlin and New York: Mouton de Gruyter.

Deutsch, Morton and Peter T. Coleman (eds). 2000. *The Handbook of Conflict Resolution. Theory and Practice*. San Francisco: Jossey-Bass.

de Waal, Frans. 2001. *The Ape and the Sushi Master. Cultural Reflections by a Primatologist*. New York: Basic Books.

Dik, Simon. 1968. *Coordination. Its Implications for the Theory of General Linguistics*. Amsterdam: North-Holland.

Dik, Simon. 1978. *Functional Grammar*. Amsterdam: North Holland.

Dik, Simon C. 1997. *The Theory of Functional Grammar. Part 1. The Structure of the Clause. Part 2: Complex and Derived Constructions*. Edited by Kees Hengeveld. 2nd, rev. edn. Berlin: Mouton de Gruyter.

Dixon, R.M.W. 1994. *Ergativity*. Cambridge: Cambridge University Press.

Dixon, R.M.W. 1997. *The Rise and Fall of Languages.* Cambridge: Cambridge University Press.

Droste, Flip G. and John E. Joseph (eds). 1991. *Linguistic Theory and Grammatical Description.* Amsterdam and Philadelphia: John Benjamins.

Dryer, Matthew. 1986. 'Primary objects, secondary objects, and antidative'. *Language* 62, 4: 808–45.

Dryer, Matthew. 1992. 'The Greenbergian word order correlations'. *Language* 68: 81–138.

Dryer, Matthew. 2005. 'What is basic linguistic theory?' http://wings.buffalo.edu/linguistics/people/faculty/dryer/dryer/blt

Du Feu, Veronica. 1996. *Rapanui.* London: Routledge.

Eckman, Fred R. 1977. 'Markedness and the contrastive analysis hypothesis.' *Language Learning* 27, 2: 315–30.

Edmondson, Jerold A. and Donald A. Burquest. 1992. *A Survey of Linguistic Theories.* Dallas, TX: Summer Institute of Linguistics.

Einstein, Albert. 1950. *The Evolution of Physics. The Growth of Ideas from Early Concepts of Relativity and Quanta.* New York: Simon and Schuster.

Erteschik-Shir, Nomi. 1979. 'Discourse constraints on dative movement'. In Talmy Givón (ed.), *Syntax and Semantics,* Volume 12. New York: Academic Press, 441–67.

Festinger, Leon. 1957. *A Theory of Cognitive Dissonance.* Stanford, CA: Stanford University Press.

Francis, Elaine J. and Laura A. Michaelis (eds). 2003. *Mismatch. Form-function Incongruity and the Architecture of Grammar.* Stanford, CA: Center for the Study of Language and Information.

Freidin, R. 1996. 'Generative grammar: principles and parameters'. In K. Brown and J. Miller (eds), 119–37.

Gass, Susan M. 1979. 'Language transfer and universal grammatical relations'. *Language Learning* 29: 327–44.

Givón, Talmy. 1979. *On Understanding Grammar.* New York and San Francisco: Academic Press.

Givón, Talmy. 1981. 'On the development of the numeral "one" as an indefinite marker'. *Folia Linguistica Historica* II, 1: 35–53.

Givón, Talmy. 1984a. *Syntax. A Functional-typological Introduction,* Volume I. Amsterdam and Philadelphia: John Benjamins.

Givón, Talmy. 1984b. 'Direct object and dative shifting: semantic and pragmatic case'. In Frans Plank (ed.), *Objects. Toward a Typology of Grammatical Relations.* London and Orlando: Academic Press, 151–82.

Givón, Talmy. 1990. *Syntax. A Functional-typological Introduction,* Volume II. Amsterdam and Philadelphia: John Benjamins.

Goldberg, Adele E. 1995. *Constructions. A Construction Grammar Approach to Argument Structure.* Chicago and London: The University of Chicago Press.

Goodman, Nelson. 1978. *Ways of Worldmaking.* Indianapolis, IN: Hackett.

Green, Georgia M. 1974. *Semantic and Syntactic Regularity.* Bloomington, IN: Indiana University Press.

Gregory, Bruce. 1988. *Inventing Reality. Physics as Language*. New York: John Wiley.

Gundel, Jeanette K., Kathleen Houlihan and Gerald Sanders. 1988. 'On the function of marked and unmarked terms'. In Hammond, E.A. Moravcsik and J.R. Wirth (eds), 285–301.

Haegeman, Liliane. 1994. *Introduction to Government and Binding Theory*. 2nd edn. Oxford and Cambridge: Blackwell.

Haiman, John. 1985a. *Natural Syntax. Iconicity and Erosion*. Cambridge: Cambridge University Press.

Haiman, John (ed.). 1985b. *Iconicity in Syntax*. Proceedings of a Symposium on Iconicity of Syntax, Stanford, 24–26 June 1983. Amsterdam and Philadelphia: John Benjamins.

Hammond, Michael, Edith A. Moravcsik and Jessica R. Wirth (eds). 1988. *Studies in Syntactic Typology*. Amsterdam and Philadelphia: John Benjamins.

Harrison, Steven: *Getting to Where You Are. The Life of Meditation*. 1999. New York: Jeremy P. Tarcher/Putnam.

Haspelmath, Martin. 1999. 'Long distance agreement in Godoberi'. *Folia Linguistica* XXXIII/2: 131–51.

Hawkins, John A. 1994. *A Performance Theory of Order and Constituency*. Cambridge: Cambridge University Press.

Hawkins, John A. 1999. 'Processing complexity and filler-gap dependencies across grammars'. *Language* 75, 2: 244–85.

Heine, Bernd, Ulrike Claudi and Friederike Hünnemeyer. 1991. *Grammaticalization: a Conceptual Framework*. Chicago: The University of Chicago Press.

Heine, Bernd and Tania Kuteva. 2002. *World Lexicon of Grammaticalization*. Cambridge: Cambridge University Press.

Hopper, Paul and Elisabeth C. Traugott. 1993. *Grammaticalization*. Cambridge: Cambridge University Press.

Hornstein, Norbert. 1999. 'Movement and control'. *Linguistic Inquiry* 30, 1: 69–96.

Horrocks, Geoffrey. 1987. *Generative Grammar*. London and New York: Longman.

Huck, Geoffrey J. and Almerindo E. Ojeda (eds). 1987. *Discontinuous Constituency*. (Syntax and Semantics, 20). Orlando, FL: Academic Press.

Hudson, Richard. 1981. 'Some issues on which linguists can agree'. *Journal of Linguistics* 17: 179–392.

Hudson, Richard. 1984. *Word Grammar*. Oxford: Basil Blackwell.

Hudson, Richard A. 1990. *English Word Grammar*. Oxford: Blackwell.

Hudson, Richard A. 1996. 'Word grammar'. In K. Brown and J. Miller (eds), 368–72.

Hurford, James. 2003. 'The interaction between numerals and nouns'. In Frans Plank (ed.), *Noun Phrase Structure in the Languages of Europe*. Berlin and New York: Mouton de Gruyter, 561–620.

Hyltenstam, Kenneth. 1984. 'The use of typological markedness conditions as predictors in second language acquisition: the case of pronominal copies in relative clauses'. In Roger Anderson (ed.), *Second Languages. A Crosslinguistic Perspective.* Rowley, MA: Newbury, 39–57.

Ioup, Georgette and Anna Kruse. 1977. 'Interference versus structural complexity as a predictor of second language relative clause acquisition'. Proceedings of the Los Angeles Second Language Research Forum. Los Angeles, CA, 48–60.

Jackendoff, Ray. 2002. *Foundations of Language. Brain, Meaning, Grammar, Evolution.* Oxford and New York: Oxford University Press.

Jackson, Hildur (ed.). 1999. *Creating Harmony. Conflict Resolution in Community.* Denmark: Gaia Trust.

Jacobs, Roderick A. and Peter S. Rosenbaum. 1968. *English Transformational Grammar.* Waltham, MA: Blaisdell.

Jacobson, P. 1996. 'Constituent structure'. In K. Brown and J. Miller, 54–67.

Jacobson, Pauline. 1987. 'Phrase structure, grammatical relations, and discontinuous constituents'. In G.J. Huck and A.E. Ojeda (eds), 27–69.

Janssen, Theo M.V. 1997. 'Compositionality'. In Johan van Benthem and Alice ter Meulen (eds), *Handbook of Logic and Language.* Amsterdam: Elsevier, 417–73.

Jeong, Ho-Won (ed.). 1999. *Conflict Resolution: Dynamics, Process and Structure.* Aldershot, Brookfield, Singapore and Sidney: Ashgate.

Johannessen, Janne Bondi. 1998. *Coordination.* New York and Oxford: Oxford University Press.

Johnson, David. 1977. 'On relational constraints on grammar'. In P. Cole and J.M. Sadock (eds), 151–78.

Jones, Linda K. 1996. 'Tagmemics'. In K. Brown and J. Miller (eds), 326–31.

Kager, René. 1999. *Optimality Theory.* (Cambridge Textbooks in Linguistics). Cambridge: Cambridge University Press.

Keenan, Edward and Bernard Comrie. 1977. 'Noun phrase accessibility and universal grammar'. *Linguistic Inquiry* 8, 1: 63–99.

Keenan, Edward and S. Hawkins. 1987. 'The psychological validity of the accessibility hierarchy'. In Edward L. Keenan (ed.), *Universal Grammar: Fifteen Essays.* London: Croom Helm, 60–85.

Kertész, András. 2004a. *Cognitive Semantics and Scientific Knowledge. Case Studies in the Cognitive Science of Science.* Amsterdam and Philadelphia: John Benjamins.

Kertész, András. 2004b. *Philosophie der Linguistik. Studien zur naturalisierten Wissenschaftstheorie.* Tübingen: Gunter Narr.

Kiss, Katalin É. 1987. *Configurationality in Hungarian.* Budapest: Akadémiai Kiadó.

Langacker, Ronald W. 1972. *Fundamentals of Linguistic Analysis.* New York: Harcourt Brace Jovanovich.

Langacker, Ronald W. 1977. 'Syntactic reanalysis'. In Charles N. Li (ed.), *Mechanisms of Linguistic Change.* Austin, TX: University of Texas Press, 59–139.

Langacker, Ronald W. 1991. 'Cognitive grammar'. In F.G. Droste and J.E. Joseph (eds), 275–306.

Langacker, Ronald W. 1995a. 'Raising and transparency'. *Language* 71, 1: 1–62.

Langacker, Ronald W. 1995b. 'Conceptual grouping and constituency in cognitive grammar'. In Linguistic Society of Korea (ed.) *Linguistics in the Morning Calm* 3: 149–72. Seoul: Hanshin.

Langacker, Ronald W. 1996. 'Cognitive Grammar'. In K. Brown and J. Miller (eds), 51–4.

Langacker, Ronald W. 1997. 'Constituency, dependency, and conceptual grouping'. *Cognitive Linguistics* 8, 1: 1–32.

Langacker, Ronald W. 1999. *Grammar and Conceptualization*. Berlin and New York: Mouton de Gruyter.

Larson, Richard. 1988. 'On the double object construction'. *Linguistic Inquiry* 19, 3: 335–91.

Laudan, Larry. 1977. *Progress and Its Problems: Toward a Theory of Scientific Growth*. Berkeley, CA: University of California Press.

Lederer, Richard. 1993. *More Anguished English*. New York: Dell.

Lehmann, Christian. 1995. *Thoughts on Grammaticalization*. München and Newcastle: LINCOM EUROPA.

Lehmann, Winfred P. (ed.). 1978. *Syntactic Typology. Studies in the Phenomenology of Language*. Austin, TX: University of Texas Press.

Li, Charles N. (ed.). 1976. *Subject and Topic*. New York: Academic Press.

Li, Charles and Sandra A. Thompson. 1976. 'Subject and topic: a new typology of language'. In Li (ed.), 491–518.

Mahmoudian, Mortéza. 1993. *Modern Theories of Language. The Empirical Challenge*. Durham and London: The Duke University Press.

Marantz, Alec. 1995. 'The Minimalist Program'. In G. Webelhuth (ed.), 349–82.

Matthews, Peter H. 1981. *Syntax*. Cambridge: Cambridge University Press.

Matthews, Stephen and Virginia Yip. 2003. 'Relative clauses in early bilingual development: transfer and universals'. In Anna Giacalone Ramat (ed.), *Typology and Second Language Acquisition*. Berlin: Mouton de Gruyter, 39–81.

Mayer, Bernard. 2000. *The Dynamics of Conflict Resolution. A Practitioner's Guide*. San Francisco: Josey Bass.

McCarthy, John J. 2002. *A Thematic Guide to Optimality Theory*. Cambridge: Cambridge University Press.

McCawley, James D. 1982a. *Thirty-million Theories of Grammar*. Chicago: University of Chicago Press.

McCawley, James. 1982b. 'Parentheticals and discontinuous constituent structure'. *Linguistic Inquiry*, 13, 1: 91–106.

Meheus, Joke (ed.). 2002. *Inconsistency in Science*. Dordrecht: Kluwer.

Mel'čuk, Igor A. 1988. *Dependency Syntax: Theory and Practice*. Albany, NY: State University of New York Press.

Merrifield, William R. *et al.* 1987. *Laboratory Manual for Morphology and Syntax.* Dallas, TX: Summer Institute of Linguistics.

Moravcsik, Edith. 1993. 'Why is syntax complicated?' In Mushira Eid and Gregory K. Iverson (eds), *Principles and Prediction. The Analysis of Natural Language. Papers in Honor of Gerald Sanders.* Amsterdam and Philadelphia: John Benjamins, 73–92.

Moravcsik, Edith. 2006. *An Introduction to Syntax. Fundamentals of Syntactic Analysis.* London and Harrisburg, PA: Continuum.

Moravcsik, Edith A. and Jessica R. Wirth (eds). 1980. *Current Approaches to Syntax.* (Syntax and Semantics, 13) New York and London: Academic Press.

Newmeyer, Frederick J. 1986. *Linguistic Theory in America.* 2nd edn. New York: Academic Press.

Newmeyer, Frederick J. 1998. *Language Form and Language Function.* Cambridge, MA: The MIT Press.

Pais, Abraham. 1994. *Einstein Lived Here.* Oxford: The Clarendon Press.

Perez-Leroux, Ana Teresa. 1995. 'Resumptives in the acquisition of relative clauses'. *Language Acquisition* 4: 105–38.

Perlmutter, David and Paul Postal. 1983. 'Toward a universal characterization of passivization'. In David M. Perlmutter (ed.), *Studies in Relational Grammar*, Volume I. Chicago: The University of Chicago Press, 3–29.

Pesetsky, David. 1995. *Zero Syntax. Experiencers and Cascades.* Cambridge and London: The MIT Press.

Plank, Frans (ed.). 1979. *Ergativity. Towards a Theory of Grammatical Relations.* London: Academic Press.

Plank, Frans. 1995. 'Ergativity'. In Joachim Jacobs, Arnim von Stechow, Wolfgang Sternefeld and Theo Vennemann (eds), *Syntax. An International Handbook of Contemporary Research*, Volume 2. Berlin: Walter de Gruyter, 1184–99.

Polinsky, Maria. 2003. 'Non-canonical agreement is canonical'. *Transactions of the Philological Society* 101, 2: 279–312.

Polinsky, Maria and Bernard Comrie. 1999. 'Agreement in Tsez'. *Folia Linguistica* XXXIII, 2: 109–30.

Popper, Karl R. 1962. 'What is dialectic?' In Karl R. Popper, *Conjectures and Refutations. The Growth of Scientific Knowledge.* New York and London: Basic Books, 312–35.

Popper, Karl R. 1965. *The Logic of Scientific Discovery.* New York: Harper & Row.

Postal, Paul. 1964. 'Underlying and superficial linguistic structure'. *Harvard Educational Review*, 34: 246–66.

Postal, Paul. 1974. *On Raising. One Rule of English and Its Theoretical Implications.* Cambridge, MA: The MIT Press.

Radford, Andrew. 1981. *Transformational Syntax. A Student's Guide to Chomsky's Extended Standard Theory.* Cambridge: Cambridge University Press.

Radford, Andrew. 1988. *Transformational Grammar. A First Course.* Cambridge: Cambridge University Press.

Radford, Andrew. 1997a. *Syntactic Theory and the Structure of English: A Minimalist Introduction.* Cambridge: Cambridge University Press.

Radford, Andrew. 1997b. *Syntax: A Minimalist Introduction.* Cambridge: Cambridge University Press.

Rescher, Nicholas. 1987. 'How serious a fallacy is inconsistency?' *Argumentation* 1: 303–15.

Rijkhoff, Jan. 2002. *The Noun Phrase.* Oxford: Oxford University Press.

Roberts, Ian. 2000. 'Current developments in generative grammar'. *The Elsevier Science Linguistics Newsletter* Winter, 5.

Sadler, Louise. 1996. 'New developments in lexical functional grammar'. In K. Brown and J. Miller (eds), 259–65.

Sadock, Jerrold M. 1987. 'Discontinuity in autolexical and autosemantic syntax'. In G. Huck and A.E. Ojeda (eds), 283–301.

Sadock, Jerrold M. 1991. *Autolexical Grammar. A Theory of Parallel Grammatical Representations.* (Studies in Contemporary Linguistics) Chicago and London: Chicago University Press.

Sag, Ivan A. 1987. 'Grammatical hierarchy and linear precedence'. In G. Huck and A.E. Ojeda (eds), 303–40.

Sag, Ivan A., Thomas Wasow and Emily M. Bender. 2003. *Syntactic Theory. A Formal Introduction.* 2nd edn. Stanford, CA: Center for the Study of Language and Information.

Sanders, Gerald A. 1972. *Equational Grammar.* The Hague: Mouton.

Schachter, Paul. 1977. 'Constraints on coordination'. *Language* 53, 1: 86–103.

Schachter, Paul and Fe T. Otanes. 1972. *Tagalog Reference Grammar.* Berkeley, CA: University of California Press.

Schachter, Stanley and Michael Gazzaniga (eds). 1989. *Extending Psychological Frontiers. Selected Works by Leon Festinger.* New York: Russell Sage.

Sells, Peter. 1985. *Lectures on Contemporary Syntactic Theories: an Introduction to Government-binding Theory, Generalized Phrase Structure Grammar, and Lexical-functional Grammar.* Stanford, CA: Center for the Study of Language and Information.

Siewierska, Anna. 1991. *Functional Grammar.* (Linguistic Theory Guides) London and New York: Routledge.

Song, Jae Jung. 2001. *Linguistic Typology: Morphology and Syntax.* Harlow: Longman.

Starosta, Stanley. 1988. *The Case for Lexicase. An Outline of Lexicase Grammatical Theory.* London and New York: Pinter.

Starosta, Stanley. 1996. 'Lexicase'. In K. Brown and J. Miller (eds), 231–41.

Stockwell, Robert P., Paul Schachter and Barbara Hall Partee. 1973. *The Major Syntactic Structures of English.* New York: Holt, Rinehart and Winston.

Tarallo, Fernando and John Myhill. 1983. 'Interference and natural language processing in second language acquisition'. *Language Learning* 33, 1: 55–76.

Tesnière, Lucien. 1959. *Éléments de Syntaxe Structurale.* Paris: Klincksieck.

Thagard, Paul. 2000. *Coherence in Thought and Action.* Cambridge, MA and London: MIT Press.

Traugott, Elizabeth Closs and Bernd Heine (eds). 1991. *Approaches to Grammaticalization.* Volume I: *Focus on Theoretical and Methodological Issues.* Volume II: *Focus on Types of Grammatical Markers.* Amsterdam and Philadelphia: John Benjamins.

Van Valin, Robert D. 2001. *An Introduction to Syntax.* Cambridge: Cambridge University Press.

Vennemann, Theo, known as Nierfeld. 1973. 'Explanation in syntax'. In John P. Kimball (ed.), *Syntax and Semantics,* Volume 2. New York, London: Seminar Press, 1–50.

Webelhuth, Gert (ed.). 1995. *Government and Binding Theory and the Minimalist Program.* Oxford and Cambridge: Blackwell.

Wood, McGee Mary. 1993. *Categorial Grammars.* (Linguistic Theory Guides) London and New York: Routledge.

Yuasa, Etsuyo. 2005. *Modularity in Language. Constructional and Categorial Mismatch in Syntax and Semantics.* Berlin and New York: Mouton de Gruyter.

Index